REVELATION:
HEARING THE LAST WORD

REVELATION:
HEARING THE LAST WORD

DAVID M. LEVY

The Friends of Israel Gospel Ministry, Inc.
P. O. Box 908, Bellmawr, NJ 08099

REVELATION: HEARING THE LAST WORD

David M. Levy

Copyright © 1999 by The Friends of Israel Gospel Ministry, Inc.
Bellmawr, NJ 08099

Sixth Printing **2018**

Library of Congress Catalog Card Number: 98-074877
ISBN 10: 0-915540-60-6
ISBN 13: 978-0-915540-60-0

Cover by Left Coast Designs, Portland, OR.
Photo, Image Bank

Visit our website at www.foi.org.

CONTENTS

PREFACE

The Book of the Revelation evokes more interest than any other book in the New Testament. People are inspired by its content, fascinated by its prophecies, and stand in awe of its mysteries. Conservative scholars believe that the Apostle John wrote the Book of the Revelation during his incarceration on the isle of Patmos around 95 A.D. It is often called the *Apocalypse*, a Greek word meaning *to uncover* or *unveil*. Unveiled in the book are the major events in God's prophetic program that must shortly come to fruition. People who take the time to read Revelation will quickly see a correlation between its prophecies and events emerging throughout the world today.

The major theme of Revelation is the Lord Jesus Christ—an unfolding of His deity, humanity, life, ministry, death, resurrection, return, judgment, and reign. The facts presented in Revelation regarding Christ's life and ministry are reason enough for all Christians, young and old, to study this book. Christ's final victory over the powers of evil and the creation of a new heaven and earth should provide great hope for believers of every generation.

On one hand, Revelation is like a magnet drawing readers to comprehend its prophetic message. On the other hand, many pastors and people shy away from a serious study of Revelation because they find the symbolic and figurative language hard to understand. When these people do interpret the symbolic language in Revelation, they often do so allegorically, stripping the text of its true meaning. Studying Revelation in this manner results in a faulty interpretation of the book's content. People studying Revelation should not read into the verses of the book any novel or mystical meanings that do not make sense within the context in which the passage is presented. Granted, the text of Revelation should be applied spiritually when applicable, but not at the expense of a proper understanding of the text's true meaning.

In order to understand the symbolic language of Revelation, the proper interpretation must be applied to each passage. The symbolic passage under consideration should be interpreted in its normal, grammatical, historical, ordinary literal sense within the context that it is written. The symbolic and figurative language in Revelation should be understood in its ordinary literal sense, unless, by doing so, it makes no sense or is illogical. Often the symbols in Revelation are interpreted within the chapter or book. Any symbols that are not explained in this way can usually be explained within the culture or custom of the time during which they were written or by studying parallel sections in other portions of the Bible. Sometimes there is not enough information given in the text to know the exact interpretation of a symbol that is to be fulfilled in the future.

Why another commentary on Revelation? It has been my experience that many commentaries written on this book are sketchy at best, allegorical in nature, too technical in their presentation, fail to deal with difficult passages, avoid specific prophetic subjects, or are too sensational in their application. World conditions have been drastically altered in recent years, making commentaries written thirty years ago dated on many of their views and applications. Those commentaries that do deal with recent events are often highly speculative, leaving the reader confused on a proper understanding of how Revelation relates to recent world events. Therefore, I felt compelled to write a new study on Revelation that would try to correct many of these problems.

This volume was written with the following purposes in mind:

1. To put the text of Revelation in a readable and understandable format, so that those interested in studying the book can adequately grasp its meaning and message.

2. To provide a verse by verse commentary on Revelation.

3. To make plain the difficult and disputed passages within the book.

4. To provide a chronological timeline of God's program so that the reader will understand the proper sequence of events throughout the book.

5. To show how the book relates to world events in the past and events emerging today.

6. To provide a detailed description of those prophetic events that must be fulfilled in the future.

7. To provide a dispensational, pretribulational, premillennial interpretation of Revelation.

8. To provide a commentary that will appeal to young Christians who are not well-versed in Scripture, as well as to mature believers who have an in-depth knowledge of Revelation.

9. To stir every believer to a deeper commitment for the Lord in light of end-time events.

10. To promote a concern for the lost souls of people who will suffer the judgments mentioned in this book.

Earlier, I mentioned that many pastors and people shy away from a serious study of Revelation. But the angel commanded John to reveal the message of Revelation for all to read and understand, in light of Christ's soon return (Revelation 22:10). God promises a blessing to all who read, receive, and respond to the prophecy of this book. John said, "Blessed is he that readeth, and they that hear the words of this prophecy, and keep those things which are written in it; for the time is at hand" (Revelation 1:3). I pray that you will receive as much insight, encouragement, and blessing in reading this book as I did in writing it.

—David M. Levy

Outline of
THE BOOK OF THE REVELATION

I. CHRIST: THINGS PAST (1:1-20)
A. Prologue (1:1-3)
B. Personal Greeting to the Churches (1:4-8)
C. Patmos Captivity (1:9)
D. Prophecy to the Churches (1:10-11)
E. Portrait of Christ (1:12-18)
F. Purpose of Communication (1:19-20)

II. CHURCHES: THINGS PRESENT (2:1-3:22)
A. Church Confronted—Ephesus (2:1-7)
B. Church Comforted—Smyrna (2:8-11)
C. Church Compromised—Pergamum (2:12-17)
D. Church Corrupted—Thyatira (2:18-29)
E. Church Crisis—Sardis (3:1-6)
F. Church Commitment—Philadelphia (3:7-13)
G. Church Complacency—Laodicea (3:14-22)

III. CONSUMMATION: THINGS PROPHESIED (4:1-22:21)
A. Prophecy Before the Tribulation (4:1-5:14)
   1. Summons from Heaven (4:1)
   2. Scene in Heaven (4:2-7)
   3. Song in Heaven (4:8-11)
   4. Sealed Scroll (5:1)
   5. Sorrowful Search (5:2-4)
   6. Savior Opens the Scroll (5:5-7)
   7. Song of Salvation (5:8-14)

B. Program in the Tribulation (6:1-16:21)
  1. Catastrophic Ruination (6:1-16:21)
     a. Six Seals (6:1-17)
     b. Saved Servants (7:1-17)
     c. Seventh Seal (8:1-6)
     d. Six Trumpets Sounded (8:7-9:21)
     e. Strong Angel with Scroll (10:1-11)
     f. Sanctuary Measured for Survival (11:1-2)
     g. Selected Witnesses Serve (11:3-6)
     h. Slain Witnesses Survive (11:7-14)
     i. Seventh Trumpet Sounded (11:15-19)
     j. Supernatural Survival of Israel (12:1-17)
     k. Satanic Beast (13:1-10)
     l. Second Beast (13:11-18)
     m. Sealed Saints with Savior (14:1-5)
     n. Sermon to the Unsaved (14:6-7)
     o. Smiting Domain of Satan (14:8-20)
     p. Scene from Heavenly Sanctuary (15:1-8)
     q. Seven Bowls of Suffering (16:1-21)

  2. Corrupt Reign (17:1-18)
     a. Mystery of the Whore (17:1-7)
     b. Monster of Wickedness (17:8-14)
     c. Murder of the Woman (17:15-18)

  3. City Razed (18:1-24)
     a. Babylon Destroyed (18:1-8)
     b. Bewailing Dirge (18:9-19)
     c. Believers Delighted (18:20-24)

  4. Christ's Return (19:1-21)
     a. Celebration in Heaven (19:1-6)
     b. Ceremony in Heaven (19:7-10)
     c. Christ Comes from Heaven (19:11-14)
     d. Christ Conqueres Heathen (19:15-21)

C. Program After the Tribulation (20:1-22:5)
  1. Christ's Reign (20:1-15)
     a. Satan Restrained (20:1-2)
     b. Savior's Rule (20:3-6)
     c. Sinners' Revolt (20:7-10)
     d. Second Resurrection and Judgment (20:11-15)
  2. Cosmos Recreated (21:1-22:5)
     a. New Creation (21:1-8)
     b. New City (21:9-22:5)
D. Proclamation of Triumphant (22:6-21)
  1. Confirming Words (22:6-7)
  2. Christ Worshiped (22:8-10)
  3. Comments to the Wicked and the Worthy (22:11-17)
  4. Christ's Warning (22:18-21)

NOTE: This outline does not always follow the outline in each chapter of the book.

REVELATION 1:1-8

The Revelation of Jesus Christ, which God gave unto him, to show unto his servants things which must shortly come to pass; and he sent and signified it by his angel unto his servant, John, Who bore witness of the word of God, and of the testimony of Jesus Christ, and of all things that he saw. Blessed is he that readeth, and they that hear the words of this prophecy, and keep those things which are written in it; for the time is at hand. John, to the seven churches which are in Asia: Grace be unto you, and peace, from him who is, and who was, and who is to come, and from the seven spirits who are before his throne; And from Jesus Christ, who is the faithful witness, and the first begotten of the dead, and the prince of the kings of the earth. Unto him that loveth us, and washed us from our sins in his own blood, And hath made us a kingdom of priests unto God and his Father, to him be glory and dominion forever and ever. Amen. Behold, he cometh with clouds, and every eye shall see him, and they also who pierced him; and all kindreds of the earth shall wail because of him. Even so, Amen. I am Alpha and Omega, the beginning and the ending, saith the Lord, who is, and who was, and who is to come, the Almighty.

1

THE REVELATION
OF JESUS CHRIST

Futurists are inundating us with articles, books, and videos on what to expect in the near future. The new millennium has rekindled an interest in the study of biblical prophecy. Many are turning to the Book of the Revelation, trying to grasp its message about the future, for failure to understand this important book will leave people in total darkness concerning their personal destiny and that of their universe.

The Book of the Revelation has given great inspiration to many people throughout the centuries. "In hours of darkness it has given courage to its readers, enabling them to endure persecution and death for the sake of Christ."[1] Others have viewed the book as a mystery. Its apocalyptic character, odd figures of speech, and unique symbolic language are seen as archaic literature. It is like an unsolvable puzzle whose meaning is unknowable or, at best, was forgotten centuries ago.

At first glance, the symbolism in Revelation seems rather confusing, a relic from a time of superstition and folklore. Most apocalyptic literature in the Bible was revealed in dreams, visions, signs, and symbols (e.g., Daniel and Ezekiel). This is the method chosen by God to reveal His prophetic program to mankind.

For more than 1,900 years, Revelation has been a battle-ground for scholars who have differed on its interpretation. They have endeavored to fashion its strange pageant into a consistent and understandable eschatology.[2]

Throughout the centuries, scholars have taken at least four approaches to the interpretation of Revelation. They are commonly called the *preterist*, *historical*, *idealist*, and *futurist* views.

- The *preterist* view holds that Revelation is not a prediction of things to come, but, rather, John was writing about events taking place in his day. He was describing the time in which he penned the book. The church was undergoing persecution at the hands of a pagan world. Although portions of Revelation addressed the church in John's day (chps. 2-3), the major portion of the book predicts future events totally unrelated to the first-century church.

- The *historical* view sees the events recorded by John as symbolically fulfilled through church history between Christ's First and Second Comings. It was highly promoted by Reformation and 19th-century theologians. This position is now considered historically unsound because most of Revelation does not apply to the church.

- The *idealist* view interprets Revelation allegorically. Those holding this position emphasize the spiritual message of Revelation: God's triumph over Satan, God's triumph over evil, and the ultimate reign of righteousness on the earth. This view sets aside the literal interpretation of Revelation and can easily lead to a fanciful or, at best, artificial interpretation of the book. It also ignores the historical meaning of Revelation.

- The *futurist* view teaches that the major portion of Revelation (chps. 4-22) describes prophetic events yet to be fulfilled. It holds that the proper principles of biblical interpretation must be applied to a study of this prophetic book to understand its meaning. It treats Revelation as a historical document, taking into consideration the cultural background and circumstances of the prophecy. The words of this prophecy are interpreted in their normal grammatical sense, which also means a proper interpretation of the literary elements of figurative and symbolic language in the book. I hold to this view.

The Revelation

John presented the central theme of his writing in verse 1: "The Revelation of Jesus Christ." Scholars have written extensively on whether John was referring to Christ as the *provider* or *content* of this book. The debate has centered on the Greek preposition *of*, which can be translated either *from* or *about*. Although the content of the book is *about* Christ (His person and program), emphasis is on Christ as the *provider* of this revelation. Thus, Christ received this revelation from "God [i.e., the Father]...to show unto his servants things which must shortly come to pass" (v. 1).

The "things which must shortly come to pass" are the prophecies set forth in Revelation. This does not mean that the prophecies will be fulfilled immediately, for more than 1,900 years have passed since the book was written. The idea of the phrase "must shortly come to pass" is that when the prophecies begin to be fulfilled, they will happen suddenly, in rapid succession, and without delay. They "must" or will, of necessity, come to pass at God's appointed time.

Christ "sent and signified" this revelation "by his angel [messenger] unto his servant, John" (v. 1). The word *signified* (Gr., *semeion*) means to *indicate* or *communicate* by means of signs and symbolic language. Throughout Revelation, angels play a major role as mediating messengers to reveal God's Word to John using signs and symbolic language.

In verse 2, John affirmed that he was the writer of this book and "bore witness [testimony]" to three things:

1. This was not his own word but the *inspired* "word of God."

2. This revelation was "the testimony of Jesus Christ," meaning a true witness that Christ Himself imparted to John.

3. Throughout the book, John indicated that he recorded "all things that he saw."

The Recipients

John addressed his message "to the seven churches which are in Asia" (vv. 4, 11). They were local assemblies in the western section of the Roman province of Asia Minor (Turkey). Although only seven churches are mentioned, probably more existed in the area. Most likely they were established through Paul's missionary outreach from Ephesus, the principal city in Asia Minor.

John does not reveal why only seven churches are mentioned. Seven is a prominent number in Revelation, emblematic of completeness or perfection. Possibly these seven churches were representative of the various types of local assemblies in John's day, as well as throughout church history.

John addressed his readers with a traditional greeting of the day: "Grace be unto you, and peace" (v. 4). The greeting speaks of what Christians experience in salvation. God's grace (unmerited favor) was manifested to believers through Christ's redeeming sacrifice on the cross. Those who put their faith in Him experience the peace *of*, *with*, and *from* God.

This greeting came to John from the *triune God*:

- God the *Father*, "who is, and who was, and who is to come" (v. 4).

- God the *Spirit*, "the seven spirits who are before his throne" (v. 4). Some hold that this refers to ministering spirits before the throne of God, but the context implies the Holy Spirit.

- God the *Son*, "And from Jesus Christ" (v. 5).

Apparently the Book of the Revelation was intended for public use in the church assembly rather than for private reading, as verse 3 indicates "he that readeth, and they that hear." This should not keep modern individuals from reading and studying the book privately (or publicly). In the first century, believers within the local church did not own personal copies of the Bible. Thus, the public reading of Scripture was crucial if they were to understand God's Word.

Verse 3 promises a threefold blessing to all who embrace the Book of the Revelation: to the *reader* ("he that readeth"), the *receivers* ("they that hear the words of this prophecy"), and the *responders* ("and keep those things which are written in it"). Six other blessings are mentioned in this book (14:13; 16:15; 19:9; 20:6; 22:7; 22:14). The Book of the Revelation commences with a blessing (1:3) and concludes with a blessing (22:7). Contrary to popular thought in many circles, Revelation is not a book to be feared, but one to be read and studied.

When John wrote "the time is at hand" (v. 3), he was not referring to clock time (Gr., *chronos*), but to a fixed season of time (Gr., *karios*). The beginning and duration of this fixed season is not stated, but the time is "at hand." The phrase *at hand* does not mean that these prophecies would be fulfilled immediately. It means that their nearness should be kept in mind, as if they are imminent, as a reminder to be prepared for what is to come. This fixed season is related to the time of Christ's Second Coming. Although Christ instructed people not to set dates concerning His coming, He did warn them to be prepared (Matthew 24:36, 42, 44).

The Redeemer

John concluded his salutation with a greeting from Christ and a glorious portrait of His worth and work. First, in His *person* Christ is "the faithful witness" (v. 5). He faithfully witnessed to the people, the priesthood of Israel, and Pilate during His life and ministry. Second, in *position* He is "the first begotten of the dead" (v. 5). That is, He retains priority in position over all who are resurrected from the dead. He was the firstfruit of those resurrected from the dead (1 Corinthians 15:20) and the first to receive a glorified body (Acts 26:23). Third, in *power* He is "the prince of the kings of the earth" (v. 5). Christ is the "KING OF KINGS, AND LORD OF LORDS" (19:16) who is given the nations as His inheritance and will rule them with a rod of iron (Psalm 2:6-9).

Fourth, Christ's *provision* to believers is threefold. The Lord's care is seen through His love, as John stated, "Unto him that loveth us" (v. 5). In the Greek text, *love* is in the present tense, not the past tense, as recorded in the King James Version. Christ has a continual, self-sacrificing, abiding love for those for whom He died. He also cleansed His own: "and washed [lit., loosed or freed] us from our sins in his own blood" (v. 5). True, Christ has cleansed believers through His shed blood, but He has also freed them. Christ paid the price to buy mankind from their slavery of sin with His own blood. He has once and for all set mankind free from the power and penalty of sin. Finally, Christ crowned the body of believers by making them "a kingdom of priests" (v. 6). Believers in the church make up a royal priesthood (5:10; 1 Peter 2:5, 9) and will reign and rule with Christ during the Millennial Kingdom (20:6). As individual priests, believers are to offer up spiritual sacrifices to God of their bodies, praise, and good works (Romans 12:1; Hebrews 13:15-16; 1 Peter 2:5). Unable to hold in his gratitude, John broke out in praise: "to him be glory and dominion forever and ever. Amen [so be it]" (v. 6).

Fifth, John *predicted* Christ's coming: "Behold, he cometh with clouds, and every eye shall see him, and they also who pierced him; and all kindreds of the earth shall wail because of him" (v. 7). The sign of Christ's coming will be His "coming in the clouds of heaven with power and great glory" (Matthew 24:30). This is not a reference to the Rapture of the church but to Christ's Second Coming. No indication is found in Scripture that every eye will see Him at the Rapture, but all will see Him at the Second Coming. All people alive on the earth will see Him come.

Some might wonder how "they...who pierced him" will see Him because they all will have died. Here, as in John 19:37 and Zechariah 12:10, the apostle is referring to all those who are against Christ and would call for His death, as did those of the first century, whether they be Jews or Gentiles. Jews called for Christ's death (Matthew 27:22-25), but Gentiles crucified Him (Luke 18:32-33). This makes *all* people responsible for His death (Acts 4:27).

At Christ's Second Coming, "all kindreds of the earth shall wail because of him" (v. 7). Israel will have the veil lifted from their eyes and will see that Jesus is their true Messiah. They will wail in repentance and grief over their sin. In contrast, wicked people the world over will wail and lament His coming because of the terror and judgment awaiting them from the Lord. Terror will fill the hearts of unsaved people, who will cry out for the mountains to fall on them in order to hide from Christ's wrath (6:16-17). John nevertheless gave affirmation and approval to the Lord's coming: "Even so, Amen" (v. 7).

Sixth, the *preeminent* Christ spoke to John for the first time: "I am Alpha and Omega, the beginning and the ending, saith the

Lord, who is, and who was, and who is to come, the Almighty" (v. 8). The Lord referred to Himself as the "I am" (v. 8), a term first used of God the Father (Exodus 3:14) to proclaim Him as the self-existent and sufficient Sovereign of the universe. Jesus also used the words "I am" in seven self-descriptions recorded in John's Gospel and ten times in Revelation. His *omniscience* is seen in the phrase "I am Alpha and Omega" (v. 8), the first and last letters of the Greek alphabet (lit., *the beginning and the end*). He is the eternal "Word" (John 1:1, 14) of God, and in Him "are hidden all the treasures of wisdom and knowledge" (Colossians 2:3) of all things. His *omnipresence* is seen in the phrase "the beginning and the ending, saith the Lord, who is, and who was, and who is to come" (v. 8). He is the one who created, controls, and will consummate all things (Ephesians 1:10; Colossians 1:16-17).[3] His *omnipotence* is seen in the words "the Almighty" (v. 8). *Almighty* is used nine times in Revelation to refer to God, who holds sway over all things as the supreme Ruler of the universe.

The readers of Revelation have been greeted with a glorious salutation from their blessed Lord. Later, John proclaimed that "the testimony of Jesus is the spirit of prophecy" (19:10). This means that the true purpose of prophecy is to provide testimony to the person and program of Jesus Christ. "Prophecy," says C. C. Ryrie, "is designed to unfold the loveliness of Jesus."[4] Christ is the central character of Revelation; all things commence and conclude in Him. He controls the conflicts and catastrophic judgments that fill the major portion of Revelation. He is the soon-coming King who will conquer His enemies and reclaim the earth. He is the one who will create a new cosmos in which will dwell the celestial city (New Jerusalem) to house righteous citizens for eternity.

Futurists may inundate us with articles, books, and videos on what to expect in the near future, but only the Book of the Revelation, sent from the triune God, has stood the test of time as the true provider and predictor of what will happen on earth.

Endnotes

[1] Merrill C. Tenney, *Interpreting Revelation* (Grand Rapids: Wm. B. Eerdmans Publishing Company, 1957), p. vii.

[2] *Ibid.*

[3] Lehman Strauss, *The Book of the Revelation* (Neptune, NJ: Loizeaux Brothers, 1964), p. 29.

[4] William MacDonald, *Believer's Bible Commentary*, *New Testament* (Nashville: Nelson, 1990), p. 1192.

REVELATION 1:9-20

I, John, who also am your brother, and companion in tribulation, and in the kingdom and patience of Jesus Christ, was in the isle that is called Patmos, for the word of God, and for the testimony of Jesus Christ. I was in the Spirit on the Lord's day, and heard behind me a great voice, as of a trumpet, Saying, I am Alpha and Omega, the first and the last; and, What thou seest, write in a book, and send it unto the seven churches which are in Asia: unto Ephesus, and unto Smyrna, and unto Pergamum, and unto Thyatira, and unto Sardis, and unto Philadelphia, and unto Laodicea. And I turned to see the voice that spoke with me. And being turned, I saw seven golden lampstands, And in the midst of the seven lampstands one like the Son of man, clothed with a garment down to the foot, and girded about the breasts with a golden girdle. His head and his hair were white like wool, as white as snow; and his eyes were like a flame of fire; And his feet like fine bronze, as if they burned in a furnace; and his voice like the sound of many waters. And he had in his right hand seven stars; and out of his mouth went a sharp two-edged sword; and his countenance was as the sun shineth in its strength. And when I saw him, I fell at his feet as dead. And he laid his right hand upon me, saying unto me, Fear not; I am the first and the last; I am he that liveth, and was dead; and, behold, I am alive for evermore, Amen, and have the keys of hades and of death.

Write the things which thou hast seen, and the things which are, and the things which shall be hereafter: The mystery of the seven stars which thou sawest in my right hand, and the seven golden lampstands. The seven stars are the angels of the seven churches; and the seven lampstands which thou sawest are the seven churches.

2

THE GLORIFIED CHRIST

What did Jesus look like in the flesh? Artists have tried to paint Him and authors have tried to describe Him. Nowhere does Scripture relate the physical appearance of Jesus during His earthly life. Isaiah wrote, "he hath no form nor comeliness, and when we shall see him, there is no beauty that we should desire him" (Isaiah 53:2). There was nothing in Jesus' human appearance to attract people to Him or make them think He was extraordinary. But Scripture does provide an awe-inspiring portrait of the glorified Christ, which John received through a vision while in captivity on the island of Patmos.

Patmos Captivity

John began by identifying with his readers and describing the setting in which he received the vision of Jesus Christ. He was a fellow believer with all those "in the kingdom" of God (v. 9). All who believe in Christ are part of God's spiritual kingdom and make up a "kingdom of priests" (v. 6). As brothers and sisters in Him, all believers who live godly lives in Christ will become "companion[s] in tribulation" (v. 9) for their faith in the Lord. John was no different. He had been banished to the "isle…called

Patmos" (v. 9) as a religious-political prisoner by Emperor Domitian in 95 A.D. John was exiled for faithfully preaching and teaching "the word of God" and for the "testimony" he manifested for "Jesus Christ" (v. 9). Patmos is a small, isolated, volcanic island, only ten miles long and six miles wide, located in the Aegean Sea. The aged apostle was forced to perform hard labor in the mines on Patmos. However, he was released by Emperor Nerva 18 months after his exile.

John was sustained during this trying time through the "patience of Jesus Christ" (v. 9). Christ provided the needed strength for the apostle to endure this extreme trial and come through it victoriously.

Jesus predicted that those in His kingdom would suffer tribulation (Mark 10:30; cp. Acts 14:22), but tribulations need not impede their walk with Christ. Often believers are brought into a closer relationship with the Lord during such trying times. John, like Peter and Paul, received his greatest revelation during a time of extreme suffering—a time when he was suffering for the gospel of Christ.

John received this vision while "in the Spirit on the Lord's day" (v. 10). This is the first of four visions John received while "in the spirit" (1:10; 4:2; 17:3; 21:10). Being *in the Spirit* is often used to describe a prophet or an apostle under the control of the Holy Spirit. The person was often in a trance or trancelike state during the time he received a vision.

The phrase *on the Lord's day* has been interpreted two ways. Some scholars hold that it refers to Sunday, the day on which Christians worship, while others hold that it refers to the *Day of the Lord*, a time of judgment revealed to John. Although modern Christians call Sunday "the Lord's day," the phrase is not used in this fashion in Scripture. True, Paul used "Lord" as an adjective in reference to "the Lord's supper" (1 Corinthians 11:20), but not in reference to a *day*. Christians regularly met for worship on "the first day of the week" (cp. Matthew 28:1; Mark 16:2, 9; Luke 24:1; John 20:1, 19; Acts 20:7; 1 Corinthians 16:2), but this time was never called "the Lord's day." The phrase did not come into use until after the first century. Thus, *the Lord's day* in verse 10 is not a reference to Sunday, but to the *Day of the Lord.* In support of this view, Dr. John Walvoord, a noted prophetic scholar writes,

> The word *Lord* in this passage is actually an adjective, used in the sense of "lordian."...Moulton and Milligan also call attention to the fact that the word is frequently used outside the Bible in the sense of "imperial" and cite Deissmann: "that the distinctive title 'Lord's day' may have been connected with the conscious feelings of protest against the cult of the Emperor with its 'Emperor's Day.' "...It is rather a reference to the day of the Lord of the Old Testament, an extended period of time in which God deals in judgment and sovereign rule of the earth. The adjective form can be explained on the ground that in the Old Testament there was no adjective form for "Lord," and therefore the noun had to be used. The New Testament term is therefore the equivalent to the Old Testament expression "the day of the Lord."...On the basis of the evidence, the interpretation is therefore preferred that John was projected forward to the future day of the Lord. It is questionable in any case whether the amazing revelation given in the entire book could have been conveyed to John in one twenty-four-hour day, and it is more probable that it consisted of a series of revelations.[1]

Thus, John recorded what he saw and heard about the future "day of the Lord." Opponents of this view point out that the vision does not mention "the day of the Lord," which refers to the end of the age and Christ's Second Coming. Rather, they say, it focuses on Christ's message to seven local churches in Asia Minor during the first century, not "the day of the Lord."[2] Scholars are equally divided on the correct interpretation.

Portrait of Christ

In this exalted state, John "heard behind [him] a great voice, as of a trumpet" (v. 10). The voice belonged to Christ, who identified Himself as "Alpha and Omega, the first and the last" (v. 11).

The Lord commanded the apostle, "What thou seest, write in a book, and send it unto the seven churches which are in Asia" (v. 11). This is the first of twelve times John was commanded to record what he saw.

Hearing the voice from behind, John turned quickly "to see the voice" (v. 12). He "saw seven golden lampstands, And in the midst of the seven lampstands one like the Son of man" (vv. 12-13). We are not told how these lampstands were shaped or what they looked like. It is possible that they had one branch arranged in a circular configuration with Christ standing in the center.

The term *Son of man* is used often in the Gospels as a reference to Christ's humanity. The glorified Christ still has a human form with identifying marks from His crucifixion.

John went on to record a sevenfold description of Christ's appearance, apparel, and authority.

1. "His head and his hair were white like wool, as white as snow" (v. 14). A hoary head was worthy of honor and conveyed the idea of wisdom and dignity. The whiteness may suggest the brightness of His heavenly glory. This image corresponds to Daniel's vision of God, when he saw "the Ancient of days," whose hair was white "like pure wool" (Daniel 7:9). White hair in

Scripture is symbolic of purity in character, dignity of age, authority as a judge, and eternality. Daniel's statement regarding the Ancient of days can also be applied to Christ.

2. Christ's face was brilliant: "his countenance was as the sun shineth in its strength" (v. 16). John's look at the glorified Lord was blinding, a reminder of Christ's transfiguration, when "his face did shine like the sun, and his raiment was as white as the light" (Matthew 17:2).

3. "His eyes were like a flame of fire" (v. 14), indicating a penetrating gaze that flashed with intelligence, righteousness, and the look of divine wrath upon the wicked.

4. The Lord's feet were "like fine bronze, as if they burned in a furnace" (v. 15). The meaning of "fine bronze" (*chalkolibanon*) is somewhat uncertain. It could be speaking of an alloy of gold and silver mixed with pure brass. His feet appeared as shining bronze fired to white heat, as in a kiln. This is symbolic of Christ's strength and stability as He treads the wicked in judgment, ultimately making His enemies His footstool (Hebrews 10:13).

5. He was "clothed with a garment down to the foot, and girded about the breasts with a golden girdle" (v. 13). The priests of the Old Testament wore long flowing robes for glory and beauty (Exodus 28:2, 4), a symbol of dignity, majesty, and divine authority. This garment is a reminder of Christ's glory, beauty, divine authority, and high priestly ministry.

6. The sound of "his voice [was] like the sound of
    many waters" (v. 15), symbolic of God's author-
    ity, power, and majesty. Those who have experi-
    enced the awesome sound and power of rushing
    water—whether the ocean or the great falls at
    Niagara—can understand John's description.

7. His speech was powerful: "out of his mouth
    went a sharp two-edged sword" (v. 16). This is a
    description of a Thracian sword—long, broad,
    heavy, and sharp on both edges. A sword is men-
    tioned six times throughout the book (1:16; 2:12,
    16; 6:8; 19:15, 21), referring to Christ's word of
    divine judgment.

In "his right hand" Christ held "seven stars" (v. 16). "The
seven stars are the angels of the seven churches" (v. 20). This is
called a "mystery" (v. 20), or a previously hidden truth in
Scripture now divinely revealed. The word *angel* means *messenger* and can refer to either an angelic being or a human being.
Some conservative scholars hold that these stars are angelic
beings and not humans for the following reasons:

- Throughout the Book of the Revelation, the Lord
  works through angels.

- The New Testament use of angels as messengers
  indicates that these are angelic beings.

- The angels are given responsibilities in the seven
  churches that surpass the abilities of human beings.

- Human leadership within these churches had
  not progressed to a state where a single person
  was in charge.[3]

Others hold that these messengers are not angelic beings, but
leaders or pastors, responsible for the spiritual welfare of the
seven churches to whom Christ directed His message. These men
were in the right hand of Christ, indicating His possession, power,

and protection over them. Scholars are divided on the correct identification of these beings. However, the second position seems to carry more weight, in light of what is recorded in the next two chapters.

John recorded the impact of the glorified Christ upon him: "And when I saw him, I fell at his feet as dead" (v. 17). He was stunned with fear and fell to the ground. Immediately the Lord laid His right hand of authority and power on John's trembling figure as He spoke, "Fear not" (v. 17), words of assurance and comfort.

The glorified Christ then identified Himself in five ways as the eternal Savior:

1. "I am the first and the last" (v. 17). He is creator and consummator, absolute Lord of all history.

2. "I am he that liveth" (v. 18). He is the resurrected Lord who eternally exists.

3. "I...was dead" (v. 18). He is the crucified Son of God who provided salvation for mankind.

4. "I am alive for evermore" (v. 18). He is expressing His eternal existence as God.

5. He controls the destiny of the departed dead, having "the keys of hades and of death" (v. 18). Christ possesses the keys because He conquered death.

Purpose of the Communication

The apostle was brought back to reality with a command from the Lord to write. In verse 19, Christ revealed a divine outline of the Book of the Revelation.

1. John was to record the *past*: "the things which thou hast seen," or the vision of Christ that he had just experienced.

2. He was to record the *present*: "the things which are," a description of the seven churches in Asia Minor (chps. 2-3).

3. He was to record *a prophecy of the future*: "the things which shall be hereafter," events revealed by Christ after His message to the seven churches (chps. 4-22).

Herein lies an important key to unlocking the order and content of future events throughout the Book of the Revelation.

Today's church needs a fresh glimpse of the glorified Christ seated at the right hand of God in all of His splendor and majesty. Like John, as finite beings, we must fall at His feet with a sense of awe and fear as we gaze on the majesty of our infinite Lord. Those who do will come away with a renewed sense of the fleshly and self-serving nature of their worship and service to Christ. The living Christ walks in the midst of the church today, weighing its worship and service. This should cause each of us to walk prudently before our omniscient Lord. Hopefully, our service will be found acceptable in His sight.

Endnotes

[1] John F. Walvoord, *The Revelation of Jesus Christ* (Chicago: Moody Press, 1966), p. 42.

[2] Walter M. Dunnett, *Lord of the Churches*, *Moody Manna* (Chicago: Moody Press, 1966), part I, p. 22.

[3] *Ibid.*, p. 23.

REVELATION 2:1-11

Unto the angel of the church of Ephesus write: These things saith he that holdeth the seven stars in his right hand, who walketh in the midst of the seven golden lampstands. I know thy works, and thy labor, and thy patience, and how thou canst not bear them who are evil; and thou hast tried them who say they are apostles, and are not, and hast found them liars; And hast borne, and hast patience, and for my name's sake hast labored, and hast not fainted. Nevertheless, I have somewhat against thee, because thou hast left thy first love. Remember, therefore, from where thou art fallen, and repent, and do the first works, or else I will come unto thee quickly, and will remove thy lampstand out of its place, except thou repent. But this thou hast, that thou hatest the deeds of the Nicolaitans, which I also hate. He that hath an ear, let him hear what the Spirit saith unto the churches: To him that overcometh will I give to eat of the tree of life, which is in the midst of the paradise of God.

And unto the angel of the church in Smyrna write: These things saith the first and the last, who was dead, and is alive. I know thy works, and tribulation, and poverty (but thou art rich); and I know the blasphemy of them who say they are Jews, and are not, but are the synagogue of Satan. Fear none of those things which thou shalt suffer. Behold, the devil shall cast some of you into prison, that ye may be tried, and ye shall have tribu-lation ten days; be thou faithful unto death, and I will give thee a crown of life. He that hath an ear, let him hear what the Spirit saith unto the churches: He that overcometh shall not be hurt of the second death.

3

THE CHURCH
CONFRONTED AND COMFORTED

"Churches are like people. No two are alike. Each has its own personality...size and shape...strength and weakness," wrote Steven Larson.[1] This is evident when reading Christ's letters to the seven churches in Revelation. Each letter is tailored to speak to the need of the church addressed.

While John was on the Isle of Patmos, Christ commanded him to record seven messages to specific churches in Asia Minor. These letters are recorded in Revelation 2 and 3 and make up the second division of the book, identified as "the things which are" (1:19).

Why were these seven churches chosen over others? Possibly because of their geographic locations. They were linked by a circular road that connected the most populous parts of the province; therefore, the letters were probably circulated to other churches within the province.

Most likely these churches provided a complete picture of the spiritual conditions common to churches in John's day and throughout history. Scholars have held various interpretations regarding the meaning of these seven churches. Primarily, the messages were given to seven literal churches existing in John's day; however, they portray seven different types of churches that have existed throughout church history. Some, like Ephesus, have left their first love for the Lord. Others, like Sardis, are spiritually dead or, like Laodicea, lukewarm at best. The same can be said of individual Christians. These letters contain warnings and counsel for every generation of believers.

Many Bible scholars assign prophetic meanings to these seven churches and their order in the narrative. Some teach a providential arrangement of the churches corresponding to the chronological development of seven stages of church history. While many parallels do exist throughout church history, there is a lack of scriptural support for this interpretation. Every period of church history has experienced the strengths and weaknesses that characterized these churches.

The message of each letter is structured in a set pattern:

1. The church and city are identified.

2. Christ's character is revealed.

3. The church is commended (except Sardis and Laodicea).

4. Compromise is condemned (except Smyrna and Philadelphia).

5. The church is counseled.

6. There is a call to commitment.

7. Compensation is promised to overcomers.

Ephesus: The Loveless Church

Ephesus was one of the oldest and largest cities in Asia. During the first century, it was a predominant city in the Roman province of Asia Minor. It was the crossroads of civilization in that day, noted for its great library, as well as its opulence and wealth. Politically, it was a free city and was home to the Roman governor of the province. Ephesus was located on the Cayster River, three miles from the Aegean Sea, and had a major harbor where ships could unload their cargo. Caravan routes from cities in the north, south, and east converged in Ephesus, making it a leading commercial center.

Religiously, the Ephesians worshiped Diana, the goddess of the woodlands and fertility (Gr., *Artemis*). The temple of Diana was one of the wonders of the world, dating back to the sixth century B.C., and religious prostitution and orgies flourished there.

Paul founded the Christian church at Ephesus, where he spent three years preaching and teaching. It became a missionary center from which all of Asia heard the gospel (Acts 19:8-10).

Christ directed His letter to "the angel [messenger] of the church of Ephesus" (v. 1). The word *messenger* refers to the *pastor* who, with the other six pastors, was said to be in the Lord's "right hand" (v. 1), a symbol of His authority and power. The Lord protected, controlled, and cared for these men and held them accountable for their ministry. Jesus "walketh in the midst of the seven golden lampstands [churches]" (v. 1) and was mindful of their spiritual condition.

The Lord commended the church in four ways.

1. He mentioned their devotion in service: "I know thy works, and thy labor, and thy patience" (v. 2).

2. He commended their deeds of righteousness: "and how thou canst not bear them who are evil" (v. 2). This church did not tolerate sin; they hated "the deeds of the Nicolaitans" (v. 6), a cult that professed faith in Christ but taught antinomianism (freedom to live without moral law) and practiced licentious living.

3. He lauded their doctrinal soundness. False apostles were not tolerated within the church (v. 2).

4. He recognized their diligence under testing: "for my name's sake hast labored, and hast not fainted" (v. 3). The church was separated from evil and sacrificially worked for the Lord with a servant's spirit.

But the Lord also had a complaint against this church: "Nevertheless, I have somewhat against thee, because thou hast left thy first love" (v. 4). Notice that they did not *lose* but had *left* (forsook) their first love for the Lord. The Ephesians had once possessed an *agape* (spiritual, self-giving) love for the Lord, but their devotion to Christ had severely eroded. He had their heads and hands, but not their hearts. When love for Christ cools, labor done in His name can become self-centered and lead to compromise and spiritual corruption.

In verse 5, the Lord counseled them concerning their condition.

- He said, "Remember, therefore, from where thou art fallen." They were to recall their past commitment and reevaluate their present compromise.

- They were to repent of their sins with contrite hearts.

- They were to repeat their "first works"; that is, serve Christ with a burning heart of love, spending time in fellowship, study, worship, and prayer.

- Their refusal to repent would cause their removal: "or else I will...remove thy lampstand out of its place" (v. 5). Loveless churches eventually lose their ability to shine in a lost world. The Ephesian church closed in the fifth century.

Compensation was promised to overcomers: "To him that overcometh will I give to eat of the tree of life, which is in the midst of the paradise of God" (v. 7). The word *overcomer* does not refer to Christians who have gained some spiritual victories in life, but to those who have accepted Christ as Savior (cp. 1

John 5:4-5). True believers are assured of eternal life; they will eat of "the tree of life" that was first mentioned in the Garden of Eden (Genesis 2:9) and is now in heaven. Those who eat of the tree will live forever (Genesis 3:22).

Smyrna: The Suffering Church

Smyrna, only 35 miles from Ephesus, was a wealthy city that rivaled Ephesus in beauty and commerce. It had well-planned harbors and a beautiful countryside surrounded by seven hills, but it was filled with the pagan temples of Apollo, Asclepia, Aphrodite, Cybelle, Emperor Tiberius, and Zeus. Although it was a free city, it gave full allegiance to the Roman Empire. Smyrna was destroyed in the seventh century B.C. and was rebuilt by Alexander the Great in the third century B.C. It was famous for its superb school of medicine.

Scripture is silent on the establishment of the church at Smyrna, but it was most likely begun by the Ephesian church.

Christ identified Himself to this church as "the first and the last, who was dead, and is alive" (v. 8). *Smyrna* means *myrrh* or *bitterness*, a sweet perfume used for embalming the dead—an appropriate reference to Christ's suffering and death. Knowledge of the Lord's suffering was a great comfort to the believers at Smyrna, who were undergoing horrible persecution.

There was no condemnation for this church, only commendation. Christ knew their "works, and tribulation, and poverty" (v. 9). Politically, they suffered persecution from the Roman Empire. Physically, they were fed to lions or set upon by wild dogs, crucified, tarred, burned at the stake, and boiled in oil. The famous Polycarp, Bishop of Smyrna, was burned at the stake in the arena at Rome around 155 A.D.

Economically, they suffered abject poverty as a result of their uncompromising commitment to Christ. They were most likely denied employment. Christian shop owners were boycotted and their homes robbed and vandalized. The Lord could easily relate to their poverty (2 Corinthians 8:9). Yet they were rich (v. 9) in Christ's love, scriptural encouragement, spiritual blessings, and the fruit of the Spirit. Paul's testimony provides a good summary of what the Christians in Smyrna were experiencing: "as poor, yet making many rich; as having nothing, and yet possessing all things" (2 Corinthians 6:10).

Religiously, many in the Jewish community were being used by Satan to blaspheme this church and the Lord. Christ said, "I know the blasphemy of them who say they are Jews, and are not, but are the synagogue of Satan" (v. 9). These people were Jews by birth, but not by faith. They were motivated by Satan to persecute and slander the church.

Satanic persecution caused some of the Smyrna believers to be imprisoned. They were "tried, and...[had] tribulation ten days" (v. 10). Commentators hold three positions on this tribulation:

1. Ten literal days of persecution.

2. Ten major Roman persecutions for the first 250 years of the church.

3. A ten-year persecution through the Emperor Diocletian.

The first position is most likely correct.

The Lord counseled the church not to fear the things they would suffer (v. 10). He assured them that He was in complete control of their circumstances. God sets limits on what Satan can do to believers. He will not allow them to be tried beyond what they are able to bear (1 Corinthians 10:13), and His grace is sufficient to carry them through any trial (2 Corinthians 12:9).

A crown was promised to those who remained faithful: "I will give thee a crown of life" (v. 10). This is the martyr's crown, given to those who are "faithful unto death" (v. 10). Again, John called on the believers to "hear what the Spirit saith unto the churches" (v. 11). The overcomer "shall not be hurt of the second death" (v. 11). No true believer will have to stand before the Great White Throne Judgment and be condemned to the lake of fire, which is the second death (20:11-15).

The Christians in Smyrna underwent crushing persecution, but throughout their experience they displayed great faith in Christ. Poor though they were, they were rich in spiritual blessings. Because of their faithful commitment to Christ, this church lived a victorious life. Christians today who are undergoing trials for their faith can glean encouragement, strength, and comfort from the testimony of this church.

Finally, the readers are challenged to take this message to heart: "He that hath an ear, let him hear what the Spirit saith unto the churches: He that overcometh shall not be hurt of the second death" (v. 11)—those who remained strong in Christ would live forever in Him.

Endnote

1 Steven J. Lawson, *Final Call* (Wheaton, IL: Crossway Books, 1994), p. 69.

REVELATION 2:12-29

And to the angel of the church in Pergamum write: These things saith he who hath the sharp sword with two edges. I know thy works, and where thou dwellest, even where Satan's throne is; and thou holdest fast my name, and hast not denied my faith, even in those days in which Antipas was my faithful martyr, who was slain among you, where Satan dwelleth. But I have a few things against thee, because thou hast there them that hold the doctrine of Balaam, who taught Balak to cast a stumbling block before the children of Israel, to eat things sacrificed unto idols, and to commit fornication. So hast thou also them that hold the doctrine of the Nicolaitans, which thing I hate. Repent, or else I will come unto thee quickly, and will fight against them with the sword of my mouth. He that hath an ear, let him hear what the Spirit saith unto the churches: To him that overcometh will I give to eat of the hidden manna, and will give him a white stone, and in the stone a new name written, which no man knoweth except he that receiveth it.

And unto the angel of the church in Thyatira write: These things saith the Son of God, who hath his eyes like a flame of fire, and his feet are like fine bronze. I know thy works, and love, and service, and faith, and thy patience, and thy works; and the last to be more than the first. Notwithstanding, I have a few things against thee, because thou allowest that woman, Jezebel, who calleth herself a prophetess, to teach and to seduce my servants to commit fornication, and to eat things sacrificed unto idols. And I gave her space to repent of her fornication, and she repented not. Behold, I will cast her into a bed, and them that commit adultery with her into great tribulation, except they repent of their deeds.

And I will kill her children with death; and all the churches shall know that I am he who searcheth the minds and hearts; and I will give unto every one of you according to your works. But unto you I say, and unto the rest in Thyatira, as many as have not this doctrine, and who have not known the depths of Satan, as they speak, I will put upon you no other burden. But that which ye have already, hold fast till I come. And he that overcometh, and keepeth my works unto the end, to him will I give power over the nations; And he shall rule them with a rod of iron; as the vessels of a potter shall they be broken to shivers, even as I received of my Father. And I will give him the morning star. He that hath an ear, let him hear what the Spirit saith unto the churches.

4

THE CHURCH COMPROMISED

" **A** new Decalogue has been adopted by the neo-Christians of our day, 'Thou shalt not disagree,' and a new set of Beatitudes too, 'Blessed are they that tolerate everything, for they shall not be made accountable for anything,' " wrote A. W. Tozer. Such attitudes are *not* new, as Tozer indicated. Compromise has been a cancer in the church from its inception. This is evident in Christ's letters to Pergamum and Thyatira denouncing tolerance of false teachers and heretical doctrine within the church.

Pergamum: The Worldly Church

Pergamum was the capital city of the Roman province in Asia. It was almost 60 miles from Smyrna and 15 miles from the Aegean Sea and had little commerce. The name comes from the word *parchment*, a type of paper. Pergamum was a center of learning, medicine, and religious books, boasting a library of 200,000 volumes. It became the home of many princes, priests, and scholars, who wished to study there. Noted for marble carving, it excelled the other six cities named in Revelation 2 and 3 in architectural beauty.

The city also was noted for its pagan religions and many heathen temples. The great altar dedicated to the chief Greek savior-god, Zeus Olympus, was located in the city, along with an altar to Athena, patron goddess of Athens. Emperor worship was practiced in Pergamum, with its first temple erected in 29 B.C. Citizens were required to burn a pinch of incense at the foot of Caesar's statue, honoring him as a god. Those who refused to do so were immediately arrested and imprisoned. They also worshiped Dionysus, the god of vegetation, and Aesculapius, the god of healing. A medical school was attached to the pagan cult of Aesculapius, and the well-known symbol of the medical profession, a serpent twined around a staff, was its insignia.

John did not reveal when or how the church in Pergamum was established. Most likely Paul or workers from Ephesus started the church. It had been established where "Satan's throne" (v. 13) had been set up; that is, the center of cultic worship. This satanic religious system had been started in Babylon by Semiramis, the wife of Nimrod. Babylon was captured by the Persians in 539 B.C., and they put a stop to this religious system. Soon it found a new home in Pergamum. Through the worship of Caesar, Zeus, Aesculapius, and other pseudo-gods, Satan had firmly established himself in the city.

Scripture indicates that Satan is "the prince of the power of the air" (Ephesians 2:2), "the god of this age" (2 Corinthians 4:4), who goes throughout the world "like a roaring lion...seeking whom he may devour" (1 Peter 5:8).

Satan therefore set up his operation in the center of learning and the healing arts, introduced idolatry, and sought to control peoples' minds through learning, their bodies through healing, and their souls through pagan religion. With the church taking its stand in the midst of Satan's dwelling place, it would only be a matter of time before conflict arose.

Christ revealed Himself as "he who hath the sharp sword with two edges" (v. 12), which refers to His judicial authority. The two-edged sword cuts in any direction. His Word is "sharper than any two-edged sword, piercing even to the dividing asunder of soul and spirit...and is a discerner of the thoughts and intents of the heart" (Hebrews 4:12). Nothing escapes the Lord's sight: All "creature[s]...are naked and opened unto the eyes" of the Lord (Hebrews 4:13), who will judge all people righteously.

The Lord commended the works of these believers who stayed faithful in the midst of such evil (v. 13). He was well aware of the conditions and pressures under which they worked as they lived out their commitment in three ways.

1. They were holding fast to His name (v. 13). There was a remnant of believers who loved the Lord and remained loyal to Him in the shadow of Satan's throne.

2. They had not "denied [His] faith" (v. 13) but were willing to confess explicit faith in Him as the only true God. In so doing, they put their lives on the line in a society controlled by Satan.

3. Christ recognized Antipas, referring to him as "my faithful martyr, who was slain among you, where Satan dwelleth" (v. 13). The name *Antipas* means *against all*. He died standing faithful to the name and doctrine of Christ, which was being opposed by satanically inspired people.

But the Lord had two complaints against the church. First, it tolerated the false "doctrine of Balaam" (v. 14). Balaam was a gifted prophet who prostituted his gift for financial gain and worldly honor. He was hired by Balak, king of Moab, to pronounce a curse on the nation of Israel. Balaam tried to curse Israel but failed on three occasions (Numbers 22:14-21) because of the restraining power of God (Numbers 23-24). Unable to curse Israel, whom God had blessed, Balaam conceived a plan to have the men of Israel enter into mixed marriages with Moabite women, thus producing spiritual compromise (Numbers 22:5; 23:8; 31:15-16). When Satan could not physically destroy the Israelites, he tried to destroy them through union with ungodly neighbors, so that Israel would no longer be separated for the Lord but would be defiled with idolatrous and immoral practices.

Christ mentioned three practices within the doctrine of Balaam that corrupted these believers.

1. Balaam tried to entice them through mixed marriages, corrupting and destroying Christian families.

2. He attempted to entice them "to eat things sacrificed unto idols" (v. 14), thus bringing in contact with idolatry.

3. He enticed them with the sexual sin of fornication, corrupting their moral purity.

These practices were condemned by the first church council in Jerusalem (Acts 15:19-20).

The Lord's second complaint was that the church tolerated "the doctrine of the Nicolaitans, which thing [He] hate[d]" (v. 15). This cult professed faith in Christ but taught antinomianism (freedom to live without moral law) and practiced licentious living. This is a picture of the church married to the world. The church is the bride of Christ and should not be unequally yoked with the dark works of this world's system.

Christ counseled the church to "Repent" (v. 16). True repentance involves three things: contrition of heart, confession of sin, and a change in conduct. He warned them that failure to repent would cause Him to come quickly and "fight against them with the sword of [His] mouth" (v. 16). He would not and will not tolerate compromise within the church by those who try to defile it.

The overcomers or conquerors are promised three things.

1. They will "eat...hidden manna" (v. 17). Christ, who is the "bread of life" (John 6:48) whom the world cannot spiritually see, provides spiritual sustenance for believers throughout eternity.

2. They will be given "a white stone" (v. 17), a symbol of Christ's assurance and acceptance to all who have not succumbed to satanic persecution.

3. They will have "a new name written, which no man knoweth except he that receiveth it" (v. 17), a symbol of the personal and intimate relationship believers will experience with the Lord in heaven.

Believers today must also heed this warning to guard against compromise in morals, false teachers, and heretical doctrine.

Thyatira:
The Doctrinally Defective Church

Thyatira, a small town about 35 miles southeast of Pergamum, was founded by Alexander the Great in 300 B.C. A military city situated in a fertile agricultural valley, it was noted for commerce, trade guilds, and craftsmen specializing in tanning, bronze, pottery, and purple dye. Although the city was not a religious center, emperor worship did exist, and each trade guild worshiped its own god. Christians most likely belonged to trade guilds, which put pressure on them to become involved in pagan worship.

Scripture does not indicate when the church was established. "Lydia, a seller of purple, of the city of Thyatira," came to the Lord under Paul's ministry in Philippi (Acts 16:14-15) and may have helped establish the church. This church, although located in the smallest city mentioned in Revelation 2 and 3, received the longest letter.

Christ described Himself as "the Son of God, who hath his eyes like a flame of fire, and his feet are like fine bronze" (v. 18). The title "Son of God" (used by the Lord only in this verse in Revelation) emphasized His deity to a city that worshiped the sun god. The words "eyes" and "feet" speak of His indignation and judgment, as mentioned in chapter 1 (cp. 1:14-15).

In verse 19, the Lord commended the church for four works:

1. Their love for Christ—not mentioned in the letters to the other churches.

2. Their service—sacrificially reaching out to others.

3. Their faith—a small group within the church was faithful and loyal to the Lord.

4. Their patience or endurance under trial—the church was not standing still but was growing and developing in its ministry, for its last works were "more than the first" (v. 19).

The Lord did, however, express major complaints against the church because they allowed "that woman, Jezebel, who calleth herself a prophetess, to teach" (v. 20). This speaks of a woman in the church whose teaching corrupted God's people, as did the Jezebel of old. Jezebel was the Phoenician princess who, after marrying King Ahab, brought Baal worship to Israel (1 Kings 16-19). This self-proclaimed prophetess counseled Christians within the church to become involved in the Roman religious practice of "fornication, and to eat things sacrificed unto idols" (v. 20). As previously mentioned, Christian workers were expected to join the trade guilds in Thyatira, where many of these immoralities were commonly practiced. Failure to participate meant losing one's livelihood and being blackballed from a trade.

Christ counseled the prophetess to repent: "And I gave her space to repent of her fornication, and she repented not" (v. 21). He patiently waited for repentance to come, but still the woman declined. God therefore brought three judgments upon her and her followers.

1. He would cast "her into a bed" (v. 22)—from her bed of immorality into a sickbed of disease and eventual death.

2. Those who "commit adultery with her" would suffer "great tribulation, except they repent" (v. 22). Following after the pseudo-teachings of this woman meant great suffering and ultimate death.

3. "I will kill her children with death [pestilence]" (v. 23). All of her followers, both the original followers and a second generation of professing believers, would suffer the same fate. Their doom left no doubt for the church that this judgment was from God: "and all the churches shall know that I am he who...will give unto every one of you according to your works" (v. 23).

The "rest in Thyatira" (the faithful remnant), who did not embrace this doctrine that had its origin in Satan's deep secrets, would not have any further burden of responsibility placed upon them from the Lord (v. 24). The Lord encouraged them not to leave the church but to "hold fast" (stand for truth without compromise) until He comes for the church (v. 25).

Two promises were made to the conquerors or overcomers who would faithfully keep Christ's works unto the end:

1. They will be given "power over the nations" (v. 26). The overcomers would be given authority to rule over the nations in the Millennium, sharing the privilege granted to Christ (Psalm 2:7-9) by God the Father (v. 27). The word "rule" in verse 27 means *to shepherd*. Believers will not only execute judgment but will administer mercy, direction, and protection to the nations during the Kingdom age.

2. They will be given "the morning star" (v. 28; cp. 22:16)—Jesus, who has given Himself to believers. The morning star shines brightly over the dark earth just before dawn. At the Rapture, Christ will appear over this dark world to take believers away before the Tribulation and will reappear to usher in the dawn of the Millennium.

Christ closed His letter to Thyatira as He did the others: "He that hath an ear, let him hear what the Spirit saith unto the churches" (v. 29).

REVELATION 3:1-13

And unto the angel of the church in Sardis write: These things saith he that hath the seven spirits of God, and the seven stars. I know thy works, that thou hast a name that thou livest, and art dead. Be watchful, and strengthen the things which remain, that are ready to die; for I have not found thy works perfect before God. Remember, therefore, how thou hast received and heard, and hold fast, and repent. If, therefore, thou shalt not watch, I will come on thee as a thief, and thou shalt not know what hour I will come upon thee. Thou hast a few names even in Sardis that have not defiled their garments, and they shall walk with me in white; for they are worthy. He that overcometh, the same shall be clothed in white raiment; and I will not blot his name out of the book of life, but I will confess his name before my Father, and before his angels. He that hath an ear, let him hear what the Spirit saith unto the churches.

And to the angel of the church in Philadelphia write: These things saith he that is holy, he that is true, he that hath the key of David, he that openeth, and no man shutteth; and shutteth, and no man openeth. I know thy works; behold, I have set before thee an open door, and no man can shut it; for thou hast a little strength, and hast kept my word, and hast not denied my name. Behold, I will make them of the synagogue of Satan, who say they are Jews, and are not, but do lie; behold, I will make them to come and worship before thy feet, and to know that I have loved thee. Because thou hast kept the word of my patience, I also will keep thee from the hour of temptation, which shall come upon all the world, to try them that dwell upon the earth. Behold, I come quickly; hold that fast which thou hast, that no man take thy crown. He that overcometh will I make a pillar in the temple of my God, and he shall go no more out; and I will write upon him the name of my God, and the name of the city of my God, the new Jerusalem, which cometh down out of heaven from my God; and I will write upon him my new name. He that hath an ear, let him hear what the Spirit saith unto the churches.

5

THE CHURCH
IN CRISES AND COMMITMENT

It has been said that many churches begin with a man, reach out with a mission, become a movement, and eventually end up a monument. The church at Sardis was spiritually dead and did end up as a monument, but the church at Philadelphia was spiritually alive and ministered for centuries. Both of these churches have an important message for us today.

Sardis: The Spiritually Dead Church

The city of Sardis was 30 miles southeast of Thyatira, the capital of the Lydian kingdom. It stood about 1,500 feet above the Hermus valley, giving the city a false sense of security over its enemies. Sardis was twice defeated—once by King Cyrus of Persia (549 B.C.) and again by Antiochus III of Syria (218 B.C.).

One thousand feet above the plains stood an impressive acropolis that housed a temple dedicated to the goddess Artemis. The worshipers of Artemis were a nature cult, dating back to the fourth century B.C. The city was noted for its impressive necropolis and the hundreds of burial mounds dotting its landscape.

Sardis was situated on five major trade routes running through Lydia. This brought great wealth to the city, which was acquired through the creation and sale of jewelry, wool, and the textile dying industry. But by the second century A.D., Sardis lay in decay, near death, only a shadow of its former glory. Today Sardis is a small village called Sart. When and how the church there was started are unknown.

Christ revealed Himself to this church as the one who "hath the seven spirits of God" (v. 1), a reference to the sevenfold fullness and perfection of the Holy Spirit that rested upon Christ (1:4; 5:6; cp. Isaiah 11:2-5). He also controls the "seven stars" (v. 1) or spiritual leaders of these churches. They are in His hand, and each will be held accountable to Him for his church's spiritual life and service. Spiritual life or deadness within the church is often governed by the spiritual life of its leadership.

The Lord gave no commendation to this church, only criticism: "I know thy works, that thou hast a name that thou livest, and art dead" (v. 1). Sardis had the look of life and a reputation for religious activity, but it lacked evidence of spiritual life. Many modern-day churches live on the spiritual reputation of days gone by but have been spiritually dead for years.

Christ counseled this church to seek spiritual healing.

- They were to "Be watchful" (v. 2), or wake up to their spiritual state. Renewal would come by recalling their original commitment and radically reversing their current conduct.

- They were to "strengthen the things which remain, that are ready to die" (v. 2). This could be done by removing false doctrine, carnal leadership, unbiblical practices, and meaningless activity. Spiritual strength is produced by getting back to the basics, spending time in God's Word and in prayer.

- The Lord called them to "Remember, therefore,
  how thou hast received and heard, and hold fast,
  and repent" (v. 3). They were to embrace the
  fundamental doctrines of the faith and repent of
  their spiritual emptiness. Failure to comply
  would bring judgment from the Lord, who would
  come upon them "as a thief," and they would
  "not know [the] hour" (v. 3) of His appearing.
  Often the Lord removes a spiritually dead church
  rather than let it continue to infect others with its
  decadence.

- The Lord made special mention of those who had
  not compromised their faith: "Thou hast a few
  names even in Sardis that have not defiled their
  garments" (v. 4). The pagan religion of Sardis for-
  bade its followers to come before the gods in garments that were stained or soiled. Those who did
  so were removed from the public ledger as citizens of Sardis.[1] Christians who soiled their garments were seen as mingling with the pagan life of
  the city and compromising with sin. Those not
  defiling their garments would "walk with [the
  Lord] in white; for they are worthy" (v. 4). They
  had gone before their God in a state of cleanliness.

Three promises were made to the conqueror:

1. "He that overcometh, the same shall be clothed
   in white raiment" (v. 5). White raiment is a symbol of purity and righteousness, the garment of
   salvation. It was symbolic of the faithful remnant that had gained spiritual victory over the
   paganism of Sardis. At the "marriage of the
   Lamb" (19:7-8), all believers will be arrayed in
   fine linen and will return to the earth with the
   Lord clothed in those garments (19:14).

2. The overcomer is recorded in the divine register: "I will not blot his name out of the book of life" (v. 5). In biblical times, the names of individuals were recorded in the city register, and after their death or departure from the city, they were erased or marked out of the book of the living.[2] The possibility of losing salvation is not mentioned here. Rather, this is an affirmation that those who are born again possess eternal life, and no person or thing can ever separate Christians from eternal life.

3. The Lord will declare the believer's name before heaven: "I will confess his name before my Father, and before his angels" (v. 5). This promises believers the assurance of eternal citizenship. Christ is their advocate before God the Father (1 John 2:1) and will acknowledge their names to the Father (cp. Matthew 10:32).

Once again, Christ challenged the readers to hear and heed His message: "He that hath an ear, let him hear what the Spirit saith unto the churches" (v. 6). This warning was especially significant to a spiritually dead church like Sardis.

Philadelphia:
The Spiritually Alive Church

The city of Philadelphia was located in the Hermus River valley about 28 miles southeast of Sardis. Founded by King Attalus of Pergamum (140 B.C.), the city transmitted the Greek language and culture to Lydia and Phrygia. It was built on a volcanic mountain range (900 feet high); thus, the city experienced many earthquakes. An earthquake in 17 A.D. destroyed Philadelphia, but it was rebuilt by Emperor Tiberius. The city prospered due to its location and its rich fertile valley. Along with its large grape industry, Philadelphia was noted for textiles and leather goods. Its high position between the coastal plains and the interior of Asia Minor made Philadelphia a strong fortress city. Because of this height and the major highways running through the city, it became an Imperial Post of the Roman Empire called "the gateway to the East." Dionysus was the major pagan god. In the fifth century, the city was nicknamed "Little Athens" because of its many festivals and pagan cults.

When and how the church at Philadelphia was established are unknown, but it prospered for many centuries, long after the area had succumbed to Islamic control. The word *Philadelphia* means *brotherly love* and is emblematic of this church.

Christ presented Himself in three ways to Philadelphia.

1. He is "holy" (v. 7). As God, Christ is holy, entirely set apart and separated from sin and sinners. Holiness is the foremost attribute of Christ because it pervades all the attributes of God and is consistent with who He is and what He does. Holiness points to Christ's majestic purity or ethical majesty.[3]

2. He is "true" (v. 7). Christ is the true God, distinct from all others. What He says is "the truth" (John 14:6), and His Word of revelation is without error. It is reliable and trustworthy. He is the source of all knowledge and truth in the universe.

3. He is the one "that hath the key of David, he that openeth, and no man shutteth; and shutteth, and no man openeth" (v. 7). The imagery of the "key of David" is mentioned in the context of Isaiah 22:20-22. Eliakim, who had replaced unfaithful Shebna as King Hezekiah's steward, was given authority over the king's house and his treasury. The key represents authority and power over the

Davidic house and kingdom. No one could reverse what Eliakim opened or shut. In like manner, Christ—who is holy, true, and of the Davidic line—possesses absolute authority to administer the spiritual and material affairs of God's kingdom.

The Lord commended the church at Philadelphia for its good works. Although they had only "a little strength," the Lord said that they "kept [His] word, and hast not denied [His] name" (v. 8). Numerically, the church was not very strong, but God had infused this faithful group with spiritual power enabling them to be true to His name in the midst of satanic opposition. Because of their faithfulness, the Lord "set before [them] an open door, and no man can shut it" (v. 8). This church had an open door for evangelizing the surrounding region because of its commitment and strategic location. God does not need naturally gifted vessels for His service (1 Corinthians 1:26-29), but yielded people through whom He can minister (2 Corinthians 4:7). Effective service does not depend upon the size of a church but upon its availability to be used.

Like the church in Smyrna, the Philadelphians were being persecuted by the "synagogue of Satan" (v. 9), but they overcame the intrusion of legalistic opposition and defeated Satan's effort to corrupt the church. They were told that the day would come when their enemies would "worship before [their] feet" (v. 9), an act symbolic of a defeated foe. Also, their enemies would come to know of Christ's great love for these believers (v. 9; cp. Ephesians 5:25).

The Lord gave this church a promise of protection: "Because thou hast kept the word of my patience, I also will keep thee from [out of] the hour of temptation, which shall come upon all the world, to try them that dwell upon the earth" (v. 10). Many people teach that the church will go through a portion or all of the Tribulation mentioned in Revelation 6-19, but the language of this verse makes it clear that the church will not go into the Tribulation. This *hour of trial* will be a time when God's wrath will be poured out upon the world. Several things verify this fact.

1. The preposition *from* (Gr., *ek*) means *out of*; that is, *out of the midst of*, a clear indication that the church will not go through any portion of the Tribulation. If the writer meant to say that the church was going *through* tribulation, he could have used a different Greek preposition, *dia*.

2. This is not just any trial, but *the hour of trial*, a specific season of Tribulation that is coming.

3. Christ promised to "keep" (protect or preserve) the church, not *in*, but *from* this season of trial.

4. Protection is granted to all believers, not just the Philadelphia church, because this time of Tribulation will come "upon all the world."

5. The phrase "to try them that dwell upon the earth" refers, not to the church, but to unbelievers who will be settled into the world's system during the Tribulation.

The Lord provided counsel to this church: "Behold, I come quickly [suddenly]; hold that fast which thou hast, that no man take thy crown" (v. 11). Those in the church were to remain faithful, rather than give in to their enemies, so that they would not lose their reward at the Bema Judgment (1 Corinthians 3:15; 2 Corinthians 5:10).

Two promises are given to the conqueror.

1. He is promised security: "Him...will I make a pillar in the temple of my God, and he shall go no more out" (v. 12). This statement was very meaningful to people who experienced frequent earthquakes. A pillar in the temple of God symbolizes salvation, spiritual stability, and the eter-

nal security of never being separated from the shelter of God's presence.

2. The signature of God will be inscribed upon him: "I will write upon him the name of my God, and the name of the city of my God, the new Jerusalem...and...my new name" (v. 12). These names inscribed upon individuals signify total identification with God and ensure them an eternal place in His kingdom.

Is your ear open to what the Spirit said to this church (v. 13)? Are you keeping God's Word, standing for His name, enduring tribulation, and walking through the open door of service?

Endnotes

1 Alan F. Johnson, *The Expositor's Bible Commentary, Revelation* (Grand Rapids: Zondervan Publishing House, 1981), vol. XII, p. 449.

2 *Ibid.*

3 Paul Enns, *The Moody Handbook of Theology* (Chicago: Moody Press, 1989), pp. 192-193).

REVELATION 3:14-22

And unto the angel of the church of the Laodiceans write: These things saith the Amen, the faithful and true witness, the beginning of the creation of God. I know thy works, that thou art neither cold nor hot; I would thou wert cold or hot. So, then, because thou art lukewarm, and neither cold nor hot, I will spew thee out of my mouth. Because thou sayest, I am rich, and increased with goods, and have need of nothing, and knowest not that thou art wretched, and miserable, and poor, and blind, and naked, I counsel thee to buy of me gold tried in the fire, that thou mayest be rich; and white raiment, that thou mayest be clothed, and that the shame of thy nakedness do not appear; and anoint thine eyes with salve, that thou mayest see. As many as I love, I rebuke and chasten; be zealous, therefore, and repent. Behold, I stand at the door, and knock; if any man hear my voice, and open the door, I will come in to him, and will sup with him, and he with me. To him that overcometh will I grant to sit with me in my throne, even as I also overcame, and am set down with my Father in his throne. He that hath an ear, let him hear what the Spirit saith unto the churches.

6

THE COMPLACENT CHURCH

The city of Laodicea was located in a fertile valley overlooking the Lycus River about 50 miles southeast of Philadelphia and 11 miles from Colosse. Laodicea was established by Antiochus II (264-261 B.C.). Named in honor of his wife Laodice, it was destined to become the capital of ancient Phrygia.

Its strategic location on a major trade route running from Ephesus to Syria enabled Laodicea to accumulate great wealth. The area was a well-known banking and money-changing center that even minted its own coins. The manufacture of expensive cloth made from a glossy black wool added to the city's wealth. Its medical school became famous for the development of an eye salve made from Phrygia powder (collyrium) that was used in the treatment of eye diseases worldwide. Laodicea was so wealthy that when a massive earthquake destroyed the city in 60 A.D., it refused aid from Rome and rebuilt at its own expense.

Antiochus the Great (III) settled two thousand Jewish families in Phrygia and Lydia after deporting them from Babylon. Although they were forbidden to send money to Jerusalem, the city magistrates did allow Jews the freedom of worship.[1]

Scripture gives no indication of when or how the church was established. Most scholars believe it was started by Epaphras (Colossians 1:7; 4:12-13). Although Paul gave no evidence of visiting Laodicea, he was aware of their spiritual struggles (Colossians 2:1) and sent greetings to the church (Colossians 4:15). He also requested that the Colossian epistle be read in the church at Laodicea (Colossians 4:16).

Christ Presented

Christ used three appositions to describe Himself to the Laodicean church.

1. He called Himself "the Amen" (v. 14). *Amen* comes from a Hebrew root word that means *certainty* or *truth*. It is often translated "so let it be" or "truly." Isaiah spoke of God as "the God of truth [lit., Amen]" (Isaiah 65:16), or the one who will keep and bring His covenant promises to pass. This title confirms Christ's absolute verity. He is "the truth" (John 14:6) and the divine standard by which all truth is measured. Therefore, what He says about this church and all churches is absolutely trustworthy and reliable (cp. 2 Corinthians 1:20).

2. He is "the faithful and true witness" (v. 14). Christ was faithful during His wilderness temptation (Matthew 4:1-11), in witnessing the truth to people of His day, and in enduring suffering and death on the cross (Philippians 2:8). Christ's comments to this church about their spiritual condition were not diluted, distorted, or double-tongued. His diagnosis was correct.

3. He is "the beginning of the creation of God" (v. 14). There is no hint in this statement, as some

maintain, that Christ was the first creature created by God, for He is the eternal Lord. The word
beginning refers to Christ's being the source of
all creation (cp. 21:6). Christ is the creator and
owner of all things, a truth that was well established in Paul's letter to the Colossians (1:15-
17)—a sober reminder to a church that neglected
to give God credit for their prosperity while
boasting of their wealth (v. 17).

Christ's Pronouncement

The Lord had no commendation for the Laodicean church but
severely censured and condemned its spiritual condition. Christ
said, "I know thy works, that thou art neither cold nor hot; I
would thou wert cold or hot" (v. 15). The Lord found some good
works in each of the other churches mentioned in Revelation, but
not one good work in this church.

They were not cold, referring to people lacking salvation,
untouched and unresponsive toward spiritual things. Nor were
they hot (boiling), referring to true believers who had received
Jesus as Savior and showed spiritual fervor in their Christian service. Christ described them as "lukewarm" (v. 16).

The word *lukewarm* also described the water supply of
Laodicea. Because the city lacked an adequate supply of good
water, it had to be piped through a system of aqueducts from the
cool springs of Colosse and the hot springs of Hierapolis. By the
time the water reached Laodicea, it was lukewarm, tepid to the
taste, and unfit to drink. Spiritually speaking, a lukewarm person
is tepid, lacking enthusiasm, halfhearted about what he or she
believes. A lukewarm person may possess some sense of duty to
the church but lacks true conviction and commitment.

Is a lukewarm person a believer? Some hold that the word
refers to carnal believers who were once fervent in their commit-

ment and witnessing for Christ but, because of sin and worldly influence, had become less fervent in their love and service for Him. Others maintain that the word refers to people who are not believers (cold) but who *profess* faith in Christ (warm) yet do not *possess* true salvation. Still others believe that lukewarm people are both of the above. Christ's words, along with the tenor of this passage, seem to teach that lukewarm people are not believers. Such people come to church, enjoy the worship and fellowship because they fill a need in their lives, but remain unregenerate. A lukewarm church is obnoxious and nauseating to Christ. He will "spew" it out of His mouth (v. 16), an act symbolic of rejection or being cut off by God (cp. Matthew 7:21-23).

The Lord revealed that wealth and worldliness had lulled this church into an attitude of self-sufficiency and self-satisfaction, producing a spirit of smug complacency. The church believed itself to be "rich, and increased with goods, and hav[ing] need of nothing" (v. 17). Such self-confidence showed a lack of true spiritual perception, which led this church to self-deception concerning its spiritual condition. In today's terminology, this church possessed a magnificent facility in which to worship, state-of-the-art equipment for ministry, a well-clothed and polished congregation that prided itself in having wealth enough to meet all its needs and wants, and a highly paid pastoral staff.

Christ revealed the true spiritual condition of this church as wanting. He saw them as "wretched" (v. 17); that is, oppressed with a burden. Wealth can become a burden to those who possess it. Paul warned that wealth can bring a snare and sorrow, not satisfaction (1 Timothy 6:9). Jesus said, "Ye cannot serve God and money" (Matthew 6:24). He saw this church as "miserable" (pitiful, v. 17). A complacent church is a pitiful sight within any community. He saw the church as "poor" (beggarly, v. 17). Although wealthy in financial and material gain, the church was spiritually bankrupt. What a contrast to the church at Smyrna, who, for the sake of Christ, was poor in this world's goods but rich spiritually. He saw the church as "blind" (nearsighted, v. 17). Wealth and materialism can blind the mind, leaving people self-deceived concerning their true spiritual condition—an irony for a city noted worldwide for producing the best remedy for treating eye diseases. He saw the church in Laodicea as "naked" (v. 17). Although they produced costly garments for others, they were spiritually naked, not clothed in the white garments of righteousness. Their spiritual poverty, blindness, and nakedness made them wretched and miserable.

Christ's Proposal

Christ counseled this church in three ways.

1. He told them to acquire spiritual riches: "buy of me gold tried in the fire, that thou mayest be rich" (v. 18). True riches are found in Christ, not in material wealth. The church needed to acquire true faith by receiving the Lord. Gold is an emblem of faith; those who possess it acquire true spiritual riches resulting in lives that glorify and honor the Lord. It must be noted that salvation cannot be purchased. In this context, to *buy* means to acquire the priceless treasure of salvation through faith in Christ (cp. Isaiah 55:1).

2. They needed to be clothed in "white raiment" so that their "nakedness" would be covered (v. 18). White raiment speaks of Christ's holiness and righteousness, which clothes all true believers, making them acceptable in God's sight.

3. The church needed its spiritual blindness healed with the salve of salvation applied by Christ, so that they could see to walk properly before Him.

Christ rebuked and chastened the lukewarm church because of His love for it (v. 19). The purpose of His chastening was to bring them to repentance. He commanded them to "be zealous...and repent" (v. 19). He wanted them to be convicted of their ways and show an enthusiastic desire to repent.

Christ's Presence

From the church that had shut Him out, Christ requested permission to enter: "Behold, I stand at the door, and knock; if any man hear my voice, and open the door, I will come in to him" (v. 20). There was still time for professing Christians to receive Christ. The point is clear: When the Lord calls a church to fervent commitment, He does so by dealing with individuals. Often the dedication of one person filled with enthusiasm for the Lord will spark revival within a church.

At Keble College in Oxford, England, there hangs a portrait of Christ entitled "The Light of the World." The painting was rendered by William Holman Hunt in 1854. Christ is pictured knocking at a door with a lantern in His hand, His hair wet with the dew of the night, anticipating that someone will answer the door. Upon finishing the painting, Hunt invited His friends to view his work. Immediately it was noticed that Hunt had forgotten to put a handle on the outside of the door. Confronted by the obvious error, Hunt replied, "True, if this were an ordinary door; but this is not an ordinary door, it is a picture of the sinner's heart and Christ is knocking, seeking admission. The handle is on the inside, for Christ cannot enter the human heart unless it is opened from the inside." Christ does not force His way or will upon the life of any individual or church. Rather, He knocks, waiting to be invited in for fellowship. The portrayal of Christ outside the door of His own church seeking entrance seems unbelievable, but it is true.

A person who opens the door of his or her heart will experience rich spiritual blessings from the Savior: "I will come in to him, and will sup with him, and he with me" (v. 20). Notice the contrast: The one who refuses His invitation is vomited out, but the one who voluntarily receives His invitation will enjoy supping with Him. The time of supping mentioned here is the main meal of the day, when families gather for intimate fellowship with each other and close friends.[2] People who have invited Christ into their lives will enjoy intimate fellowship with Him. They will feast on the spiritual food that only the Lord can supply.

Christ's Promise

To the conqueror Christ promised, "To him that overcometh will I grant to sit with me in my throne, even as I also overcame, and am set down with my Father in his throne" (v. 21). Overcoming believers will share the throne of their overcomer, the Lord Jesus Christ.[3] Jesus overcame the world through suffering and death (John 16:33) and is now seated at the right hand of God the Father (Mark 16:19). A joint reign with Christ is mentioned a number of times throughout Revelation (1:6, 9; 2:26-27; 5:10; 20:4-6). Christ has promised His disciples that they will eat and drink at His table in the Kingdom. All believers are joint heirs with Christ (Romans 8:17). During the Millennium, Christ will establish His throne on the earth (Matthew 25:31; Luke 1:32), and all believers will reign with Him for a thousand years (20:6). Can there be any greater reward than this?

Once again the Lord concluded His message with a command for the church to listen: "He that hath an ear, let him hear what the Spirit saith unto the churches" (v. 22). Although grace has its limits, the day of grace has not ended. There is still time for lukewarm people to invite Christ into their hearts.

In her hymn, "Let Jesus Come Into Your Heart," Mrs. Lelia Morris penned an appropriate response to those who are tired of the load of their sin and desire a new life to begin. She wrote,

> Just now, your doubtings give o'er;
> Just now, reject Him no more;
> Just now, throw open the door;
> Let Jesus come into your heart.

Endnotes

[1] William White, Jr., *The Zondervan Pictorial Encyclopedia of the Bible*, *Laodicea* (Grand Rapids: Zondervan Publishing House, 1976), vol. III, p. 877.

[2] Alan F. Johnson, *The Expositor's Bible Commentary*, *Revelation* (Grand Rapids: Zondervan Publishing House, 1981), vol. XII, p. 459.

[3] Walter M. Dunnett, *Lord of the Churches*, *Moody Manna* (Chicago: Moody Press, 1966), part II, p. 30.

REVELATION 4:1-11

After this I looked and, behold, a door was opened in heaven; and the first voice that I heard was, as it were, of a trumpet talking with me; which said, Come up here, and I will show thee things which must be hereafter. And immediately I was in the Spirit and, behold, a throne was set in heaven, and one sat on the throne. And he that sat was to look upon like a jasper and a sardius stone; and there was a rainbow round about the throne, in sight like an emerald. And round about the throne were four and twenty thrones, and upon the thrones I saw four and twenty elders sitting, clothed in white raiment; and they had on their heads crowns of gold. And out of the throne proceeded lightnings and thunderclaps, and voices; and there were seven lamps of fire burning before the throne, which are the seven spirits of God. And before the throne there was a sea of glass like crystal; and in the midst of the throne, and round about the throne, were four living creatures full of eyes in front and behind. And the first living creature was like a lion, and the second living creature like a calf, and the third living creature had a face like a man, and the fourth living creature was like a flying eagle. And the four living creatures had each of them six wings about him, and they were full of eyes within; and they rest not day and night, saying, Holy, holy, holy, Lord God Almighty, who was, and is, and is to come. And when those living creatures give glory and honor and thanks to him that is seated on the throne, who liveth forever and ever, The four and twenty elders fall down before him that is seated on the throne, and worship him that liveth forever and ever, and cast their crowns before the throne, saying, Thou art worthy, O Lord, to receive glory and honor and power; for thou hast created all things, and for thy pleasure they are and were created.

7

GOD'S THRONE REVEALED

Questions about heaven are always at the center of a believer's thinking, especially questions dealing with the appearance of and activities in heaven. Through the eyes of John, believers are permitted a gaze on the awe-inspiring spiritual realities surrounding God and His throne. In Revelation 4, the apostle tried to put into words the indescribable glory he saw in heaven.

A brief review is necessary to understand the setting of Revelation 4. In Revelation 1, John received a vision of the glorified Christ, called "the things which thou hast seen" (1:19). In Revelation 2 and 3, Christ revealed His final message to the church on earth, called "the things which are" (1:19). Beginning with Revelation 4, John received a second vision unveiling future events that make up the third division of this book (chps. 4-22), appropriately identified as "the things which shall be hereafter" (1:19).

The words "After this" (v. 1), meaning *after these things*, indicate that this is a new division in Revelation. The second mention of "things which must be hereafter" (v. 1) differs in function from the first. It places the fulfillment of prophecies mentioned in Revelation 4-22 after the church age. This interpretation is supported by the following reasons:

1. The word *church* is not used in this section (chps. 4-18) about the Tribulation period.

2. There is no indication that the events mentioned during the Tribulation have any literal fulfillment in the church age.

3. There is evidence in this section that the church is already in heaven when the Tribulation prophecies are being fulfilled.

Christ promised that the church would be kept from going into or through any portion of the Tribulation that is to come upon the entire earth (3:10). Therefore, it is reasonable to conclude that the church will be removed from the earth before the events that "must be hereafter" occur.

Summoned to Heaven

John said, "I looked and, behold, a door was opened in heaven; and the first voice that I heard was, as it were, of a trumpet talking with me; which said, Come up here" (v. 1). The word *behold* draws the reader's attention to a specific door that was opened in heaven to provide access for John. The voice is that of Christ (cp. 1:8, 10-11), who summoned John before God's throne. "Immediately" the apostle "was in the Spirit" (v. 2) and saw a throne set in heaven.

Was John caught up bodily, or only in his spirit? Most likely the Holy Spirit took possession of John's senses. He was caught up into heaven and could hear and see what was happening before God's throne, although he was physically on the earth.

Scene in Heaven

Instantly John saw "a throne...set in heaven" (v. 2).
Central to everything happening in chapters 4 and 5 is God's
throne. What the apostle saw is organized around four prepo-
sitional phrases: "*on* the throne" (v. 2), "*round* about the
throne" (vv. 3-4), "*out of* the throne" (v. 5), and "*before* the
throne" (v. 6). John, speaking in symbolic language, provided a sevenfold description of God's throne and the activities
surrounding it.

First, John saw the sovereign God of the universe sitting
"on the throne" (v. 2). This must be God the Father, for Christ
took the scroll (5:7) from the right hand (5:1) of the one seated
on the throne. John gave no anthropomorphic description of
the one sitting on the throne. He could not do so because God
the Father is Spirit and does not possess a body as we know it.
John saw no form because no one has seen God at any time
(John 1:18; cp. Exodus 33:20). He simply reported, "he that sat
was to look upon like a jasper and a sardius stone" (v. 3). The
jasper stone is similar to a brilliant diamond, and the sardius
stone is similar to a blood-red ruby. John saw a sparkling light
like that of a blue-white diamond mingled with the bright light
from a blood-red stone like a ruby, producing a flashing blaze
of glorious color.

Second, surrounding the throne was "a rainbow" that looked
"like an emerald" (v. 3). This was not a multicolored bow, an
atmospheric condition such as we see today. The rainbow symbolizes God's mercy, grace, and covenant promises in the midst
of divine judgment (cp. Genesis 9:13).

Third, John saw a "sea of glass like crystal" (v. 6) before
the throne. The sea of glass functioned as a mirror, reflecting
the many brilliant colors flashing from God's throne. No
meaning is given for the sea of glass. Some commentators
have tied its symbolic meaning to the laver (a large basin used

for ceremonial cleansing in the Tabernacle and Temple), but such typology seems fanciful. Others teach that it symbolizes peace in heaven compared with turbulence on the earth—again, highly doubtful. Most likely the sea of glass, reflecting the glory and majesty of God, is symbolic of His purity, holiness, and separation from creation.

Fourth, John heard and saw, proceeding from God's throne, "lightnings and thunderclaps, and voices" (v. 5). These are symbolic of the awesomeness of God's presence and divine power (cp. Exodus 19:16). Throughout Revelation, these sights and sounds signal the rising storm of God's wrathful judgment to be poured out on a sinful world (8:5; 11:19; 16:18).

Fifth, John saw "seven lamps of fire burning before the throne, which are the seven spirits of God" (v. 5). These were not the lampstands already mentioned (1:12, 20), but torches blazing perpetually before the throne of God, representing the Holy Spirit in His fullness and perfection. Although the Holy Spirit has no physical form, He was often manifested in various forms throughout the New Testament. At Jesus' baptism, He descended upon Him like a dove (Matthew 3:16). At Pentecost, He appeared as cloven tongues of fire (Acts 2:3) sitting on each person in the upper room. Here the Spirit is symbolized by blazing torches of fire, representing God's wrath and judgment ready to be poured out on the ungodly.

Sixth, John saw "four and twenty elders sitting" around the throne, "clothed in white raiment; and they had on their heads crowns of gold" (v. 4). Scholars differ on whether these elders are angels, church saints, or representatives of Israel and the church. Many believe the elders are angels, based on a variant reading of the Greek text in Revelation 5:9-10. (For an in-depth description of this position, see Dr. Renald Showers, *Those Invisible Spirits Called Angels* [Bellmawr, NJ: The Friends of Israel Gospel Ministry, Inc., 1997], pp. 38-42).

To say that a portion of the elders represents Israel does not seem to be a correct interpretation. The elders are pictured in their glorified bodies before God's throne while the Great Tribulation is taking place on the earth. Scripture teaches that the redeemed in Israel will be resurrected after the Great Tribulation (Daniel 12:12-13), just before Christ's return to the earth. There are clues within the text that seem to indicate that the 24 elders represent the church:

- There is no mention of the church on the earth during the Tribulation.

- The term *elder* is used frequently throughout the New Testament for leaders in the church.

- The elders are clothed in "white raiment" (v. 4), the garments worn by the church saints in heaven (19:8).

- They are wearing "crowns [Gr. *stephanos*] of gold" (v. 4), a victor's crown, symbolic of honor and reward.

- The crowns and the white raiment give evidence that the elders have already been judged and rewarded by Christ. This is not applicable to angels or Old Testament believers.

- There is a distinction made between the angels, Tribulation saints (Jewish and Gentile), and the elders in Revelation 7:11, 14.

- The elders are pictured in heaven while the Great Tribulation is taking place on the earth (7:13-14). David divided the Levitical priesthood into 24 courses (1 Chronicles 24) to represent the complete priesthood. In like manner, the 24 elders stand for the completed church, which is identified in Scripture as "a royal priesthood" (1 Peter 2:9).

Seventh, John saw "in the midst of the throne, and round about the throne...four living creatures [beings]" (v. 6). These creatures looked like a lion, a calf, a man, and a flying eagle. Each was full of eyes in front, behind, and within, and each had six wings. They praised God continually, day and night, without rest (vv. 6-8). These living creatures are mentioned several times in Revelation (4:9; 5:8, 11, 14; 6:1).

Scholars are divided on who and what the living creatures represent. Some see them as angels. Others believe they may represent the attributes of God: majesty, strength, intelligence, and divine vigilance. Still others see them as reflecting four aspects of Christ's ministry in the Gospels. In addition, some see them as representing Israel during their wilderness wandering. Four of the tribes, whose tents were pitched in order around the Tabernacle, had the same symbols on their banners: Judah, a lion; Ephraim, an ox; Reuben, a man; and Dan, an eagle (Numbers 2:2). The most reasonable view is that John saw some type of angelic beings, although they do not seem to be "angels" (5:11). Such living creatures were seen by Ezekiel (Ezekiel 1:5-14), and he called them cherubim (Ezekiel 10:14-22). They are also similar to the seraphim mentioned in Isaiah 6:2-3. Angels vary greatly in appearance. Most likely these living creatures are of some order of angels whose sole function is to give attention to God. They are in a position of watchfulness (nothing is hidden from their sight) to guard God's throne and are swift (six wings) to execute His will and work. They praise God day and night, honoring His purity, power, and preeminence.

Songs in Heaven

John heard two songs being sung by the host of heaven. The first was sung by the "four living creatures," who acknowledged God's worthiness. They acknowledged His purity, singing, "Holy, holy, holy" (v. 8). This threefold adoration suggests praise to the triune God—Father, Son, and Holy Spirit (cp. Isaiah 6:3)—whose nature is separate from sin. They acknowledged God's power by singing "Lord God Almighty" (v. 8). He is the omnipotent sovereign of the universe. They acknowledged His perpetuity: "who was, and is, and is to come" (v. 8). He is the eternal God who stands above time and space, having no beginning or end, no past or future—everything is in the present tense to Him. They gave God perpetual praise—"glory and honor and thanks" (v. 9)—for His divine attributes and worthiness.

The second song was sung by the "four and twenty elders" (v. 10), who acknowledged not only God's worthiness, but also His works in creation. The 24 elders praised God whenever the four living beings praised Him. They were submissive to God as sovereign of the universe. They "fall down before him that is seated on the throne" (v. 10). They worshiped Him in two ways.

1. They "cast their crowns before the throne" (v. 10). These crowns typify the rewards given to the overcomers at the Judgment Seat of Christ. Believers will receive various crowns for faithful service during their lives on earth. The elders realized that any merit they had received was not due to their own worthiness, but to God's. They gave testimony to this fact by laying their crowns before God's throne.

2. They offered Him praise for His work in creation. He alone is worthy "to receive glory and honor and power" (v. 11). God deserves such praise from His creation because it owes its very existence to Him. God alone has "created all things, and for thy pleasure they are and were created" (v. 11), sang the elders.

Let us, along with the host of heaven, humbly bow in adoration and praise to our great God for who He is and what He has done.

REVELATION 5:1-14

And I saw in the right hand of him that sat on the throne a scroll written within and on the back, sealed with seven seals. And I saw a strong angel proclaiming with a loud voice, Who is worthy to open the scroll, and to loose its seals? And no man in heaven, nor in earth, neither under the earth, was able to open the scroll, neither to look on it. And I wept much, because no man was found worthy to open and to read the scroll, neither to look on it. And one of the elders saith unto me, Weep not; behold, the Lion of the tribe of Judah, the Root of David, hath prevailed to open the scroll, and to loose its seven seals. And I beheld and, lo, in the midst of the throne and of the four living creatures, and in the midst of the elders, stood a Lamb as though it had been slain, having seven horns and seven eyes, which are the seven spirits of God sent forth into all the earth. And he came and took the scroll out of the right hand of him that sat upon the throne. And when he had taken the scroll, the four living creatures and four and twenty elders fell down before the Lamb, having every one of them harps, and golden bowls full of incense, which are the prayers of saints. And they sang a new song, saying, Thou art worthy to take the scroll, and to open its seals; for thou wast slain, and hast redeemed us to God by thy blood out of every kindred, and tongue, and people, and nation; And hast made us unto our God a kingdom of priests, and we shall reign on the earth. And I beheld, and I heard the voice of many angels round about the throne and the living creatures and the elders, and the number of them was ten thousand times ten thousand, and thousands of thousands, Saying with a loud voice, Worthy is the Lamb that was slain to receive power, and riches, and wisdom, and strength, and honor, and glory, and blessing. And every creature that is in heaven, and on the earth, and under the earth, and such as are in the sea, and all that are in them, heard I saying, Blessing, and honor, and glory, and power be unto him that sitteth upon the throne, and unto the Lamb forever and ever. And the four living creatures said, Amen. And the four and twenty elders fell down and worshiped him that liveth forever and ever.

8

THE SCROLL WITH SEVEN SEALS

In Revelation 4, John presented a description of what he saw and heard in his heavenly vision. He saw God the Father seated on His throne and heard the host of heaven offering Him continual worship. In Revelation 5, the apostle narrowed his focus to a scroll in the right hand of God and a search for one qualified to open its seals and reveal its message. This chapter is extremely important because it provides a fitting introduction to the revelation of God's program to be unfolded in chapters 6 to 22.

The Sealed Scroll

John wrote, "And I saw in the right hand of him that sat on the throne a scroll written within and on the back, sealed with seven seals" (v. 1). In the first century, scrolls were made of papyrus and sheep or goat skin sewn together, and often averaged 15 feet in length. The scroll that John saw had writing on both sides, indicating a full or comprehensive message.

This scroll had "seven seals" (v. 1). It was common in the first century for a person in authority to seal an important document so that its contents would remain secret. Roman law required a last will and testament to be sealed seven times, as illustrated in the wills of Caesar Augustus and Emperor Vespasian.[1] Such documents were sealed with wax or clay and could be opened only by a qualified person.

What does the content of the scroll represent? Various answers have been given to this question. Some scholars believe it represents the New Covenant of the promised kingdom. Others teach that it is a testament or will assuring believers that they have an inheritance reserved for them by God. Another teaching identifies it as the Lamb's book of life mentioned numerous times in the Book of the Revelation. Still others view it as God's redemptive program predicted in the Old Testament and fulfilled in the New Testament. Many believe that it represents Christ's title deed to planet Earth. Although the last view is partially true, the scroll's contents represent much more. Yet another view asserts that the scroll represents a history of the future. It reveals the judgments of God to be poured out on the earth, Christ's Second Coming to rightfully inherit and implement the title deed of redemption to planet Earth, and His righteous rule in the Millennial Kingdom. This last view best describes the scroll's contents.[2]

Sorrowful Search

John saw "a strong angel...with a loud voice" (v. 2) making a proclamation in heaven. Some scholars have identified the angel as Gabriel (cp. Daniel 8:16; 9:21; Luke 1:19, 26). Others believe he is the archangel Michael, who will play a major role in end-time events (Daniel 12:1-3). The text provides no indication of the angel's identity. The loud sound of the angel's voice, vibrating throughout heaven, denotes authority, urgency, and the importance of what he is about to announce.

The angel's proclamation is in the form of a question: "Who is worthy to open the scroll, and to loose its seals?" (v. 2). After a universal search, "no man in heaven, nor in earth, neither under the earth [the underworld], was able to open the scroll, neither to look on it [look into its contents]" (v. 3).

John's response was sorrowful. He said, "And I wept much, because no man was found worthy to open and to read the scroll, neither to look on it" (v. 4). This implies that John continually wailed in an uncontrollable, loud voice. Scholars have proposed three aspects for the apostle's sorrow. Some believe he wept over the moral inability of mankind to open the scroll. Others believe he wept because the world would never know the contents of the scroll—"things which must be hereafter" (4:1). Still others believe he wept because, without the scroll being opened, God's program would not be fulfilled.[3] Although the third answer seems the most reasonable, the text simply states that he wept because "no man was found worthy to open and to read the scroll."

Immediately an elder consoled John and commanded him, "Weep not," because one had been found "to open the scroll, and to loose its seven seals" (v. 5). The elder's words turned John from sorrow to joy.

The Savior Takes the Scroll

Three descriptions are given for the one who is qualified to open the seven-sealed scroll. First, he is "the Lion of the tribe of Judah" (v. 5). This reference originated in Genesis 49:9, where Judah was called a lion. The lion is considered king of the beasts because of his majestic dignity, strength, courage, and ability to rule over his domain. Christ is from the tribe of Judah (Matthew 1:2; Hebrews 7:14), is majestic and strong, and, after His Second Coming, He will reign as King over the earth.

Second, the one qualified to open the scroll is from "the Root of David" (v. 5; cp. 22:16). This is a reference from Isaiah 11:1, 10, linking Christ to the Davidic line (cp. 2 Samuel 7:12-16). But

Christ is greater than His father David (Matthew 22:41-46) and will one day sit on David's throne to rule in the Kingdom age (Luke 1:32-33).

Third, the one qualified to open the scroll is identified as "a Lamb" (v. 6). The Lamb is Christ, pictured in three ways:

1. The Lamb is standing in "the midst of the throne" (v. 6). Christ has stepped down from His throne at the Father's right hand and moved in front of God the Father to receive the scroll (v. 7).

2. The Lamb looks as if it "had been slain" (v. 6), although it is still standing. Christ is often portrayed in the New Testament as a slain lamb (John 1:29; Acts 8:32; 1 Peter 1:18-19; Revelation 13:8) who still possesses the scars of His death (the crucifixion).

3. The Lamb has "seven horns and seven eyes, which are the seven spirits of God sent forth into all the earth" (v. 6). This is a picture of Christ in the fullness of His omnipotence, omniscience, and omnipresence. Twenty-eight times in the Book of the Revelation, Christ is referred to as a Lamb.

The symbols of a lamb and a lion seem to be incongruous, but in reality they complement each other, representing Christ's vicarious redemptive work on behalf of mankind and His victorious resurrection and rule. The elder announced that the one qualified "hath prevailed to open the scroll, and to loose its seven seals" (v. 5). The word *prevail* means *to overcome, to conquer,* or *be victorious.* Christ secured the right to open the scroll based on His Messianic office, holiness, and redemptive death on the cross.

Christ stepped forward "and took the scroll out of the right hand of him that sat upon the throne" (v. 7). He alone has the credentials and is qualified to implement God's wrath and redemptive program recorded in the sealed scroll.

There is a parallel between Christ's qualification to take the scroll and loose its seal with that of the kinsman-redeemer (see the account of Ruth and Boaz found in the Old Testament book of Ruth). Like the kinsman-redeemer, Christ paid the redemptive price to regain the title deed to mankind's lost inheritance. In the future, He will take possession of His inheritance (the earth) and exercise sovereign rule over it.[4]

Song of Salvation

When Christ took the scroll, "the four living creatures and four and twenty elders fell down before the Lamb" (v. 8) in worship. This is evidence that Christ is God, for heavenly beings would never worship anything less. The elders possessed "harps, and golden bowls full of incense, which are the prayers of saints" (v. 8). Harps were used in the Old Testament (Psalm 33:2; 98:5; 147:7) and in heaven (14:2; 15:2) to offer praise and adoration to God. In the Old Testament Tabernacle and Temple, the altar of incense stood next to the veil in the center of the holy place, separating it from the holy of holies, where God manifested His presence. The high priest burned incense on the altar, and it ascended to God, symbolic of the prayers of God's people (Psalm 141:2). The same is true in this instance (8:3-4).

The heavenly host sang "a new song" (v. 9) to the Lamb, celebrating His redemptive work. The word *new* does not mean new in time or origin, but new in the sense of its nature—something previously unknown and unprecedented. Christ's accomplishment in redemption was superior in value to the Old Testament revelation. A new work of redemption calls for a new song. This new song revealed five marvelous insights:

    1. The Redeemer is "worthy" (v. 9) to open the sealed scroll on the basis of His sacrifice. In being "slain" (v. 9), He opened the way for worldwide redemption.

2. The ransom price was paid through His blood
   (v. 9). Worthiness is not based on mankind's
   performance but on Christ's personal blood
   sacrifice (1 Peter 1:18-19), which made it possible for God's grace and mercy to be manifested to mankind.

3. A representative group "out of every kindred,
   and tongue, and people, and nation" (v. 9)
   was redeemed.

4. As a result of mankind's redemption, God has
   formed the church into a royal "kingdom of
   priests" (v. 10; 1 Peter 2:9).

5. The church will rule and "reign on the earth"
   (v. 10) with Christ during the Millennial
   Kingdom.

In light of this, it is no wonder that heaven breaks out in praise to
the Lord, who has provided all this for His creation.

This introductory section of the second vision concludes with
a revelation of heavenly praise pouring forth from creation. The
participants are "many angels...living creatures...elders...ten
thousand times ten thousand, and thousands of thousands" (v. 11)
of beings around God's throne. The number is incalculable (cp.
Daniel 7:10) and is meant to be so. This heavenly host offers a
sevenfold symphony of praise to the "Lamb that was slain" (v.
12). He is "Worthy...to receive power, and riches, and wisdom,
and strength, and honor, and glory, and blessing" (v. 12). This
doxology recognizes the infinite, incalculable, and intrinsic
power that Christ eternally possesses in Himself.

Moreover, the praise emanating from heaven builds to a
crescendo of worship as every creature in the universe gives
"Blessing, and honor, and glory, and power...unto him [God the
Father] that sitteth upon the throne, and unto the Lamb [Christ]
forever and ever" (v. 13) "Every creature," including the

demonic world and unsaved humanity, will ultimately praise Christ as Lord (cp. Philippians 2:9-11). Again, combining praise to both God the Father and the Lamb proves that Christ is God. This fourfold expression of praise will be manifested throughout eternity.

John concluded this section with the "four living creatures" saying, "Amen," whereupon the "four and twenty elders fell down and worshiped" (v. 14). This is a fitting conclusion to an awesome introduction of the third section of Revelation—the "things which must be hereafter" (4:1).

Endnotes

[1] John F. Walvoord, *The Revelation of Jesus Christ* (Chicago: Moody Press, 1966), p. 113.

[2] Robert L. Thomas, *Revelation 1-7, An Exegetical Commentary* (Chicago: Moody Press, 1992), pp. 376-379.

[3] *Ibid.*, p. 366.

[4] For a full discussion of the kinsman-redeemer in relation to Christ and the sealed scroll, see: Renald Showers, *Maranatha: Our Lord, Come!* (Bellmawr, NJ: The Friends of Israel Gospel Ministry, Inc., 1995), pp. 80-82, 85, 87-89, 91, 94-95, 104.

REVELATION 6:1-17

And I saw when the Lamb opened one of the seals, and I heard, as it were, the noise of thunder, one of the four living creatures saying, Come. And I saw and, behold, a white horse; and he that sat on him had a bow; and a crown was given unto him, and he went forth conquering, and to conquer. And when he had opened the second seal, I heard the second living creature say, Come. And there went out another horse that was red; and power was given to him that sat on it to take peace from the earth, and that they should kill one another; and there was given unto him a great sword. And when he had opened the third seal, I heard the third living creature say, Come. And I beheld and, lo, a black horse; and he that sat on him had a pair of balances in his hand. And I heard a voice in the midst of the four living creatures say, A measure of wheat for a denarius, and three measures of barley for a denarius, and see thou hurt not the oil and the wine. And when he had opened the fourth seal, I heard the voice of the fourth living creature say, Come. And I looked and, behold, a pale horse, and his name that sat on him was Death, and Hades followed with him. And power was given unto them over the fourth part of the earth, to kill with sword, and with hunger, and with death, and with the beasts of the earth. And when he had opened the fifth seal, I saw under the altar the souls of them that were slain for the word of God, and for the testimony which they held. And they cried with a loud voice, saying, How long, O Lord, holy and true, dost thou not judge and avenge our blood on them that dwell on the earth? And white robes were given unto every one of them; and it was said unto them that they should rest yet for a little season, until their fellow servants also and their brethren, that should be killed as they were, should be fulfilled.

And I beheld, when he had opened the sixth seal and, lo, there was a great earthquake, and the sun became black as sackcloth of hair, and the moon became like blood; And the stars of heaven fell unto the earth, even as a fig tree casteth her untimely figs, when she is shaken of a mighty wind. And the heaven departed as a scroll when it is rolled together; and every mountain and island were moved out of their places. And the kings of the earth, and the great men, and the rich men, and the chief captains, and the mighty men, and every slave, and every free man, hid themselves in the dens and in the rocks of the mountains, And said to the mountains and rocks, Fall on us, and hide us from the face of him that sitteth on the throne, and from the wrath of the Lamb; For the great day of his wrath is come, and who shall be able to stand?

9

SIX OF SEVEN SEALS OPENED

" **N**ever in all history have men spoken so much of the end-times, yet been so shrouded in ignorance of God's impending doomsday," said Carl F. H. Henry. Be assured that those who study Revelation 6 and what follows it will not be shrouded in ignorance of God's impending judgment.

Revelation 5 ends with Christ's holding the sealed scroll. This scroll contains Christ's title deed to the earth by right of creation and redemption. The judgments mentioned in this scroll are divided into three groups: seals (6:1-17; 8:1), trumpets (8:7-9:21; 11:15), and bowls (16:1-19:21), with an interlude between each section.

Before examining the text, two important questions must be addressed:

1. Will the seal judgments be fulfilled in the future, or, were they fulfilled in the past? There is no historic evidence pointing to a past fulfill-ment of these seals. Scripture indicates that they will be fulfilled in the third division of Revelation, called "the things which shall be hereafter" (1:19; cp. 4:1).

2. When in the future will the six seals be fulfilled? They will be fulfilled during the first
half of Daniel's 70th week, a seven-year period that begins with the Antichrist's "confirm[ing] the covenant with many for one
week" (Daniel 9:27).

These seals parallel the conflicts mentioned by Jesus in
Matthew 24—false christs (Matthew 24:5; Revelation 6:1-
2), war (Matthew 24:6-7; Revelation 6:3-4); famine
(Matthew 24:7; Revelation 6:5-6), death (Matthew 24:7-9;
Revelation 6:7-8), martyrdom (Matthew 24:9-10; Revelation
6:9-11), and earthquakes (Matthew 24:7; Revelation 6:12)—
and are called "the beginning of sorrows [birth pangs]"
(Matthew 24:8). The seven seals are revealed chronologically, covering the entire judgment period concurrently. This
is often illustrated by a telescope comprising three sections
(the largest containing the two inner sections); that is, seven
trumpets proceed from the seventh seal, and seven bowls
proceed from the seventh trumpet. Nothing is read from the
scroll; with the opening of each seal, John is given a vivid,
symbolic description of literal events that will take place on
the earth.

Horsemen Coming

The Rider on the White Horse

Still viewing what is taking place in heaven, John
watched the Lamb (Christ) open the first seal. Immediately
the sound of "thunder" roared throughout heaven, as "one of
the four living creatures [said], Come" (v. 1). Who did the
living creature address? It cannot be Christ; He is the one
opening the seal. It cannot be John; he is already present and
viewing what is taking place before God's throne. It must be

the four horsemen who are summoned to "Come" (v. 1; cp. vv. 2, 3, 5, 7).

John watched as a white horse appeared, and its rider was given "a bow; and a crown" (v. 2). Who is the rider and what does he represent? Answers have varied: a Roman emperor, the personification of judgment, the victorious proclamation of the gospel, the triumph of militarism during the Tribulation, Christ, or the Antichrist.[1]

Most scholars believe the rider is either Christ or the Antichrist. But the rider cannot be Christ, according to other Scriptures. This rider is given a temporary victor's "crown [*stephanos*]" (v. 2), whereas Christ is wearing "many crowns [*diadems*]" (19:12) as King at His Second Coming. Christ will carry a sword, not a bow. Christ will not initiate war but will end war at His coming. Lastly, Christ will appear at the end, not the beginning, of the Tribulation. This rider has the markings of a counterfeit (Antichrist) who arrives on the world stage at the beginning of the Tribulation. Carrying a bow (v. 2) without arrows suggests that he has already conquered (v. 2) by powerful means in the beginning of his rise to power. The Antichrist will be given a victor's crown as world leader, but for only "forty and two months" (13:5).

The Rider on the Red Horse

When the second seal was opened, a red horse appeared, and "power was given to him that sat on it to take peace from the earth" (v. 4). The color red is symbolic of war and bloodshed. International conflict and internal civil war (Matthew 24:6-7) will take place during the first half of the Tribulation, for "they…kill one another" (v. 4). Although war will be waged worldwide during the first half of the Tribulation, Israel will not be involved because of protection provided by the Antichrist.

The Rider on the Black Horse

When the third seal was opened, a black horse appeared with its rider carrying "a pair of balances" (v. 5). This represents famine, which usually follows war (cp. Matthew 24:7b). The "balances" (scales) were used to weigh out the cost of food: "A measure [quart] of wheat for a denarius [16 cents, a day's wage], and three measures of barley for a denarius" (v. 6). The cost of food for one day will be a day's wage. The rider was instructed to "hurt not the [olive] oil and the wine" (v. 6), meaning that luxury items, affordable only to the rich, will not be touched. Thus, the famine will affect the lower and middle classes, but the rich will continue to enjoy their luxurious lifestyle.

The Rider on the Pale Horse

When the fourth seal was opened, "a pale [yellowish green] horse" appeared with "Death" (v. 8) as its rider. An awesome destruction of life will ensue in the first half of the Tribulation, when the rider is given power to kill a "fourth part of the earth...with sword [war]...hunger [famine]...death [plague], and with the beasts of the earth" (v. 8). The mention of "Hades follow[ing] with him" (v. 8) leaves no doubt that those who are slain will be unsaved people, who will be cast into hell until they stand before the Great White Throne Judgment (20:11-15). This is only the beginning of the Tribulation that is to come upon the earth.

Human Cry

When the Lamb "opened the fifth seal, [John] saw under the altar the souls of them that were slain for the word of God, and for the testimony which they held" (v. 9). These are believers who received the Lord during the first half of the Tribulation

(Matthew 24:9, 13-14) but were martyred for their confession and commitment to Christ (7:14). They are pictured "under the altar" in God's heavenly Temple without their resurrected bodies. Whether this altar is a reference to the brazen altar, the altar of incense (cp. 8:3; 9:13), or some other altar in heaven (11:1; 14:18; 16:7) is uncertain.

They cried, "How long, O Lord...dost thou not judge and avenge our blood on them that dwell on the earth?" (v. 10). The martyred saints recognize that it is God who will punish the wicked (cp. Romans 12:19; 2 Thessalonians 1:8), but they want to know when. They are not given an answer but are told to "rest yet for a little season" (v. 11). Vengeance will come upon the wicked after the martyrdom of their "fellow servants" and "brethren" is "fulfilled" (v. 11). During the interim, they are provided with "white robes" (v. 11) symbolizing their salvation, righteousness, and victory. This verse sheds light on the state of believers after death. Those in heaven are conscious, at rest, and aware of a future judgment upon their slayers. The white robes provided for these saints indicate that they will possess some type of intermediate bodies before they receive their resurrected bodies. There is a set number of believers appointed for martyrdom during the Tribulation. God has determined the time and manner of death for believers.

Some would argue that the first five seals are not speaking of *God's wrath* upon mankind, but mankind's *wrath* upon mankind. They reason that the word *wrath* is not mentioned until the sixth seal in relation to "the day of his [the Lord's] wrath" (v. 17). Renald Showers provides evidence to the contrary:

1. Absence of the word *wrath* does not prove that the first five seals will not involve God's Day of the Lord wrath.

2. All seven seals are part of a common pattern, purpose (function), and program in preparation for Christ to take possession of the earth.

3. Revelation portrays Christ as the judge and ruler over of the world, exercising God's wrath in all seven seals to destroy His foes and restore and rule over His theocratic Kingdom on earth.

4. An examination of the first five seals provides specific evidence that they too will involve the wrath of God.[2]

Heaven and Earth Convulse

When the Lamb opens the sixth seal, heaven and earth will begin to convulse.

- A "great earthquake" (v. 12) will be felt worldwide as volcanic eruptions cause a shift in the earth's crust. This will be the first of several earthquakes experienced throughout the Tribulation (8:5; 11:13, 19; 16:18). "Every mountain and island were moved out of their places" (v. 14). These earthquakes will not disappear until the seventh bowl judgment is poured out (16:20).

- "The sun became black as sackcloth of hair" (v. 12), producing a terrifying darkness worldwide.

- The cosmic disturbances taking place in heaven and on earth will cause the moon to appear red "like blood" (v. 12).

- Meteors will shower the earth like a fig tree dropping its fruit prematurely in a windstorm, when "the stars of heaven [fall] unto the earth" (v. 13).

- "The heaven departed [ripped apart] as a scroll when it is rolled together" (v. 14). Heaven will first be divided in the middle, then rolled up like a scroll in opposite directions. This is not the same departing of the heavens mentioned elsewhere in Revelation (20:11; 21:1).

People from every stratum of society, "kings...great men...rich men...chief captains...mighty men...every slave, and every free man, hid themselves in the dens and in the rocks of the mountains" (v. 15) from the events manifested in the sixth seal. They will cry out in terror "to the mountains and rocks, Fall on us, and hide us from the face of him that sitteth on the throne [God the Father], and from the wrath of the Lamb" (v. 16). All six seals will have a cumulative effect on these people, causing them to believe that "the great day of his [God's] wrath is [has] come" (v. 17).

John is not saying that this is the great "Day of the Lord" wrath, but he has simply recorded the response of these people. Their evaluation is both right and wrong concerning the Day of the Lord wrath. They are right in believing that this is God's wrath. Dr. Thomas states,

> The verb *helthen* ("has come") is aorist indicative, referring to a previous arrival of the wrath, not something that is about to take place. Men see the arrival of this day at least as early as the cosmic upheavals that characterize the sixth seal (6:12-14), but upon reflection they probably recognize it was already in effect with the death of one-fourth of the population (6:7-8), the worldwide famine (6:5-6), and the global warfare (6:3-4). The rapid sequence of all these events could not escape public notice, but the light of their true explanation does not

dawn upon human consciousness until the severe phenomena of the sixth seal arrive.

Sproule raises the possibility, without endorsing it, that [*helthen*] is a dramatic aorist that would give no time indication for the beginning of the great day of wrath (John A. Sproule, *In Defense of Pre-Tribulationism* [Winona Lake, Ind.; BMH, 1980], pp. 54-55). The only time an aorist indicative speaks of something future or something about to happen, however, is if it is a dramatic aorist (H. E. Dana and Julius R. Mantey, *A Manual Grammar of the Greek New Testament* [New York: Macmillan, 1927], p. 198), a futuristic aorist (BDF, par. 333 [2]), or a proleptic aorist (Nigel Turner, *Syntax*, vol. 3 of *A Grammar of New Testament Greek* [Edinburgh: T. & T. Clark, 1963], p. 74). Some contextual feature must be present to indicate clearly these exceptional usages. No such feature exists in the context of the sixth seal, so these special uses are not options here. Rosenthal cites a use of the same verb form in Rev. 19:7 to demonstrate its futuristic connotation (*Pre-Wrath Rapture*, pp. 166-67), but this usage is in one of the heavenly songs that often in the Apocalypse utilize proleptic aorists (e.g., Rev. 11:15-19). His citation of [*helthen*] in Mark 14:41 is not relevant to the sixth seal, because the historical context of that passage clearly refers to Christ's coming crucifixion. The verb in Rev. 6:17 must be a constantive aorist looking back in time to the point in the past when the great day of wrath arrived.[3]

Thus, the people correctly recognize that what is happening in all six seals is God's wrath upon mankind (cp. Isaiah 2:10-22). In the broad sense, all six seals will involve the Day of the Lord wrath.

On the other hand, these people are wrong in assuming that this is "the great day of his [the Lord's] wrath" (v. 17) predicted to come at the end of the Tribulation. They are wrong for the following reasons.

1. The great Day of the Lord wrath will not take place until the seventh seal is opened, at which time the armies of the world will gather in Israel for Armageddon (16:12-16).

2. The cosmic disturbances related to the great Day of the Lord will take place during the pouring out of the bowl judgments.

3. In the time of the sixth seal, people will flee to the mountains to hide from God's wrath, but in the great and terrible Day of the Lord, they will stand with the Antichrist in defiance against the Lord. This will take place at the end of the Tribulation.[4]

Thus, the sixth seal is connected with events taking place in the first half of the Tribulation.

Those in the Tribulation ask, "who shall be able to stand?" (v. 17). The answer is known only by those who have put their faith in Christ as Savior.

Endnotes

[1] Robert L. Thomas, *Revelation 1-7, An Exegetical Commentary* (Chicago: Moody Press, 1991), pp. 420-421.

² Renald Showers, *Maranatha: Our Lord, Come!* (Bellmawr, NJ: The Friends of Israel Gospel Ministry, Inc., 1995), pp. 110-112.

³ Thomas, *op. cit.*, pp. 457-458, 460.

⁴ Showers, *op. cit.*, pp. 120-121.

REVELATION 7:1-17

And after these things I saw four angels standing on the four corners of the earth, holding the four winds of the earth, that the wind should not blow on the earth, nor on the sea, nor on any tree. And I saw another angel ascending from the east, having the seal of the living God; and he cried with a loud voice to the four angels, to whom it was given to hurt the earth and the sea, Saying, Hurt not the earth, neither the sea, nor the trees, till we have sealed the servants of our God in their foreheads. And I heard the number of them which were sealed; and there were sealed an hundred and forty and four thousand of all the tribes of the children of Israel. Of the tribe of Judah were sealed twelve thousand. Of the tribe of Reuben were sealed twelve thousand. Of the tribe of Gad were sealed twelve thousand. Of the tribe of Asher were sealed twelve thousand. Of the tribe of Naphtali were sealed twelve thousand. Of the tribe of Manasseh were sealed twelve thousand. Of the tribe of Simeon were sealed twelve thousand. Of the tribe of Levi were sealed twelve thousand. Of the tribe of Issachar were sealed twelve thousand. Of the tribe of Zebulun were sealed twelve thousand. Of the tribe of Joseph were sealed twelve thousand. Of the tribe of Benjamin were sealed twelve thousand. After this I beheld and, lo, a great multitude, which no man could number, of all nations, and kindreds, and peoples, and tongues, stood before the throne, and before the Lamb, clothed with white robes, and palms in their hands, And cried with a loud voice, saying, Salvation to our God who sitteth upon the throne, and unto the Lamb. And all the angels stood round about the throne, and about the elders and the four living creatures, and fell before the throne on their faces, and worshiped God, Saying, Amen! Blessing, and glory, and wisdom, and thanksgiving, and honor, and power, and might be unto our God forever and ever. Amen. And one of the elders answered, saying unto me, Who are these who are arrayed in white robes? And from where did they come? And I said unto him, Sir, thou knowest. And he said to me, These are they who came out of the great tribulation, and have washed their robes, and made them white in the blood of the Lamb. Therefore are they before the throne of God, and serve him day and night in his temple; and he that sitteth on the throne shall dwell among them. They shall hunger no more, neither thirst any more; neither shall the sun light on them, nor any heat. For the Lamb who is in the midst of the throne shall feed them, and shall lead them unto living fountains of waters; and God shall wipe away all tears from their eyes.

10

THE TRIBULATION SAINTS

Revelation chapter 7 opens with the phrase, "And after these things" (v. 1), indicating that John was about to receive a new vision. This vision is an interlude between the sixth and seventh seals and does not advance the chronology of Revelation. The interlude could easily be omitted without any interruption in the progression of the seals' being opened, but inclusion of this chapter is extremely important. It provides details surrounding the sealing of Jewish believers, as well as the salvation, slaughter, and heavenly service of Gentile believers mentioned in the fifth seal (6:9-11).

Preparation Before Sealing

Before the sealing of Jewish believers, John saw "four angels" positioned on the "four corners [major points on the compass] of the earth" (v. 1). They were sent to restrain the "four winds" (agents of God's judgment) struggling to blow their destructive fury over the earth (v. 1).

John beheld a fifth "angel ascending from the east, having the seal of the living God" (v. 2). Scholars have tried to identify this angel as Christ, the Holy Spirit, an archangel, or some specially prepared messenger from God. Such views are highly speculative, having no scriptural foundation. He is simply "another" (v. 2) of the same kind of angel, distinguished from the other four only by his exalted mission to seal the 144,000 Jewish men.

The fifth angel commanded the other four angels in a loud voice, "Hurt not the earth, neither the sea, nor the trees, till we have sealed the servants of our God in their foreheads" (v. 3). The angel's loud cry indicated the importance and urgency of his command to hold back judgment until the servants of God were sealed. The seal is the name of God the Father written on their foreheads (14:1). No reason is given for this sealing. Most likely it is to protect them from death by the Antichrist's persecution and natural disaster during the Great Tribulation. This is validated by their appearance with Christ on Mount Zion after His return to earth (14:1).

People Saved

John recorded the number sealed as "an hundred and forty and four thousand of all the tribes of the children of Israel" (v. 4). John did not see the sealing, but he "heard" (v. 4) that the number was 144,000 (12,000 from each tribe of Israel), which should be interpreted literally. This has no reference to a spiritual Israel, represented by the church, or a superspiritual group of individuals who will be guaranteed a place in heaven because of their faithful service to God on earth. The term *Israel* must refer to the physical descendants of Abraham, Isaac, and Jacob. The fact that the 12 tribes are singled out during the Tribulation indicates that this is speaking of a literal, physical Israel.

Although there are 12 tribes listed in verses 5 through 8, some substitutions have been made. For example, Dan is eliminated and Levi is added to the list, while Ephraim is replaced by Joseph. Many reasons have been given for the substitutions. Most scholars believe that Dan and Ephraim were omitted because of their continual promotion of idolatry in Israel (1 Kings 12:28-30). Later it will be shown that God will use the 144,000 Jewish believers to preach throughout the world during the Tribulation. For this reason, many scholars believe God has chosen to substitute the idolatrous tribes of Dan and Ephraim with Levi and Joseph.

Some have asked how the identity of the 12 tribes can be confirmed, since the genealogical records were destroyed when the Romans invaded Jerusalem in 70 A.D. While it is true that mankind is unable to identify who belongs to which tribes, God knows, and He is responsible for this sealing.

Persecution of the Saints

The words "After this" used again in verse 9 indicate that John received a second vision in chapter 7. He saw "a great multitude, which no man could number, of all nations, and kindreds, and peoples, and tongues...before the throne, and before the Lamb" (v. 9). Who is this multitude of people? They are not the 144,000 mentioned earlier. The first group is exclusively Jewish, whereas this new multitude is a mixture of Gentile and Jewish believers. This group is a vast multitude of people who became believers during the Tribulation, many of whom died violent deaths.

How did they become believers? It could not have been through the witness of the church. There is no indication that the church is on earth during the seven-year period of the Tribulation. In fact, one of the "elders" (v. 13), representing the church in heaven, asked, "Who are these who are arrayed in white robes? And from where did they come?" (v. 13). Scripture makes it clear that the "gospel of the kingdom shall be preached in all the world for a witness unto all nations; and then shall the end come" (Matthew 24:14). This preaching is not done during the church age but during the seven-year Tribulation period (Matthew 24:21). These people heard the message in one of three ways.

1. God's two witnesses "shall prophesy a thousand two hundred and threescore days [during the first three and one-half years of the Tribulation]" (11:3).

2. An angel "having the everlasting gospel to preach unto them that dwell on the earth, and to every nation, and kindred, and tongue, and people" (14:6) will fly above the earth proclaiming his message.

3. It is possible that the *sheep people* (saved Gentiles), who come to the Lord during the Tribulation, will do so through the witness of Jewish people (the 144,000) who are scattered worldwide because of persecution by the Antichrist. These saved Gentiles will have housed, clothed, fed, visited in prison, and provided medical care to the Lord's brethren (Jews) during the Tribulation (Matthew 25:31, 35-40) and will have heard of their salvation.

The elder answered his own question: "These are they who came out of the great tribulation [continually keep coming out], and have washed their robes, and made them white in the blood of the Lamb" (v. 14). They became believers in Christ and were made spiritually pure through His blood.

A great multitude of those who come to the Lord will be martyred for their faith during the Great Tribulation.

1. They are pictured standing "before the throne, and before the Lamb" (v. 9) in heaven.

2. Their attire provides information about their sta-
    tus. They are "clothed with white robes" (v. 9),
    the attire of the redeemed, symbolic of the right-
    eousness and holiness of God.

3. They are holding "palms in their hands" (v. 9),
    symbolic of peace, joy, and victory.

4. They will sing the song of salvation, "saying,
    Salvation to our God who sitteth upon the throne,
    and unto the Lamb" (v. 10). The song of salva-
    tion indicates deliverance from sin through the
    blood of the Lamb for those who do not accept
    the mark of the beast or worship his image (14:9-
    12) during the Tribulation.

The phrase "cried with a loud voice" (v. 10) means that
these believers continually, without stopping, praised the
Father and the Son for the great salvation they experienced.
This prompted "the angels...round about the throne" (v. 11)
to fall on their faces before God and worship Him. Although
the angels do not experience salvation, they desire to know
about it (1 Peter 1:12) and rejoice over each sinner who
repents (Luke 15:10). Once again they offered up a sevenfold doxology, similar to the one expressed earlier:
"Blessing, and glory, and wisdom, and thanksgiving, and
honor, and power, and might be unto our God forever and
ever. Amen" (v. 12; cp. 5:12).

The elder's questions, "Who are these who are arrayed in
white robes? And from where did they come?" (v. 13), must
still be answered. John replied, "Sir, thou knowest" (v. 14).
John could not identify the group. This may seem strange, but
upon reflection, it is not difficult to understand his lack of
insight. The location of the group is in heaven, making its
identification difficult. John was projected into the time of the
Great Tribulation, of which he had little or no understanding.
The number of people was vast, making discernment among

them impossible. Their different racial and national backgrounds must have been confusing to the apostle. Any or all of these reasons could have prevented John from identifying these people.

Apparently John needed more information concerning the elder's questions.[1] The elder responded by answering, "These are they who came out of the great tribulation, and have washed their robes, and made them white in the blood of the Lamb" (v. 14). They are the saints who were martyred for their faith during the Great Tribulation.

Perpetual Service

The Tribulation saints are pictured standing before "the throne of God, and serv[ing] him day and night in his temple" (v. 15). The type of service they offer is not indicated, but the word *serve* means *to perform worshipful service*. Thus, they perform a priestly service connected with offering prayer and praise to God. Their service is carried out continually in the Temple of God, "day and night" (v. 15). Because heaven has no day or night, some scholars interpret this as a reference to the Millennial Temple (Ezek. 40-44) on earth during the Kingdom age. This is a weak interpretation, offering no textual proof. The phrase *day and night* is an idiomatic expression used to indicate that they continually serve in God's Temple without the physical limitations experienced by priests on earth.

These saints enjoy three provisions from God.

1. They receive protection from the Lord: "he that sitteth on the throne shall dwell among them" (v. 15). The protection and fellowship are in contrast to what they experienced during the Great Tribulation.

2. Earthly privation is replaced with heavenly pro-
    vision: "They shall hunger no more, neither
    thirst any more; neither shall the sun light on
    them, nor any heat" (v. 16). The privations they
    were forced to endure during the Great
    Tribulation will be eliminated (cp. Matthew
    25:42-43). "The Lamb who is in the midst of the
    throne shall feed them, and shall lead them unto
    living fountains of waters" (v. 17). Christ, who
    is standing in the midst of the throne (between
    God the Father and the saints), will shepherd
    these saints in heaven, supplying and satisfying
    all their spiritual needs.

3. Past sorrows will be replaced with eternal sereni-
    ty: "and God shall wipe away all tears from their
    eyes" (v. 17). There is no hint that this refers to
    sorrow in heaven over the loss of opportunity to
    serve the Lord on earth. These tears will be shed
    by the saints who suffered trials and tribulation
    for the sake of their faith in Christ during the
    Great Tribulation. There will be no tears for the
    saints in eternity (21:4).

Many will succumb to the deluded lies of the Antichrist
and give him total allegiance during the Tribulation. At the
same time, one of the greatest revivals in history will ensue
when multitudes of Jews and Gentiles throughout the world
receive Christ.

Revelation chapter 7 will be of great comfort to the
Tribulation saints at that time. They will know that their struggles against the satanic onslaughts of the Antichrist will be
replaced by the comfort of the Shepherd of their souls, who will
wipe away every tear of sorrow and meet all their spiritual needs.
What a picture of God's divine grace and mercy in the midst of
His wrath and judgment!

Endnote

[1] Robert L. Thomas, *Revelation 1-7, An Exegetical Commentary* (Chicago: Moody Press, 1992), p. 495.

REVELATION 8:1-9:21

And when he had opened the seventh seal, there was silence in heaven about the space of half an hour. And I saw the seven angels who stood before God, and to them were given trumpets. And another angel came and stood at the altar, having a golden censer; and there was given unto him much incense, that he should offer it with the prayers of all saints upon the golden altar which was before the throne. And the smoke of the incense, which came with the prayers of the saints, ascended up before God out of the angel's hand. And the angel took the censer, and filled it with fire from the altar, and cast it upon the earth; and there were voices, and thunderclaps, and lightnings, and an earthquake. And the seven angels who had the seven trumpets prepared themselves to sound.

The first angel sounded, and there followed hail and fire mixed with blood, and they were cast upon the earth; and the third part of trees were burnt up, and all green grass was burnt up. And the second angel sounded, and, as it were, a great mountain burning with fire was cast into the sea; and the third part of the sea became blood; And the third part of the creatures which were in the sea, and had life, died; and the third part of the ships were destroyed. And the third angel sounded, and there fell a great star from heaven, burning as though it were a lamp, and it fell upon the third part of the rivers, and upon the fountains of waters. And the name of the star is called Wormwood; and the third part of the waters became wormwood; and many men died of the waters, because they were made bitter. And the fourth angel sounded, and the third part of the sun was smitten, and the third part of the moon, and the third part of the stars, so that the third part of them was darkened, and the day shone not for a third part of it, and the night likewise.

And I beheld, and heard an angel flying through the midst of heaven, saying with a loud voice, Woe, woe, woe, to the inhabiters of the earth by reason of the other voices of the trumpet of the three angels, which are yet to sound!

And the fifth angel sounded, and I saw a star fall from heaven unto the earth; and to him was given the key of the bottomless pit. And he opened the bottomless pit, and there arose a smoke out of the pit, like the smoke of a great furnace; and the sun and the air were darkened by reason of the smoke of the pit. And there came out of the smoke locusts upon the earth, and unto them was given power, as the scorpions of the earth have power. And it was commanded them that they should not hurt the grass of the earth, neither any green thing, neither any tree, but only those men who have not the seal of God in their foreheads. And to them it was given that they should not kill them, but that they should be tormented five months; and their torment was like the torment of a scorpion, when he striketh a man. And in those days shall men seek death, and shall not find it; and shall desire to die, and death shall flee from them. And the shapes of the locusts were like horses prepared unto battle; and on their heads were, as it were, crowns like gold, and their faces were like the faces of men. And they had hair like the hair of women, and their teeth were like the teeth of lions. And they had breastplates, as it were breastplates of iron; and the sound of their wings was like the sound of chariots of many horses running to battle. And they had tails like scorpions, and there were stings in their tails; and their power was to hurt men five months. And they had a king over them, who is the angel of the bottomless pit, whose name in the Hebrew tongue is Abaddon, but in the Greek tongue hath his name Apollyon. One woe is past and, behold, there come two woes more hereafter.

And the sixth angel sounded, and I heard a voice from the four horns of the golden altar which is before God, Saying to the sixth angel who had the trumpet, Loose the four angels who are bound in the great river, Euphrates. And the four angels were loosed, who were prepared for an hour, and a day, and a month, and a year, to slay the third part of men. And the number of the army of the horsemen were two hundred thousand thousand; and I heard the number of them. And thus I saw the horses in the vision, and them that sat on them, having breastplates of fire, and of jacinth, and brimstone; and the heads of the horses were like the heads of lions, and out of their mouths issued fire and smoke and brimstone. By these three was the third part of men killed, by the fire, and by the smoke, and by the brimstone, which issued out of their mouths. For their power is in their mouth, and in their tails; for their tails were like serpents, and had heads, and with them they do hurt. And the rest of the men who were not killed by these plagues yet repented not of the works of their hands, that they should not worship demons, and idols of gold, and silver, and bronze, and stone, and wood, which neither can see, nor hear, nor walk. Neither repented they of their murders, nor of their sorceries, nor of their fornication, nor of their thefts.

11

THE TRUMPET JUDGMENTS

When the seventh seal was opened, "there was silence in heaven about the space of half an hour" (8:1). This seventh seal contains the seven trumpet and seven bowl judgments. These judgments are similar to but do not retrace or overlap the seal judgments mentioned in Revelation 6. The trumpets follow the six seals chronologically and begin at the middle of Daniel's 70th week, often called the *Great Tribulation*. As one author aptly stated, "It is not the silence of rest and peace, but the ominous quiet in preparation for God's wrath ready to be poured out in quick succession."

Prayer for Judgment

John saw "the seven angels who stood before God...given seven trumpets" (v. 2). They should not be identified with the seven spirits of God (5:6) nor with the angels who will pour out the seven bowl judgments. Trumpets were used in Israel to announce feast days, ceremonial processions, war, and to warn of the coming Day of the Lord. "Another angel" appeared before John standing "at the altar, having a golden censer; and there was given unto him much incense, that he should offer it with the prayers of all saints upon the golden altar" (v. 3). The text does not identify this eighth angel, but he is an angel, not Christ functioning in His intercessory ministry. This angel does not intercede for saints; he simply offers up incense with the saints' prayers. The word *another* refers to another of the same kind of angel as those previously mentioned. The text clearly says that this is an angel, not Christ.

Some scholars have questioned whether the altar mentioned in verses 3a and 5 is the brazen altar from which coals of fire are taken to burn incense on the golden altar (v. 3b). There is no indication that the altar in verse 3a is a *burnt altar*. The offering of incense is taken from the Old Testament worship, when the high priest burned incense on the golden altar in the Tabernacle. A thick cloud of smoke filled the Tabernacle, symbolic of Israel's offering prayer and worship to God (Exodus 30:34-38).

The prayers rising to heaven are cries from Tribulation saints asking God for deliverance and the destruction of their enemies (vv. 3-4). The smoke is *not the same* as the prayers; rather, it ascended "*with* the prayers of the saints" (v. 4, italics added).

After the offering of prayer, "the angel took the censer, and filled it with fire from the altar, and cast it upon the earth" (v. 5). In response, John heard the sound of "voices, and thunderclaps, and lightnings, and an earthquake" (v. 5) proceeding from the throne of God, symbolic of His authority, power, and approval of the imminent judgment about to be poured out on the earth. The seven angels were thus prepared to announce the coming judgments (v. 6).

Perils of Judgment

The First Trumpet

When "The first angel sounded [his trumpet]...there followed hail and fire mixed with blood, and they were cast upon the earth" (v. 7; cp. Exodus 9:22-26). Some find it difficult to comprehend how hail, fire, and blood can be mixed together and rained upon the earth. They must remember that this is a supernatural event orchestrated by God from heaven. The earth was affected in two ways. The "third part of trees was burnt up, and all green grass was burnt up" (v. 7). Some translations add "a third of the earth was burned up," indicating that all of the earth's vegetation was destroyed by this event. Others see a contradiction between "all" green grass being burned up (v. 7) and the grass not being hurt in the fifth trumpet judgment (9:4). The problem is solved by the understanding that the grass will grow back after being burned.

The Second Trumpet

When "the second angel sounded...a great mountain burning with fire was cast into the sea" (v. 8). Most likely this is a huge meteor. The result is threefold: A third part of the sea became literal blood (v. 8; cp. Exodus 7:19-21); "the third part of the creatures which were in the sea, and had life, died" (v. 9); "the third part of the ships were destroyed" (v. 9). This will greatly impact the world ecologically and economically, considering that three-fourths of the earth's surface is water.[1]

The Third Trumpet

When "the third angel sounded...there fell a great star from heaven, burning as though it were a lamp" (v. 10). This star is named "Wormwood" (v. 11), a strong-smelling and extremely bitter-tasting plant that grows in many varieties throughout the Middle East. In Scripture, it is a symbol of bitterness, sorrow, calamity, and divine punishment (see Jeremiah 9:15; 23:15; Lamentations 3:15). The star polluted a third part of the fresh water, "rivers," and "fountains [springs]" (v. 10), making them unfit for human consumption.

Although the plant wormwood is not normally a fatal poison, many of those who drink the water poisoned by "Wormwood," the fallen star, will die (v. 11).

The Fourth Trumpet

When the fourth angel sounded, the third part of the sun, moon, and stars was smitten, "so that the third part of them was darkened, and the day shone not for a third part of it, and the night likewise" (v. 12; cp. Exodus 10:21-22). This judgment will greatly affect agricultural production, animal life, and mankind's physical, psychological, and social health.

During this fourth trumpet judgment, John "beheld, and heard an angel [some translations read *eagle*] flying through the midst of heaven, saying with a loud voice, Woe, woe, woe, to the inhabiters of the earth by reason of the other voices of the trumpet of the three angels, which are yet to sound!" (v. 13). The *woes* distinguish these last three trumpet judgments as more severe than the previous four because they will greatly increase the destruction about to be unleashed on the earth. The phrase *inhabiters of the earth* (lit., *earth dwellers*) is used throughout Revelation in reference to unbelievers who are against God and follow the demonic intents of the Antichrist.

The Fifth Trumpet

When the fifth angel sounded, John "saw a star fall from heaven unto the earth" (9:1). The star is an intelligent being of some sort because he is announced as an individual: "to him" (v. 1) and "he" (v. 2). Scholars are divided as to whether this individual is an angel, a special messenger from God, a fallen angel, or even Satan himself. Textual evidence seems to indicate that this is an angel sent from God to release demonic beings from the bottomless pit to punish unbelievers on the earth.

When the bottomless pit was opened, "there arose a smoke...like the smoke of a great furnace," so thick that "the sun and the air were darkened" (v. 2). Throughout Revelation, smoke is associated with judgment, doom, and torment. Coming out of the pit will be a swarm of locusts (v. 3; cp. Exodus 10:12-20) that almost defy description. Their very appearance, not to speak of their ability to torment, will strike terror in the hearts of all people. They have crowns like gold on their heads, faces like a man, hair like a woman, teeth like a lion, breasts like breastplates of iron, motion in their wings sounding like many horses running to battle, and tails and stingers like a scorpion (vv. 7-10). Unlike real locusts, they do not feed on grass or any green thing. John used the words "as" or "like" to describe these creatures, signifying the difference of the creatures from the insects. They are demonic spirits from the pit and are so vile that they have been chained there for centuries.

Their king is named "Abaddon" in Hebrew and "Apollyon" in Greek (v. 11), both meaning *destroyer*. Most scholars identify him as Satan, but a case can be made for an unnamed demonic angel who is in charge of the bottomless pit. Satan is the prince of the power of the air (Ephesians 2:2; 6:12) and will not come in contact with the bottomless pit until he is cast into it during Christ's thousand-year reign (20:1-3).

God put a number of limitations on the locusts. They cannot hurt "the grass...neither any green thing, neither any tree" (v. 4). They cannot hurt those who have the seal of God in their foreheads. This would exempt the 144,000 Jewish men (7:4-8), and possibly all believers, from being tormented by the locusts during this judgment (cp. Exodus 8:22-23). They can torment but cannot kill their victims (v. 5). They are allowed to torment their victims for five months only (vv. 5, 10).

The agony and duration of their sting will be so painful that people will seek death by suicide to be relieved of the torment, but "death shall flee from them" (v. 6). With the end of the locust plague, one woe is past and two more are yet to come (v. 12).

The Sixth Trumpet

When the sixth trumpet sounded, John "heard a voice from the four horns of the golden altar which is before God" (v. 13). The prayers of the persecuted saints were offered to God at this altar (8:3-5), and the judgment of the sixth trumpet is linked to these prayers. The voice commanded the sixth angel to "Loose the four angels who are bound in the great river, Euphrates" (v. 14). Obviously these are wicked angels loosed to carry out their mission of God's appointed wrath on mankind. They "were prepared for an hour, and a day, and a month, and a year, to slay the third part of men" (v. 15). God has a precise period of time during which to carry out His program of wrath on a designated portion of people. On this occasion, His goal is not torment but death.

Without any explanation, John revealed that "the army of the horsemen were two hundred thousand thousand [200 million]" (v. 16). This gives the impression that they are connected in some way to the four wicked angels. Is the army composed of men or demons? The description of the horses and their riders gives the impression that it is a supernatural army of demonic beings. The emphasis is on the horses, not the riders. The power to kill comes from the horses' mouths, by which they killed the third part of men (v. 18) by "fire, and by the smoke, and by the brimstone" (v. 18), and with their tails, which were like serpents' tails with heads to wound men (v. 19).

Remarkably, "the rest of the men who were not killed by these plagues...repented not" (v. 20). The trumpet judgments failed to produce contrition of heart, confession of sin, or a change in conduct or cardinal beliefs. Such depraved people remain defiant against God and under the delusion of demonic power (see 2

Thessalonians 2:9-11), of whom Pharaoh of Egypt is a classic illustration. They did not repent "of the works of their hands...idols of gold, and silver, and bronze, and stone, and wood, which neither can see, nor hear, nor walk" (v. 20). They did not repent of the "worship [of] demons" (v. 20); that is, the unclean spirits represented by their idols. The very demons who were agents inflicting widespread death under the sixth trumpet were the objects of their worship.[2] They did not repent of their wicked walk, "murders...sorceries...fornication, nor of their thefts" (v. 21). The word *sorceries* (*pharmakia*) refers to the use of drugs and witchcraft for the purpose of casting magic spells or divinations. Demonic practices of witchcraft are often associated with mind-altering drug use, especially today. The sins mentioned here are growing at an alarming rate worldwide.

Those without Christ during the Great Tribulation will suffer the wrath of the trumpet judgments. Scripture clearly teaches, "now is the day of salvation" (2 Corinthians 6:2). Those who come to Christ today will not be exposed to the terrors of the trumpet judgments tomorrow.

Endnotes

[1] Warren W. Wiersbe, *The Bible Exposition Commentary, Galatians* (Wheaton: Victor Books, 1989), vol. 11, p. 593.

[2] Robert L. Thomas, *Revelation 8-22, An Exegetical Commentary* (Chicago: Moody Press, 1995), p. 53.

REVELATION 10:1-11

And I saw another mighty angel come down from heaven, clothed with a cloud; and a rainbow was upon his head, and his face was as though it were the sun, and his feet like pillars of fire. And he had in his hand a little scroll open; and he set his right foot upon the sea, and his left foot on the earth, And cried with a loud voice, as when a lion roareth; and when he had cried, seven thunders uttered their voices. And when the seven thunders had uttered their voices, I was about to write; and I heard a voice from heaven saying unto me, Seal up those things which the seven thunders uttered, and write them not. And the angel whom I saw standing upon the sea and upon the earth lifted up his hand to heaven, And swore by him that liveth forever and ever, who created heaven and the things that are in it, and the earth and the things that are in it, and the sea and the things which are in it, that there should be delay no longer; But in the days of the voice of the seventh angel, when he shall begin to sound, the mystery of God should be finished, as he hath declared to his servants, the prophets. And the voice which I heard from heaven spoke unto me again, and said, Go and take the little scroll which is open in the hand of the angel who standeth upon the sea and upon the earth. And I went unto the angel, and said unto him, Give me the little scroll. And he said unto me, Take it, and eat it up; and it shall make thy belly bitter, but it shall be in thy mouth sweet as honey. And I took the little scroll out of the angel's hand, and ate it up; and it was in my mouth sweet as honey, and as soon as I had eaten it my belly was bitter. And he said unto me, Thou must prophesy again about many peoples, and nations, and tongues, and kings.

12

ANGEL WITH A LITTLE SCROLL

There are a number of interludes throughout the judgment portions of Revelation. One is presented between the sixth and seventh seals in Revelation 7, and a second is presented between the sixth and seventh trumpets in Revelation 10:1-11:14. These interludes do not advance the chronology of Revelation, but they do provide detailed information about other events taking place in relation to the seal, trumpet, and bowl judgments. Interludes also provide comfort to believers by showing God's sovereign control over earthly events, His judgment of the wicked, and ultimate victory in His redemptive program for mankind and planet Earth. Revelation 10 centers on a mighty angel holding a little scroll. It is the beginning of a long interlude that leads to the seventh trumpet judgment.

The Angel's Appearance

The scene in Revelation 10 shifts from heaven to earth, as John sees "another mighty angel come down from heaven" (v. 1). The apostle gives a vivid description of the angel's appearance. First, he is "clothed with a cloud" (v. 1). Angels often ascend and descend on clouds. Clouds not only enhance the dignity and glorious appearance of angels, but are often associated with angels and the Lord when they come on a mission of judgment. Nine of the twenty occurrences of clouds in the New Testament are connected with scenes of judgment (Matthew 24:30; 26:64; Mark 13:26; 14:62; Luke 21:27; Revelation 1:7; 14:14, 15, 16).[1]

Second, the angel has "a rainbow...upon his head" (v. 1). An emerald rainbow appeared earlier around God's throne (4:3), but the angel wears a multicolored rainbow as a headdress. The rainbow symbolizes God's mercy, grace, and covenant promises in the midst of divine judgment (cp. Genesis 9:13).

Third, "his face was as though it were the sun" (v. 1). Like Christ (1:16), the angel's face radiated glory and majesty. This is because he has been in the presence of God and is marked with delegated authority from God (cp. Exodus 34:29). Angels often radiate glory when they appear (Luke 24:4; Revelation 18:1).

Fourth, "his feet [were] like pillars of fire" (v. 1). Fire throughout Revelation symbolizes judgment, and this angel's mission is to announce God's coming judgment. His "right foot [was] upon the sea, and his left foot on the earth" (v. 2), symbolizing the power and authority the angel has over the earth. The angel's huge size and stance on both the sea and the earth, mentioned three times in Revelation 10 (vv. 2, 5, 8), emphasize that God's judgment will not be limited to a specific area, but will be worldwide.

Fifth, "he had in his hand a little scroll open" (v. 2). The Greek word "scroll" (*biblion*) in 5:1 is different from the "little scroll" (*biblaridion*). This seems to distinguish the little scroll from the seven-sealed scroll of 5:1. Although the message in the little scroll is not stated, many theologians have speculated on its content. Because there are similarities between the two scrolls, some scholars believe that the little scroll should be identified with the earlier scroll as the title deed to the earth. Both scrolls are fully opened, and each is associated with a strong angel. But there is no indication that the little scroll represents the title deed to the earth. Others teach that the little scroll contains the prophecies mentioned in chapters 12-22, whereas the seven-sealed scroll contains the prophecies of chapters 1-11. This is not probable because the little scroll would have more content than the seven-sealed scroll, making it larger, not smaller. Also, the seven-sealed scroll contains all of the prophecies mentioned in chapters 6-22. Still others teach that the little scroll contains the immediate contents of 11:1-13 because it is little and unrelated to the seven-sealed scroll. This position is too limited in scope. It would also have to be larger. The content of the little scroll, although not stated, must relate in some way to a portion of the seven-sealed scroll, the bitter prophecies of "the mystery of God [that] should be finished" (v. 7), and John's commission to "prophesy again about many peoples, and nations, and tongues, and kings" (v. 11).[2]

Sixth, the angel "cried with a loud voice, as when a lion roareth" (v. 3). The volume and power of the angel's cry were similar to a lion's roar, which would command immediate attention and emphasize the importance of what is about to be said. In response to the angel's cry, "seven thunders uttered their voices" (v. 3; cp. 4:5). The voices contained further revelation concerning the perfect judgment of God about to be manifested to the apostle.

John understood the revelation that was being articulated by the seven thunders because he was "about to write" (v. 4) what he heard. Instantly, John "heard a voice from heaven saying...Seal up those things which the seven thunders uttered, and write them not" (v. 4). The voice is not identified, but in all likelihood it is the voice of God the Father or Jesus Christ instructing John not to write the revelation of the seven thunders. This revelation was specifically for the apostle, and not for the world. Speculation on this revelation is useless. Daniel (Daniel 12:9) and Paul (2 Corinthians 12:4) had the same experience. John received more revelation concerning the future than he was permitted to reveal. What he wrote is exactly what God wanted mankind to know about the future. The revelation given to John, which he was not to reveal, must have prepared the apostle in some way for what was to follow concerning God's future program.

Who is the mighty angel described in the first four verses? The characteristics of this angel lead many commentators to say that he is Christ. Some do so on the basis of the Christophanies in the Old Testament, where Christ appeared as the "angel of the LORD" (Genesis 16:6-13; 24:7; 31:11, 13; Judges 6:22). Others hold this position because of an earlier description of Christ in Revelation. This view is untenable for a number of reasons.

1. Nowhere in Revelation is Christ identified as an angel; He is *Lord over all the angels.*

2. Christ was never called the "angel of the LORD" after He took on humanity.

3. This angel is described as "another mighty angel [of the same kind]" (v. 1), similar to the angel in 5:2.

4. This angel came "down from heaven" (v. 1), but there is no indication in Scripture that Christ will return to the earth before His Second Coming.

5. It is evident that this angel cannot be Christ because he "swore by him that liveth forever and ever, who created heaven and the things that are in it, and the earth and the things that are in it, and the sea and the things which are in it" (v. 6). Christ, who is God, would not swear by God. This view has the angel (Christ) swearing by God, implying that God is greater than the angel (Christ).

6. Some identify this angel as Gabriel or Michael. This is highly unlikely because no name is given to the angel.

7. Others identify him with the "strong angel" of 5:2 because he speaks with a loud voice. Again, it is doubtful that this is the same angel. Although this angel is similar to other angels mentioned in Revelation, there is little evidence that he has been previously revealed.

The Angel's Affirmation

John saw the angel "standing upon the sea and upon the earth [who] lifted up his hand to heaven" (v. 5). The purpose of this was to take a solemn oath. The angel "swore by him that liveth forever and ever, who created heaven and the things that are in it, and the earth and the things that are in it, and the sea and the things which are in it" (v. 6). God, who has created all things in the earth and sovereignly controls His creation, has the divine prerogative and authority to control the time of its creation.

The angel announced "that there should be delay no longer" (v. 6). The word *delay* is sometimes rendered *time*. This cannot be referring to the end of time and the beginning of eternity because the thousand-year reign of Christ has not been announced (see Revelation 20), and it must be lived out before the beginning of the eternal state. In other words, "it does not refer to time as a succession of chronological events. Rather, it means that time has run out; that is, there will be no further delay"[3] in the unveiling and fulfillment of "the mystery of God" (v. 7). "The mystery of God" refers to hidden truth concerning God's program that is about to be divinely revealed through John. This hidden truth deals with the coming bowl judgments, which will be poured out with the blowing of the seventh trumpet, as well as all of the events yet to be revealed concerning the institution of the Millennial Kingdom and the new heaven and new earth. Thus, there should be no delay in revealing the remainder of God's program; it "should be finished" (v. 7) or brought to completion.

The Apostle's Assignment

God spoke again from heaven, instructing John to "Go and take the little scroll which is open in the hand of the angel who standeth upon the sea and upon the earth" (v. 8). This is the third time in Revelation 10 that the angel is identified as the one standing "upon the sea and upon the earth" (cp. vv. 2, 5), indicating his complete power over the earth to carry out God's revealed program.

John said to the angel, "Give me the little scroll" (v. 9), in obedience to God's command. The angel complied and instructed John to "eat" (v. 9) the scroll. The apostle said, "I took the little scroll out of the angel's hand, and ate it up; and it was in my mouth sweet as honey, and as soon as I had eaten it my belly was bitter" (v. 10). Eating the scroll suggests the idea of devouring and digesting the *knowledge* of the contents of the little scroll's revelation. The revelation concerning future events was sweet to John's taste, but when he digested its message, it was bitter or sharp in his stomach. Both Ezekiel (Ezekiel 2:9-10; 3:1-4) and Jeremiah (Jeremiah 15:16-18) had the same experience when they received God's message. Often the Word of God is sweet to the taste or pleasant to the ears, but its message, once understood, can produce pain and anguish in the soul. God's Word is a two-edged sword. It contains the sweet message of deliverance to believers and the bitter message of judgment and damnation to unbelievers (Hebrews 4:12).[4]

Upon digesting the scroll, John is instructed to "prophesy

again about many peoples, and nations, and tongues, and kings" (v. 11). The apostle is commissioned to reveal the scroll's contents to the world. John has no choice; he "must" obey the directive of God's will and faithfully minister the revelation. This commission to reveal the future is not new to John, for he is to "prophesy again" (cp. 1:19).

The subject of John's future pronouncement involves four groups. These groups are the objects of the prophecy, not the audience.

1. The "many people" include the next three categories but indicate that the scope of John's prophecy will extend far beyond his geographical sphere to include the masses of mankind.

2. It will be directed specifically to the "nations"— that is, the Gentile world separated by national boundaries, laws, and traditions.

3. It will go to those people who are divided by "tongues" or languages.

4. The prophecies yet to be pronounced will have a special focus and message to specific "kings" throughout the world (cp. 16:14; 17:10, 12; 18:9).

Like John, believers must devour and digest the contents of Revelation in order to send a warning to a lost world concerning future events. To those who reject the message in unbelief, it will be forever bitter, producing anguish and fear. To those who heed the message and put their faith in Christ, God's Word will be forever sweet.

Endnotes

[1] Robert L. Thomas, *Revelation 8-22, An Exegetical Commentary* (Chicago: Moody Press, 1995), p. 61.

[2] *Ibid.*, pp. 62-63.

[3] *Ibid.*

[4] Lehman Strauss, *The Book of the Revelation* (Neptune, NJ: Loizeaux Brothers, 1964), pp. 207-208.

REVELATION 11:1-19

And there was given me a reed like a rod; and the angel stood, saying, Rise, and measure the temple of God, and the altar, and them that worship in it. But the court, which is outside the temple, leave out, and measure it not; for it is given unto the nations, and the holy city shall they tread under foot forty and two months. And I will give power unto my two witnesses, and they shall prophesy a thousand two hundred and threescore days, clothed in sackcloth. These are the two olive trees, and the two lampstands standing before the God of the earth. And if any man will hurt them, fire proceedeth out of their mouth, and devoureth their enemies; and if any man will hurt them, he must in this manner be killed. These have power to shut heaven, that it rain not in the days of their prophecy; and have power over waters to turn them to blood, and to smite the earth with all plagues, as often as they will. And when they shall have finished their testimony, the beast that ascendeth out of the bottomless pit shall make war against them, and shall overcome them, and kill them. And their dead bodies shall lie in the street of the great city, which spiritually is called Sodom and Egypt, where also our Lord was crucified. And they of the peoples and kindreds and tongues and nations shall see their dead bodies three days and a half, and shall not permit their dead bodies to be put in graves. And they that dwell upon the earth shall rejoice over them, and make merry, and shall send gifts one to another, because these two prophets tormented them that dwelt on the earth. And after three days and a half the spirit of life from God entered into them, and they stood upon their feet, and great fear fell upon them who saw them. And they heard a great voice from heaven saying unto them, Come up here. And they ascended up to heaven in a cloud, and their enemies beheld them. And the same hour was there a great earthquake, and the tenth part of the city fell, and in the earthquake were slain of men seven thousand; and the remnant were terrified, and gave glory to the God of heaven. The second woe is past and, behold, the third woe cometh quickly. And the seventh angel sounded; and there were great voices in heaven, saying, The kingdom of this world is become the kingdom of our Lord, and of his Christ, and he shall reign forever and ever. And the four and twenty elders, who sat before God on their thrones, fell upon their faces, and worshiped God, Saying, We give thee thanks, O Lord God Almighty, who art, and wast, and art to come, because thou hast taken to thee thy great power, and hast reigned. And the nations were angry, and thy wrath is come, and the time of the dead, that they should be judged, and that thou shouldest give reward unto thy servants, the prophets, and to the saints, and them that fear thy name, small and great, and shouldest destroy them who destroy the earth. And the temple of God was opened in heaven, and there was seen in his temple the ark of his covenant; and there were lightnings, and voices, and thunderclaps, and an earthquake, and great hail.

13

MESSENGERS WITH A MANDATE

The long interlude between the sixth and seventh trumpets is continued from Revelation 10. In the last verse of that chapter, John was instructed that he must prophesy again about many peoples, tongues, and nations. His prophecy was to describe major events that will take place during the last half of the Great Tribulation, as God thwarts the nations' attempt to destroy His plan and purpose for Israel and the world. Three aspects of these events—the Tribulation Temple, the two witnesses, and the seventh trumpet—are revealed in Revelation 11.

Temple Measured

Sometime before the midpoint of the Tribulation, Israel will build a Temple in Jerusalem and restore the Levitical worship system. John was given "a reed like a rod" and instructed by the angel to "Rise, and measure the temple of God, and the altar, and them that worship in it" (v. 1). Many scholars believe that the Temple, altar, and worshipers are being measured for preservation and protection. It is probable that this is to show that they are God's unique possession, in response to "the court" and "the holy city [Jerusalem]," which are "given unto the nations" to be trodden "under foot forty and two months" (v. 2) during the Tribulation.

Although Israel maintains control over Jerusalem today, such will not be the case during the Great Tribulation. That period will begin with the Antichrist's making a covenant with Israel for seven years (the "one week" of Daniel 9:27). This seven-year period is divided into two equal parts of three and a half years each. Israel will live in peace, protected by the Antichrist, during the first three and a half years, but at the mid-point of the Tribulation, he will take over Jerusalem and the Temple. He will tread both Jerusalem and the Temple under foot for 42 months—the last three and a half years of the Tribulation. This is substantiated by Jesus' prophecy in Luke 21:24. "The times of the Gentiles" began during the reign of Nebuchadnezzar of Babylon and will not be fulfilled until the Second Coming of Christ (v. 15).

Two Messengers

Abruptly, John is introduced to God's "two witnesses," who "shall prophesy a thousand two hundred and threescore days, clothed in sackcloth" (v. 3). Who are these witnesses?

Some believe they represent the church because they are called "lampstands" (v. 4). Although lampstands represent the church earlier in Revelation (1:20), this position is unlikely here because the church is not mentioned or alluded to during the Tribulation. It is clear from the text that these witnesses are individuals for the following reasons:

1. The definite article "my" before "two witnesses" (v. 3).
2. They are dressed in "sackcloth" (v. 3).
3. They are killed (v. 7).

4. Their bodies lie in the street (v. 8).

5. They are resurrected (v. 11).

6. They ascend into heaven (v. 12).

Others identify the two witnesses as Enoch and Elijah because they both were translated into heaven without dying. Those holding this position point out Hebrews 9:27, "it is appointed unto men once to die." Thus, Enoch and Elijah would suffer death during the Tribulation. This interpretation is untenable. Christians who are alive on the earth when the Rapture of the church occurs will not suffer death (1 Thessalonians 4:17), nor will the believers who survive the Great Tribulation (Matthew 25:33-34). Although Elijah exhibited the miraculous gifts manifested by these two witnesses (v. 6), Enoch did not.

Still others identify the two witnesses as Moses and Elijah for the following reasons:

1. Moses represents the Law and Elijah the prophets.

2. Both performed the miracles mentioned in verse 6.

3. Both are called prophets.

4. Both appeared with Jesus during His transfiguration.

5. There is some mystery concerning the death of Moses (Deuteronomy 34:5-6; Jude 9), and Elijah was translated without seeing death (2 Kings 2:11).

6. Scripture indicates that Elijah must come "before the coming of the great and terrible day of the LORD" (Malachi 4:5).

7. Both had a message of judgment.

This teaching has several difficulties. It is evident that Moses did die (Deuteronomy 34:5-6), and this position would require him to die a second time. It could be argued that this is not a problem because all of the people whom Jesus raised from the dead died a second time (i.e., Lazarus). Another objection is that John the Baptist fulfilled the prophecy concerning Elijah by coming "in the spirit and power of Elijah" (Luke 1:17). Jesus said, "But I say unto you, That Elijah is come already....Then the disciples understood that he spoke unto them of John the Baptist" (Matthew 17:12-13). Jesus also said, "And if ye will receive it, this is Elijah [referring to John the Baptist], who was to come" (Matthew 11:14). If Israel had repented and received Jesus as the Messiah, John would have fulfilled this prophecy. But Israel did not repent, so the prophecy still must be fulfilled. John's ministry was *like* Elijah's, but he denied *being* Elijah (John 1:21) and did not restore all things.

A number of teachers believe the two witnesses will not be figures from the past but will exhibit a ministry similar to Moses and Elijah's. This position has merit because the text does not identify the two witnesses. If the witnesses are from the past, Moses and Elijah seem to be the best candidates.

The witnesses are described as "two olive trees, and the two lampstands standing before...God" (v. 4). Their mission is similar to that of Joshua, the high priest, and Zerubbabel, the civil leader (Zechariah 4:2-3, 11-14), who were raised up as lights (lampstands), ready to implement their prophetic witness through power supplied by the Holy Spirit. The two witnesses will be endowed with miraculous power enabling them "to shut heaven, that it rain not in the days of their prophecy; and have power over waters to turn them to blood, and to smite the earth with all plagues, as often as they will" (v. 6). They will be protected from death until their ministry is completed. If anyone tries to harm them, "fire proceedeth out of their mouth, and devoureth their enemies" (v. 5). The enemies of Moses and Elijah were also destroyed by fire.

"When they shall have finished their testimony, the beast that ascendeth out of the bottomless pit shall make war against them...and kill them" (v. 7). Some scholars believe that the "beast" is Satan, while others teach that it is the Antichrist. Satan is referred to in Revelation as the dragon, not as a beast. The beast coming out of the bottomless pit is the Antichrist, who is empowered by Satan to kill the two witnesses. Their dead bodies will be left lying "in the street of the great city [Jerusalem], which spiritually is called Sodom [symbol of immorality] and Egypt [symbol of oppression and slavery]" (v. 8). The authorities will not "permit their...bodies" to be buried for "three days and a half," so that the "peoples and kindreds and tongues and nations" (v. 9) can see them lying in the street. Leaving a body unburied was the greatest contempt and humiliation that could be shown in biblical times.

The unbelieving earth dwellers will "rejoice" over their deaths by "mak[ing] merry, and...send[ing] gifts one to another" (v. 10). Such a celebration over these godly prophets is fiendish and childish, indicating the total depravity and hatred for Tribulation believers.[1] The reason for their celebration is clear: No more will they be "tormented" (v. 10) by the godly prophets' miracles of judgment (vv. 5-6) and their message of repentance. The world will hate God's messengers and their message (Hebrews 11:35-38), but although they may silence the messengers, they cannot silence the message.

"After three days and a half" (v. 11), while the earth dwellers are rejoicing, God will vindicate His messengers by raising them from the dead. The prophets' resurrection will cause "great fear [panic]" (v. 11), terrorizing the unbelieving world. Immediately the prophets will hear "a great voice from heaven saying unto them, Come up here" (v. 12). Their enemies will witness the prophets' ascension as they are caught "up to heaven in a cloud" (v. 12).

In "the same hour" in which the witnesses ascend into heaven, "a great earthquake" will destroy a "tenth part" of

Jerusalem, resulting in the death of "seven thousand" people (v. 13). The remaining population of the city will become panic-stricken and give "glory to the God of heaven" (v. 13). Will the remnant giving glory to God actually come to faith in Christ, or simply acknowledge His awesome power because of the earthquake? The text provides no indication that they will become believers. If true repentance were to be the result, God's judgment most likely would be postponed, or at least delayed. John records that this is not the case: "The second woe is past and, behold, the third woe cometh quickly" (v. 14).

Trumpet Mentioned

The blowing of the seventh trumpet introduces the third woe and contains the seven bowl judgments, which are not poured out upon the earth until later (16:1ff). Again, heaven is opened and John hears a multitude of voices declaring, "The kingdom of this world is become the kingdom of our Lord, and of his Christ, and he shall reign forever and ever" (v. 15). The phrase "is [lit., has] become" views Christ's future rule over this world as already accomplished. Christ will reclaim rule over the kingdoms of this world at His Second Coming. This will settle the question of who is the sovereign ruler over planet Earth.

Upon hearing this, "the four and twenty elders...fell upon their faces, and worshiped God" (v. 16) by giving Him "thanks" (v. 17). They thank God for who He is: "O Lord God Almighty, who art, and wast, and art to come" (v. 17). They thank God for His worldwide rule: "because thou hast taken to thee thy great power, and hast reigned" (v. 17). They thank God for His wrath upon the ungodly: "And the nations were angry, and thy wrath is come [lit., came]" (v. 18). This is the fulfillment of God's wrath that will be poured out upon the nations (Psalm 2:1-6, 8-9), who will set themselves against Christ at His Second Coming. He will destroy them with the word of His mouth when He treads "the winepress of the fierceness and wrath of Almighty God" (19:15). They thank God for judging the wicked: "that they should be judged" (v. 18). They thank God for rewarding the works of the righteous: "and that thou shouldest give reward unto thy servants, the prophets, and to the saints, and them that fear thy name, small and great" (v. 18). Some see the last two praises as a twofold time of judgment, where God will judge the wicked at the Great White Throne Judgment (20:10-14) and provide rewards to the righteous at the Bema Judgment (2 Corinthians 5:10). It is better to interpret this verse as a general statement about God's judgment on the wicked and the righteous. Finally, they thank God for judging worldwide wickedness: "destroy them who destroy the earth" (v. 18). God will destroy every kind of wickedness on the earth before setting up the Millennial Kingdom (19:17-21).

At the conclusion of this praise hymn, John reports, "the temple of God was opened in heaven, and there was seen in his temple the ark of his covenant" (v. 19). This is not the ark of the covenant translated to heaven before the destruction of Solomon's Temple, but the original ark in God's Temple. The Tabernacle fixtures were patterned after things in heaven (cp. Exodus 25:40; Hebrews 9:23).

The descriptions of "lightnings, and voices, and thunderclaps, and an earthquake, and great hail" (v. 19) are a fitting conclusion to the sounding of the seventh trumpet, whose judgments will soon be poured out upon the earth (cp. 15:5-16:21).

Today, we sense that the world is moving swiftly toward a time of judgment. Like the two witnesses, we in the church are messengers with a mandate to proclaim the message of repentance and judgment to our generation—while there is still time.

Endnote

[1] Robert L. Thomas, *Revelation 8-22, An Exegetical Commentary* (Chicago: Moody Press, 1995), p. 96.

REVELATION 12:1-17

And there appeared a great wonder in heaven—a woman clothed with the sun, and the moon under her feet, and upon her head a crown of twelve stars. And she, being with child, cried, travailing in birth, and pained to be delivered. And there appeared another wonder in heaven; and, behold, a great red dragon, having seven heads and ten horns, and seven crowns upon his heads. And his tail drew the third part of the stars of heaven and did cast them to the earth; and the dragon stood before the woman who was ready to be delivered, to devour her child as soon as it was born. And she brought forth a male child, who was to rule all nations with a rod of iron; and her child was caught up unto God, and to his throne. And the woman fled into the wilderness, where she hath a place prepared by God, that they should feed her there a thousand two hundred and threescore days. And there was war in heaven; Michael and his angels fought against the dragon, and the dragon fought and his angels, And prevailed not, neither was their place found any more in heaven. And the great dragon was cast out, that old serpent, called the Devil and Satan, who deceiveth the whole world; he was cast out into the earth, and his angels were cast out with him. And I heard a loud voice saying in heaven, Now is come salvation, and strength, and the kingdom of our God, and the power of his Christ; for the accuser of our brethren is cast down, who accused them before our God day and night. And they overcame him by the blood of the Lamb, and by the word of their testimony; and they loved not their lives unto the death. Therefore rejoice, ye heavens, and ye that dwell in them. Woe to the inhab-

iters of the earth and of the sea! For the devil is come down unto you, having great wrath, because he knoweth that he hath but a short time. And when the dragon saw that he was cast unto the earth, he persecuted the woman who brought forth the male child. And to the woman were given two wings of a great eagle, that she might fly into the wilderness, into her place, where she is nourished for a time, and times, and half a time, from the face of the serpent. And the serpent cast out of his mouth water like a flood after the woman, that he might cause her to be carried away by the flood. And the earth helped the woman, and the earth opened her mouth and swallowed up the flood which the dragon cast out of his mouth. And the dragon was angry with the woman, and went to make war with the remnant of her seed, who keep the commandments of God, and have the testimony of Jesus Christ.

14

ISRAEL'S TRAVAIL AND TRIUMPH

Satan's attempts to annihilate the Jewish people throughout the centuries are well documented in biblical and secular history. Throughout history, demonically inspired despots like Haman and Hitler, filled with fanatical hatred, have attempted genocide of the Jewish people. The Jews often stand before their history in sober silence, stunned and numbed by the unmitigated brutality that their eyes have seen but that their minds find difficult to believe. Penetrating pictures of the Holocaust of World War II continually parade across the television screens and minds of America, reminding the viewers of Satan's relentless attempts to eradicate world Jewry. In Revelation 12, Satan's strategy is unmasked as he tries to annihilate Israel during the second half of the Tribulation period, known as "the time of Jacob's trouble" (Jeremiah 30:7).

Participants in the Conflict

God drew back the clouds of heaven and revealed to John the participants in this conflict. John saw "a great wonder in heaven—a woman clothed with the sun, and the moon under her feet, and upon her head a crown of twelve stars" (v. 1).

Some scholars believe that this is the virgin Mary, but this is impossible because the woman is referred to as a "wonder," literally, *a sign*. The same imagery is presented in Joseph's dream, where the sun, moon, and stars represent Jacob, Rachel, and the tribes of Israel (Genesis 37:9-11). Others believe that the woman represents the church. This cannot be correct either because Israel, not the church, gave birth to the "child" (vv. 2, 5), who is Jesus, the Messiah. Thus, we must conclude that the woman spoken of in this chapter is none other than Israel.

The woman who, "being with child, cried, travailing in birth, and pained to be delivered" (v. 2), is not a picture of the virgin Mary giving birth, as some teach. This is a picture of Israel's travail in bringing forth Jesus the Messiah, as Satan attempted to thwart the birth through the iron heel of Roman oppression and the insanity of a paranoid Herod (Matthew 2:16-18).

John saw "another wonder [sign] in heaven...a great red dragon" (v. 3). The red dragon is symbolic of Satan (v. 9), who is described by various names throughout this chapter. The phrase "a great red dragon" (v. 3) presents him as a cruel monster and a bloody murderer. He is called "that old serpent" (v. 9) because he beguiled Eve in the Garden of Eden. He is called "the Devil" (v. 9) because he is a slanderer. "Satan" (v. 9) describes him as an adversary who opposes God and His program and goes about trying to deceive the whole world. He is called "the accuser of our brethren" (v. 10) because his current work is to bring reproach on believers before God's throne.

The dragon is described as "having seven heads and ten horns, and seven crowns upon his heads" (v. 3). The seven heads represent seven consecutive evil world empires controlled by Satan and leading up to the revival of the Roman Empire. The ten horns represent the ten-nation confederacy that comes out of the seventh head, which is the revived Roman Empire controlled by

Satan during the Great Tribulation. The seven crowns upon his heads indicate the fullness of Satan's authority and his rule over nations, which he will give to the beast (the Antichrist) during the Great Tribulation (13:2). The Antichrist is simply a pawn in the hands of Satan to carry out his devilish program of world supremacy during this time.

At one time, the dragon wielded great power and authority over "the stars of heaven" (v. 4). It is clear from other passages that the "stars" here represent angelic beings (see 9:1). In the past, Satan and his angels engaged in a heavenly conflict that resulted in their removal from heaven: "And his tail drew the third part of the stars of heaven and did cast them to the earth" (v. 4). The stars are one-third of the angelic host of heaven who followed Satan during his rebellion, when he attempted to usurp authority over God and His throne (see Isaiah 14:12-17). Not all of these fallen angels are loose today; some are so vile that they must be chained in hell until the day of judgment (Jude 6; 2 Peter 2:4). Although Satan's work is limited to the atmosphere of the earth, he still has access to God's throne (v. 10; Job 1-2) until he is removed a second time during the Tribulation (v. 9).

"The dragon stood before the woman [Israel]...to devour her child [Jesus] as soon as it was born" (v. 4). Satan recognized that Jesus' birth was a threat to his illegal possession and control of the earth. Long before Israel was a nation, it was prophesied that Satan would try to cut off the woman and her seed (Genesis 3:15). He tried to cut off Christ's lineage by the death of Abel (Genesis 4); polluting the godly line of Seth (Genesis 6); producing a pseudo-son of promise in Ishmael (Genesis 16); destroying Israel in Egypt (Exodus 1) and in Persia (Esther 3:8-15); trying to kill Christ in Bethlehem (Matthew 2:16) and Nazareth (Luke 4:28-29), and succeeding at His crucifixion (Matthew 27:33-50). But Christ defeated Satan through that very crucifixion (Hebrews 2:14).

Clearly, the "male child, who was to rule all nations with a rod of iron" (v. 5) is Jesus Christ. After His birth, ministry, death, and resurrection, He ascended back to heaven and is seated on the right hand of God, where Satan cannot touch Him.

Unable to destroy Christ, Satan centered his attack on the woman. "The woman fled into the wilderness, where she hath a place prepared by God, that they should feed her there a thousand two hundred and threescore days" (v. 6). This is the last three and one-half years of the Great Tribulation, when God will protect Israel from being exterminated by the Antichrist.

John saw a fourth person, Michael the archangel (v. 7), whose ministry is to oversee and protect the nation of Israel. The text reveals that "Michael and his angels fought against the dragon [Satan], and...his angels [demons]" (v. 7). Michael gained the victory over Satan and cast him out of heaven onto the earth, thus forever excluding him from access to God (vv. 8-9). This is the first of three judgments on Satan. He will be bound and sealed in the bottomless pit during the Kingdom age (20:1-3) and finally cast into the lake of fire to be tormented forever (20:10). The time of this battle, although not given, must be sometime before the middle of the Tribulation. This conclusion parallels Michael's defense of Israel during the Great Tribulation (Daniel 12:1).

Satan's removal from heaven produced a victorious hymn of praise. Although John does not identify the "loud voice" (v. 10) that he heard, it most likely comes from God, angels, the 24 elders, and the martyred Tribulation saints who are under the altar.

The hymn is divided into three stanzas.

1. Praise is given to celebrate the completion of God's program: "Now is come salvation, and strength, and the kingdom of our God, and the power of his Christ; for the accuser of our

brethren is cast down" (v. 10). Thus, Satan is defeated and the earth is delivered from his control as God manifests His strength in establishing the Millennial Kingdom under Christ's authoritative reign.

2. Praise is offered for the victory of the saints who "overcame him [Satan] by the blood of the Lamb" (v. 11). Christ's shed blood provided salvation and standing for the saints before God and protected them from Satan's accusations. They also overcame Satan "by the word of their testimony" (v. 11)—that is, confession of faith in Jesus Christ and His Word before the world. The strength of their commitment is seen in the statement, "they loved not their lives unto the death" (v. 11). These believers were willing to give up their lives for what they believed, even if it meant suffering the violent death of a martyr.

3. Those in heaven are encouraged to "rejoice" (v. 12) over Satan's expulsion and exile to the realm of the earth, but the earth is given a warning: "Woe to the inhabiters of the earth and of the sea! For the devil is come down unto you, having great wrath, because he knoweth that he hath but a short time" (v. 12). The world, already under the wrath of God, must now face the uncontrollable anger of Satan as he pours out the most irrational hatred possible upon humanity. Why such intense wrath? Satan knows "that he hath but a short time" to accomplish his objectives before being cast into the bottomless pit.

Preserved Through Conflict

Once Satan is cast out of heaven, he will give his full attention to "persecut[ing] the woman who brought forth the male child" (v. 13). His intense hatred of Israel will reach its climax during the Great Tribulation, as he tries to do everything in his power to destroy them. Satan knows that if he can destroy Israel, he can thwart God's program, keeping it from coming to its ultimate fruition.

But the miraculous hand of God will be upon Israel in the midst of Satan's plot to destroy them, providing a way for them to escape: "And to the woman were given two wings of a great eagle, that she might fly into the wilderness, into her place, where she is nourished for a time, and times, and half a time, from the face of the serpent" (v. 14). Some scholars believe that this refers to a massive airlift to safety, similar to the May 1991 Operation Solomon, when 14,400 Ethiopian Jews were flown to safety in Israel within 24 hours on El Al Airlines. However, the term "eagles' wings" (Exodus 19:4) was used to describe Israel's flight from Egypt without the assistance of an airlift. The phrase simply indicates that Israel's flight to safety will be swift and supernatural.

Scripture does not identify the location of "the wilderness" (v. 14) where God will protect and nourish this remnant of Jewish people. Many believe it will be in the area of Edom because this country will escape the wrathful destruction of the Antichrist during the Tribulation (Daniel 11:41). This could well be the place because Christ will come to Edom upon His return to take vengeance on the people of Bozrah and possibly to deliver a remnant of Jewish believers (Isaiah 63:1-6).

Satan, in one last effort to exterminate Israel, will send "water like a flood after the woman" (v. 15) to destroy her. Israel will be spared from Satan's tactic when God sends an earthquake to swallow up the flood (v. 16). The text indicates that the water is *like* a flood, making it difficult to tell if the flood should be interpreted literally or figuratively. Israel has been spared from water twice—at the Red Sea (Exodus 14:13-31) and at the Jordan River (Joshua 3). This flood most likely figuratively refers to Satan's dispatching a huge army to destroy the fleeing Israelites near the midpoint of the Tribulation (see Ezekiel 38-39).

Being unable to destroy Israel will intensify Satan's anger, causing him "to make war with the remnant of her seed, who keep the commandments of God, and have the testimony of Jesus Christ" (v. 17). These are the 144,000 Jewish people who will become believers during the Tribulation (7:4-8) and will be scattered worldwide to testify of their faith in Jesus Christ. They will be victorious over Satan's attempt to destroy them (14:1-5). Although the Devil will be unable to totally exterminate Israel, two-thirds of the Jewish population will be killed during the Tribulation (Zechariah 13:8).

Knowing that his time is short, Satan will step up his persecution of Israel in these latter days. Today, Satan's strategy to proliferate a legacy of hatred against Israel is like a wound that never heals. Like the prophets of old, we must warn Israel of their impending travail and stand with the nation as it approaches the birth pains of the Tribulation. And, like the prophets of old, we must bring to Israel the comforting message that there is hope and victory in Jesus, the Messiah.

REVELATION 13:1-10

And I stood upon the sand of the sea, and saw a beast rise up out of the sea, having seven heads and ten horns, and upon his horns ten crowns, and upon his heads the name of blasphemy. And the beast which I saw was like a leopard, and his feet were like the feet of a bear, and his mouth like the mouth of a lion; and the dragon gave him his power, and his throne, and great authority. And I saw one of his heads as though it were wounded to death; and his deadly wound was healed, and all the world wondered after the beast. And they worshiped the dragon who gave power unto the beast; and they worshiped the beast, saying, Who is like the beast? Who is able to make war with him? And there was given unto him a mouth speaking great things and blasphemies, and power was given unto him to continue forty and two months. And he opened his mouth in blasphemy against God, to blaspheme his name, and his tabernacle, and them that dwell in heaven. And it was given unto him to make war with the saints, and to overcome them; and power was given him over all kindreds, and tongues, and nations. And all that dwell upon the earth shall worship him, whose names are not written in the book of life of the Lamb slain from the foundation of the world. If any man have an ear, let him hear. He that leadeth into captivity shall go into captivity; he that killeth with the sword must be killed with the sword. Here is the patience and the faith of the saints.

═══ 15 ═══

THE COMING WORLD RULER

Attempts to identify the beast of Revelation have been numerous. Throughout church history, suggested candidates have been Judas, Nero, a Roman Pope, Hitler, Mussolini, Kennedy, Kissinger, and many others. To properly identify the beast, we must study what the Bible records about his nature, character, and government.

Two beasts are mentioned in Revelation 13, one from the sea (v. 1) and another from the earth (v. 11). The beast from the sea has been identified by many scholars as the Antichrist, while the beast from the earth has been identified as the false prophet. This chapter focuses on the beast "out of the sea."

His Appearance

John wrote, "And I stood upon the sand of the sea, and saw a beast rise up out of the sea" (v. 1). In some translations, the word "I" is translated "he" because of a variance in the Greek word. If the translation "he" is correct, it refers to the dragon (Satan), not John, who is standing upon the "sand of the sea." Although scholars are divided on the correct reading, neither alters the interpretation of the chapter.

The beast will rise "up out of the sea" (v. 1), indicating that he will come from the *sea* of Gentile humanity, over whom he will usurp authority. The term *beast* is indicative of his ferocious nature, putting him in a league with Satan. It is clearly stated that the beast is a man (v..18) who comes out of the abyss (11:7; 17:8), indicating that he will be raised up by Satan.

John described him as having "seven heads and ten horns, and upon his horns ten crowns, and upon his heads the name of blasphemy" (v. 1). Some scholars interpret the "seven heads" as kings from the revived Roman Empire ruling simultaneously (as sub-rulers) under the beast during the Tribulation. Others see the "seven heads" as successive world empires of the past leading up to the final Roman Empire (cp. 17:10-12). The second interpretation is more tenable. The "ten horns" are ten kings within the confederacy of the revived Roman Empire (17:12) who will be ruled by the beast during the Tribulation.

The beast's appearance, described in verse 2, is identical to a combination of three of the beasts mentioned in Daniel 7:3-8, but in reverse order.

1. "His mouth like the mouth of a lion" is symbolic of Nebuchadnezzar and speaks of majesty, power, and ferocity.

2. "His feet...like the feet of a bear" are symbolic of the Medo-Persian Empire and speak of strength, stability, and tenacity—the ability to crush its prey at will.

3. He was "like a leopard," a symbol of the Grecian Empire under Alexander the Great, who swiftly moved through the Middle East conquering the known world at will.

He will be energized by the "dragon" (Satan), who "gave

him his power, and his throne, and great authority." Thus, the beast will be a pawn in the hand of Satan and will possess greater authority and power than all successive world empires before him.

His Affliction

John saw one of the beast's "heads as though it were wounded to death; and his deadly wound was healed" (v. 3; cp. vv. 12, 14). There is disagreement among scholars about whether the beast will actually die from his fatal wound and later be resurrected, or whether he will survive a deathbed affliction without actually dying. Some people believe that this passage refers to the resurrection of someone like Judas Iscariot or Adolf Hitler. Both scenarios are highly unlikely because Scripture does not record that Satan has been given power to raise anyone from the dead. It is also doubtful that God would allow one such as Judas or Hitler to return from the dead because the wicked will not be resurrected until the Great White Throne Judgment (20:11-15). The text says "as though it were wounded to death," giving the distinct impression that the beast will be near death but will not die.

Others believe that an assassination attempt will be made on the beast but that he will be completely restored to health and power. Still others believe that the deadly wound refers to the Roman Empire that never died, and not to the beast himself. That is, the imperial form of the Roman Empire received a fatal wound centuries ago but will be "healed" (restored) and will reemerge into a ten-nation European confederation. Because the beast is referred to as a composite empire by the description of its parts (13:3; 17:7-8), it is reasonable to believe that this is speaking about raising up the empire and not its leader. Often the leader and his empire are used interchangeably in Scripture or are identified together. Thus, the word "beast" refers to both the

Antichrist and his empire—the king and his kingdom. Taken as a whole, it seems that verse 3 refers to the empire being healed, and not its leader.

The beast's healing will cause worldwide amazement: "and all the world wondered after the beast" (v. 3). This wonderment will turn into worship of "the dragon" and "the beast" (v. 4). Those who worship them will have no love for the truth of Christ and His saving message. For this reason, God will send them strong delusions so that they will believe the lie of Satan (2 Thessalonians 2:10-11). They will be completely turned over to devil worship. Satan will finally realize a portion of his long-sought desire to receive worldwide worship from God's creation. People will give full allegiance to this beast, who is the Antichrist, because of his authoritative personality. The masses will admire his power, wisdom, leadership, and military might to rule the world. The world will ask, "Who is like the beast?" (v. 4). The expected answer is, No one!

His Authority

The beast will seem invincible: "Who is able to make war with him?" (v. 4). Again, the answer is, "No one!" Satan will give him the necessary authority to be a world conqueror (v. 2). In fact, he will honor only "the god of fortresses" (Daniel 11:38). God alone has the power to destroy him.

Most world dictators have proven to be persuasive speakers, able to motivate the masses to their political ideology. The Antichrist will be no exception. Like Adolf Hitler, he will able to mesmerize the whole nation with his inspiring speeches. Who will give the Antichrist "a mouth" to speak such "great things and blasphemies" (v. 5; cp. Daniel 7:8, 11, 20)? Some teach that Satan will give him this authority, based on verse 2. Others believe that God will permit him to carry out his vile pronouncements and program of persecution. The latter teaching seems more plausible because the Antichrist's power will be limited to "forty and two months" (v. 5). God granted similar permissions in other portions of Revelation (6:4, 8; 7:2; 9:5). In all probability, if Satan gives power to the Antichrist, it will not be limited. Verse 6 lists three ways in which the beast will blaspheme God:

1. He will blaspheme God's name by casting direct aspersion on His person.

2. He will blaspheme His Tabernacle by speaking against His dwelling place.

3. He will blaspheme those who dwell (tabernacle) in heaven—the saints and the angelic host who, along with Michael the archangel, will cast Satan out of heaven (12:7-9, 12).

His Aggression

The Antichrist will be given power "to make war with the saints, and to overcome them" (v. 7). Multitudes will be killed during the Great Tribulation (13:15; 20:4). Although they will be martyred for their faith, they will come forth victorious in the end (12:11; 17:14). There will, however, be a host of Jewish (12:6, 14-16) and Gentile (Matthew 25:32-33) believers who will survive his wrath.

The Antichrist's power will become worldwide by the middle of the Tribulation, for "power was given him over all kindreds, and tongues, and nations" (v. 7). He will receive global worship, for "all that dwell upon the earth shall worship him, whose names are not written in the book of life" (v. 8). Only a remnant of "elect" believers (Matthew 24:24) will escape being drawn into worship of the Antichrist.

Those who worship the beast will not have their "names...written in the book of life of the Lamb slain from the foundation of the world" (v. 8). The word "written" is in the perfect tense, indicating that their names will *never* be in the book of life. Thus, all who worship the beast or take his mark will be eternally lost and destined for damnation in the lake of fire (14:9-11). The question must be asked, If the book of life contains the names of all people born into the world, does God then blot out the names of the unsaved at their death? Or, does the book contain only the names of the redeemed, who will never be blotted out? Most likely the latter view is correct.

The phrase "foundation of the world" (v. 8) has been interpreted in two ways. Some read the phrase in its given order: "the Lamb slain from the foundation of the world." Others connect the phrase to the "book of life written from the foundation of the world." The latter interpretation is preferable. Thus, John is referring to the book of life written from the foundation of the world. This position is supported by Revelation 17:8.

An invitation is given to those living in the Great Tribulation: "If any man have an ear, let him hear" (v. 9). People are to hear the warning previously given concerning the Antichrist's war against the saints, his attempt to gain worldwide worship as God, and his coming captivity and death, as mentioned in verse 10. Earlier, those in the church are given a similar call to "hear what the Spirit saith unto the churches" (2:7, 11, 17, 29; 3:6, 13, 22). Notice that the phrase "unto the churches" is conspicuously absent in verse 9. This is another indication that the church will be raptured before the Tribulation.

The phrase "He that leadeth into captivity shall go into captivity; he that killeth with the sword must be killed with the sword" (v. 10) is better understood, "If any man is for captivity, into captivity he goes. If any man is to be killed by the sword, he must be killed by the sword." Scholars have differed on the interpretation of this verse. Some take it to mean that divine judgment will be poured out on the beast and his army who will kill the Tribulation saints. This promise of punishment for their tormentors will provide encouragement to the saints—who will be undergoing severe persecution—to be patient and faithful during this time. Others believe the verse is teaching that the Tribulation saints will in no way escape persecution and martyrdom by the beast and his army. Thus, they are warned of their coming martyrdom and urged to submit to such persecution in the providence of God, for he was given power and authority (vv. 5, 7, 14, 15) to be victorious over them. A similar incident was prophesied to Judah by Jeremiah prior to their captivity in Babylon (Jeremiah 15:2; 43:11). The captivity and death of Judah would be inevitable and inescapable. Under such tribulation, the saints are exhorted to exercise "patience" (endurance and steadfastness) and "faith" (faithfulness, v. 10) in their commitment to the Lord. A glimmer of hope shines through this dismal prediction: God is sovereignly in control of the situation and has limited this persecution by the Antichrist to 42 months.

Attempts are still being made to identify the beast. Will the church ever be able to identify the Antichrist? No. Scripture indicates that the church will be raptured off the earth before the Tribulation and the revelation of the Antichrist.

John has presented a glimpse of the Antichrist's rise to worldwide rule through the revived Roman Empire. Satan and his forces will be the impetus providing this beast with his power, authority, and kingdom. This will be Satan's final attempt to acquire worldwide worship and supremacy for himself.

REVELATION 13:11-18

And I beheld another beast coming up out of the earth; and he had two horns like a lamb, and he spoke like a dragon. And he exerciseth all the power of the first beast before him, and causeth the earth and them who dwell on it to worship the first beast, whose deadly wound was healed. And he doeth great wonders, so that he maketh fire come down from heaven on the earth in the sight of men, And deceiveth them that dwell on the earth by the means of those miracles which he had power to do in the sight of the beast, saying to them that dwell on the earth, that they should make an image to the beast, that had the wound by a sword, and did live. And he hath power to give life unto the image of the beast, that the image of the beast should both speak, and cause that as many as would not worship the image of the beast should be killed. And he causeth all, both small and great, rich and poor, free and enslaved, to receive a mark in their right hand, or in their foreheads, And that no man might buy or sell, except he that had the mark, or the name of the beast, or the number of his name. Here is wisdom. Let him that hath understanding count the number of the beast; for it is the number of a man; and his number is six hundred threescore and six.

16

THE COMING WORLD PROPHET

Jesus predicted that many false Christs and prophets will appear in the last days. The two beasts mentioned in Revelation 13 are the final unveiling of Jesus' prophecy that will take place during the Great Tribulation. The first beast is the world political ruler popularly identified as the Antichrist (13:1-10). The second beast is a religious leader identified as the false prophet (16:13; 19:20; 20:10). This chapter focuses on the second beast.

His Appearance

John wrote, "And I beheld another beast coming up out of the earth" (v. 11). The word *another* (Gr., *allo*) means *another of the same kind*. He will possess the same kind of nature, character, power, and ferocity as the first beast but will function in a supporting role as the false religious prophet.

Three phrases in verse 11 describe the second beast.

　　1. He will come "up out of the earth." Some interpret the word *earth* as referring to Israel. They reason that because the first beast rising from the sea is identified as a Gentile, the second beast

coming out of the earth must be a Jewish prophet
from Israel. This is highly unlikely because he
will promote the satanic program of the dragon
and the first beast, who will try to annihilate the
Jewish people (12:13-17). Nothing is revealed in
Scripture about the second beast's ethnicity or
racial identity.

2. "He had two horns like a lamb." In Scripture,
horns indicate power and ruling authority.
Thus, his appearance will be a counterfeit
(imitation) of Christ. Christ as a Lamb (5:6)
had seven horns; the false prophet has only
two horns, indicating that he has less power
than Christ. He appears lamb-like—defenseless and mild-natured, as was Christ at His first
coming. But he will actually be a wolf in
sheep's clothing, ready to devour all who will
not obey his commands.

3. "He spoke like a dragon." Although docile in
appearance, his speech will be subtle, seductive, and satanic, structured to lead people
away from belief in Christ and into the cun-
ning, corrupt worship of the Antichrist.[1] His
word will be law, and those who defy it will
pay with their lives.

Some commentators try to identify the second beast as the
Antichrist because of his lamb-like qualities, his appearance,
and his miracle-working power—all of which imitate Christ.
The two horns, they claim, suggest that the false prophet is both
the Antichrist and the world religious leader who will consolidate apostate Catholicism and Protestantism under his ecclesiastical leadership as head of the apostate church. This claim
cannot be substantiated in light of Scripture. Clearly the first
beast is the Antichrist, and the false prophet is subservient to

him. The second beast is identified as a prophet, not a leader of the one-world church. Although he will convince or coerce the unbelieving world to worship the Antichrist through his miracle-working power, there is no direct indication that he is the ecclesiastical head of the one-world church or the Pope of the Roman Catholic Church.

His Authority

Satan will infuse the second beast with the same great authority he will give to the first beast. "And he exerciseth all the power of the first beast" (v. 12). The word *exerciseth* (Gr., *poieo*) appears eight times in verses 12 to 18 and means *to do, to cause, to make.* By exercising great power, the false prophet will consolidate worldwide religion, economy, and commerce (vv. 13-17) under his control. Notice the chain of authority: The first beast will promote Satan's desire for worldwide domination and worship; the second beast will promote the first beast's desire for the same by manifesting "great wonders" (v. 13).

Through manifesting those "great wonders," the false prophet will use satanic deception (2 Thessalonians 2:9-11) to lead unsaved people to worship the first beast and his idolatrous image as God (2 Thessalonians 2:4). His miraculous healing of the first beast from its "deadly wound" (v. 12) will help persuade people to worship the beast. This will not include the remnant of Jewish people who will flee into the wilderness to escape the Antichrist's wrath (12:13-17) nor true Gentile believers.

Some commentators see an analogy in this pseudoreligious system imitating the triune God: the dragon (Satan) representing God the Father, the first beast (Antichrist) representing Jesus Christ the Son, and the second beast (the false prophet) representing the Holy Spirit.

His Activities

The false prophet will possess supernatural power from Satan, which he will use to function as a miracle worker. "And he doeth great wonders [lit., signs], so that he maketh fire come down from heaven on the earth in the sight of men" (v. 13). These miracles will not be like those of the Egyptian magicians (Exodus 7:11-12) or Simon the sorcerer (Acts 8:9-12), who used trickery. They will be like that of Elijah, who called down fire from heaven during his confrontation with the prophets of Baal (1 Kings 18:38-39). Satan, working through the false prophet, may try to imitate the miracle of the two prophets who used fire from their mouths to devour their enemies (11:5), especially Elijah. Satan was behind the fire sent from heaven to destroy Job's sheep (Job 1:16), although those who reported the incident said it was from God. Satan has limited power and can only perform the miracles that God will allow.

The miracle-working power of the false prophet will be so convincing that he "deceiveth them that dwell on the earth by the means of those miracles which he had power to do in the sight of the beast" (v. 14). The unsaved world will be completely and continually captivated by his miraculous power, signs, and lying wonders. Jesus warned that these signs and wonders will be so compelling "that, if it were possible, they shall deceive the very elect" (Matthew 24:24).

The unsaved world will be duped into constructing "an image to the beast, that had the wound by a sword, and did live" (v. 14). Dr. John Walvoord provides a plausible explanation of this phrase.

> The beast is both the empire and its ruler. As ruler he is the symbol of the empire and the executor of its power. Though the wound by the sword apparently refers to the decline of the

historic Roman Empire and its revival is indicated by the expression "did live," the man
who serves at the head of the empire is the
symbol of this miraculous restoration....The
image is the center of the false worship and the
focal point of the final state of apostasy, the
acme of the idolatry which has been the false
religion of so many generations.[2]

The image erected by the people will seem to take on life:
"And he [the false prophet] hath power [lit., was given power] to
give life unto the image" (v. 15). Commentators are divided on
whether this image actually will have life or only the appearance
of life. Some believe that God will allow the false prophet to
give life to the image because of its ability to speak and cause the
death of those not worshiping it. Others believe that the word *life*
(lit., *breath* or *spirit*) refers only to an appearance of life, similar
to a computerized figure, and not to life itself. It has been documented that trickery, magic, and ventriloquism were used in the
first century to gain a following and worship by pseudoreligion-
ists (Acts 13:6-12; 16:16; 19:13-20).

Not much is told about this image—whether its power will
be natural or supernatural, how long it will appear to have life,
or any other characteristics that it will possess. The image
will demand the death of everyone who will not worship it (v.
15). Many true believers will refuse to worship it and will pay
with their lives (7:9, 14; 20:4). A similar progression occurred
when Nebuchadnezzar erected an image of gold and demand-
ed all people to bow in worship to it or be killed in the fiery
furnace (Daniel 3:1-7).

The false prophet will reorganize the world's population
under the Antichrist's control. "And he causeth all...to
receive a mark in their right hand, or in their foreheads" (v.
16). "All" (except believers, 20:4) will receive an identifying
mark as a sign of allegiance, regardless of their social stand-

ing ("small and great"), substance ("rich and poor"), or status ("free and enslaved") [v. 16]. Scripture does not say what the mark will be, but many speculative answers have been presented. The word *mark* (Gr., *charagma*) was used in the first century. It referred to the imprint from an imperial seal of the Roman Empire bearing the name and date of the emperor and used on official documents or coins. This mark is a visible brand or tattoo signifying ownership, loyalty, and protection—similar to that given to soldiers, slaves, and those who worshiped the emperor in the first century.[3]   Just as the 144,000 Jewish believers will be sealed, indicating God's protection (7:4), those who worship the beast will receive an identifying mark.

Through this mark, the false prophet will regulate the economy and commerce, not only in the revived Roman Empire, but worldwide. "And...no man might buy or sell, except he that had the mark" (v. 17). With the opening of the third seal, much of the world's population (excluding the wealthy) will have trouble acquiring food for survival (6:5-6). During the second half of the Tribulation, survival will be almost impossible without the beast's mark. "The name of the beast, or the number of his name" (v. 17) is in apposition with "the mark." The name, whether written in letters or numbers, is the same as "the mark."

Ancient peoples—such as the Jews, Greeks, and Romans—assigned numbers to the letters of their alphabets (called *gematria* in Hebrew). To understand the mark, one must be able to properly calculate the number 666, "for it is the number of a man; and his number is six hundred threescore and six" (v. 18). Thus, one could supposedly take the letters of a person's name, add up the numerical equivalent, and determine if it came to 666. Past attempts to identify the Antichrist in this manner have not yielded any positive results, and the same is true today.

Speculation on the meaning of this number and whom it identifies has been endless throughout church history. Many theories have been advanced: a Roman emperor, such as Nero; a future Roman Pope; a resurrected Judas or Hitler; humankind, which falls short of perfection (seven is the number of *perfection*, six is the number of *man*, displaying man's imperfection); the satanic system of the world in opposition to God's people; an unholy trinity of Satan, the Antichrist, and the false prophet; or a future man who will not be recognized until the time of the Tribulation.

The last of these interpretations seems most probable for two reasons:

1. John wrote, "Here is wisdom. Let him that hath understanding count the number of the beast" (v. 18). It seems that the wisdom and understanding needed to identify the beast will not be given until the time of the Tribulation. No generation has yet been able to properly identify the Antichrist.

2. More importantly, the church will not need the wisdom or understanding to identify the Antichrist because it will be raptured before the Tribulation begins.

John has revealed a pervasive satanic system that will control the world during the Great Tribulation. Discerning believers are acutely aware that seeds of this movement are being sown today and could blossom in the very near future. Jesus not only warned of pseudochrists and prophets, but admonished, "Take heed that no man deceive you" (Matthew 24:4). In other words, beware of the times so that you will not be led into deception. We must take this warning seriously and admonish others to do likewise.

Endnotes

[1] Robert L. Thomas, *Revelation 8-22, An Exegetical Commentary* (Chicago: Moody Press, 1995), p. 173.

[2] John F. Walvoord, *The Revelation of Jesus Christ* (Chicago: Moody Press, 1966), p. 207.

[3] Thomas, *op. cit.*, p. 181.

REVELATION 14:1-20

And I looked and, lo, a Lamb stood on Mount Zion, and with him an hundred forty and four thousand, having his Father's name written in their foreheads. And I heard a voice from heaven, like the voice of many waters, and like the voice of a great thunder; and I heard the voice of harpers harping with their harps. And they sang, as it were, a new song before the throne, and before the four living creatures and the elders; and no man could learn that song but the hundred and forty and four thousand, who were redeemed from the earth. These are they who were not defiled with women; for they are virgins. These are they who follow the Lamb wherever he goeth. These were redeemed from among men, the first fruits unto God and to the Lamb. And in their mouth was found no guile; for they are without fault before the throne of God.

And I saw another angel fly in the midst of heaven, having the everlasting gospel to preach unto them that dwell on the earth, and to every nation, and kindred, and tongue, and people, Saying with a loud voice, Fear God, and give glory to him; for the hour of his judgment is come; and worship him that made heaven, and earth, and the sea, and the fountains of waters. And there followed another angel, saying, Babylon is fallen, is fallen, that great city, because she made all nations drink of the wine of the wrath of her fornication. And the third angel followed them, saying with a loud voice, If any man worship the beast and his image, and receive his mark in his forehead, or in his hand, The same shall drink of the wine of the wrath of God, which is poured out without mixture into the cup of his indignation; and he shall be tormented with fire and brimstone in the presence of the holy angels, and in the presence of the Lamb; And the smoke of their torment ascendeth up forever and ever; and they have no rest day nor night, who worship the beast and his image, and whosoever receiveth the mark of his name. Here is the patience of the saints; here are they that keep the commandments of God, and the faith of Jesus. And I heard a voice from heaven saying unto me, Write, Blessed are the dead who die in the Lord from henceforth. Yea, saith the Spirit, that they may rest from their labors, and their works do follow them.

And I looked and, behold, a white cloud, and upon the cloud one sat, like the Son of man, having on his head a golden crown, and in his hand a sharp sickle. And another angel came out of the temple, crying with a loud voice to him that sat on the cloud, Thrust in thy sickle, and reap; for the time is come for thee to reap; for the harvest of the earth is ripe. And he that sat on the cloud thrust in his sickle on the earth, and the earth was reaped. And another angel came out of the temple which is in heaven, he also having a sharp sickle. And another angel came out from the altar, who had power over fire, and cried with a loud cry to him that had the sharp sickle, saying, Thrust in thy sharp sickle, and gather the clusters of the vine of the earth; for her grapes are fully ripe. And the angel thrust in his sickle into the earth, and gathered the vine of the earth, and cast it into the great winepress of the wrath of God. And the winepress was trodden outside the city, and blood came out of the winepress, even unto the horse bridles, by the space of a thousand and six hundred furlongs.

17

THE VICTORIOUS CHRIST

The conflict between good and evil is vividly described in Revelation 13 and 14. In chapter 13, the two beasts reap a harvest of souls through deception and persecution, in what could be called the darkest period of world history. In Revelation 14, John is given a vision of Christ's victorious triumph over evil as He thrusts in His sickle of judgment to destroy Satan's rule over the earth. This parenthetical chapter previews a series of seven proleptic visions to be fulfilled in the last half of the Tribulation.

Victory Assured

John sees "a Lamb [standing] on Mount Zion, and with him an hundred forty and four thousand" (v. 1). This is the same group of Jewish believers mentioned in Revelation 7:4, who will be saved, sealed, and kept safe throughout the Tribulation. Some commentators teach that the 144,000 will be in heaven with the Lord, but the text clearly teaches that they will stand with the Lord on Mount Zion in Jerusalem after His Second Coming. John sees the "Father's name written in their foreheads" (v. 1), denoting ownership and guaranteeing their protection throughout the seven years of the

Tribulation. They have come through the Great Tribulation victoriously and are ready to enter the Millennial Kingdom in their natural bodies.

The apostle provides a graphic description of the 144,000 Jewish believers. They are virgin men who have not been "defiled with women" (v. 4). They are loyal to Christ, willing to "follow the Lamb" (v. 4) wherever He leads them. They are "first fruits unto God and to the Lamb" (v. 4) who are saved at the beginning of the Tribulation. There is no "guile" (deceit) in their mouths, "for they are without fault [blemish] before the throne of God" (i.e., in God's sight, v. 5). They possess a sterling character and commitment to the Lord, giving them the needed strength to stand against the Antichrist's demonic program.

The apostle "heard a voice from heaven, like the voice of many waters, and like the voice of a great thunder" (v. 2). In all likelihood, this is the voice of God the Father. John also heard other voices coming from heaven that sounded like many melodious harps (v. 2).

The "new song" that John heard "before the throne" of God could not be learned by any man "but the hundred and forty and four thousand, who were redeemed from the earth" (v. 3). The phrase "And they sang" (v. 3) refers to the singing of an unidentified group in heaven, but the words are intelligible to the 144,000 who stand triumphantly on Mount Zion after the Tribulation. Speculation on the identity of these singers in heaven ranges from an innumerable group of unidentified angels (cp. 5:11) to the martyred Tribulation saints (7:9-13). The theme and content of the song are not revealed, but it seems to be a song of praise, sung in celebration of Christ's victorious triumph over the earth following His Second Coming, just before the Millennial Kingdom begins.

Vengeance Announced

In the verses that follow, six angels appear to announce various phases of God's final judgment on the ungodly world system that has been set up and controlled by Satan. There has been much discussion about the identity of "another angel" (v. 6) because no angel is mentioned thus far in this section. Most likely John is connecting this angel with the ones in 8:3, 10:1, and 11:15, or the angels associated with Michael in 12:7.

The first angel flew "in the midst of heaven, having the everlasting gospel to preach unto them that dwell on the earth" (v. 6). The word *gospel* means *good news* and is used in different ways throughout Scripture. There is the "gospel of God" (Romans 1:1), the "gospel of Christ" (Galatians 1:7), the "gospel of the kingdom" (Matthew 24:14), and the "everlasting gospel" (14:6). What is the "everlasting gospel"? In context, the "everlasting [eternal] gospel" is the proclamation that men need to fear God and give Him glory and worship in light of the impending judgment that is ready to fall upon the world (v. 7). It is God's last call of grace concerning the opportunity for people to believe in God. It should be noted that there is no call to repent of sin or invitation to receive Christ in this gospel. To the contrary, the content of this gospel is judgment.

Embracing the second view, Dr. John Walvoord writes:

> The expression "the everlasting gospel," actually without the article ("everlasting gospel") is an arresting phrase. It is everlasting in the sense that it is ageless, not for any specific period. Ordinarily, one would expect this to refer to the gospel of salvation. In verse 7, however, the content of the message is quite otherwise, for it is an announcement of the hour of judgment of God and the command to worship Him....The everlasting gospel seems to be neither the gospel of grace nor the gospel of the

kingdom, but rather the good news that God at last is about to deal with the world in righteousness and establish His sovereignty over the world. Throughout eternity God will continue to manifest Himself in grace toward the saints and in punishment toward the wicked. To refer to the gospel of grace as an everlasting gospel is to ignore the context and usage of the term.[1]

According to this position, it will be good news to the believers who suffered under Satan's wrath during the Great Tribulation—good news of their impending deliverance and reward. But to the unsaved world who refused to put their faith in Christ and worship the God of creation, it is bad news of coming "judgment" (v. 7). This is the first time the word *judgment* is used in Revelation. This judgment is for a specific "hour" (v. 7), or a fixed time, and "is come" (v. 7), or already on the way. This will be the last opportunity for unsaved people to turn to Christ.

A second angel followed saying, "Babylon is fallen, is fallen, that great city, because she made all nations drink of the wine of the wrath of her fornication" (v. 8). The announcement of Babylon's fall anticipates the coming judgment that will be poured out on that wicked city. Other nations who participate in Babylon's religious and political corruption will suffer the same judgment. "Fallen" is mentioned twice to emphasize the certainty of Babylon's destruction. Although the fall will come near the end of the Great Tribulation, John speaks of it as already having taken place. Various views are held concerning Babylon's role during the Tribulation. Some believe that Babylon refers to a literal city yet to be rebuilt in Iraq. Others believe it refers to the city of Rome. Still others believe it refers to the religious practices of ancient Babylon that will be manifest through a one-world religious and political system that will emerge from the area of Rome.

A third angel followed saying, "If any man worship the beast and his image, and receive his mark in his forehead, or in his hand, The same shall drink of the wine of the wrath of God" (vv. 9-10). Those who worship the beast or take his mark during the Tribulation will be sealed to damnation with no possibility of salvation. Such people will not be shown mercy while on earth or at the Great White Throne Judgment. Their torment is "without mixture [undiluted]...with fire and brimstone...forever and ever" (vv. 10-11) in the lake of fire (cp. 20:15). They will not experience any reprieve from their suffering, for "they have no rest day nor night" (v. 11).

Scripture does not teach the concept of purgatory, where the soul goes to an intermediate place for purging and cleansing from sin in readiness for eternal union with God in heaven. Neither is the concept of the annihilation of the body, soul, or spirit taught in Scripture. Although the suffering of the damned is described as visible "in the presence of the holy angels, and in the presence of the Lamb" (v. 10), this will only be temporary until the new heaven is brought forth.

At this point in the chapter, there is an abrupt transition from those who will be eternally tormented to faithful believers suffering for their commitment to Christ during the Great Tribulation. John writes, "Here is the patience of the saints; here are they that keep the commandments of God, and the faith of Jesus" (v. 12). The warning of damnation to those who follow the beast will be a great assurance to faithful believers. The word of encouragement will strengthen the weak in faith who might consider succumbing to the Antichrist's worldwide control. Those believers will realize that martyrdom for their faith is far better than eternal death and suffering in the lake of fire.

Commitment to Christ during the Tribulation will mean martyrdom for many true believers, but there will be blessings at the time of their deaths. John "heard a voice from heaven saying...Write, Blessed are the dead who die in the Lord from henceforth" (v. 13). This is the second of seven beatitudes mentioned in Revelation. The Holy Spirit is announcing a special blessing and reward for those who are martyred for their loyalty to and love for the Lord. They are given "rest from their labors [troubles]" (v. 13; cp. 6:11). Note the contrast: Faithful believers will have rest from their troubles, but the damned will have no rest, day or night, forever (v. 11). The Holy Spirit assures believers that "their works do follow them" (v. 13). Everything done for Christ will be justly acknowledged and richly rewarded.

Vision of Armageddon

The last section of this chapter describes God's judgment poured out at the end of the Tribulation. John wrote, "I looked and, behold, a white cloud, and upon the cloud one sat, like the Son of man, having on his head a golden crown, and in his hand a sharp sickle" (v. 14). This is Christ poised to bring judgment. His crowned head symbolizes that He is victor over the earth. The sharp sickle in His hand indicates readiness to carry out His judicial role in pouring out divine wrath and judgment on the ungodly at the end of the Tribulation.

The first three angels announced that judgment would be forthcoming, but the fourth angel commanded the Lord to accomplish it: "Thrust in thy sickle, and reap; for the time is come for thee to reap; for the harvest of the earth is ripe" (v. 15). This is not a dual harvest—reaping the elect to heaven and the wicked to hell—as some hold, but judgment on the ungodly. The word *ripe* indicates that this judgment is long past due. The phrase *the time is come* indicates that God has a specific appointed hour in which He will execute divine wrath, and not before. At the signal of the fourth angel, the Son of Man "thrust in his sickle…and the earth was reaped" (v. 16). The wicked are destroyed.

Then a fifth angel appears "out of the temple which is in heaven" carrying "a sharp sickle" (v. 17). This indicates that the Lord will use angels to help carry out destruction on the ungodly during this time.

A sixth angel exhorts the fifth angel to "gather the clusters of the vine of the earth" (v. 18). The altar from which the angel departs is the golden altar of incense (8:3) where the prayers of the saints were offered and divine judgment dispensed. His "power over fire" (v. 18) speaks of a purging judgment that will be poured out in response to the saints' prayers. Hearing the call to reap the fully ripened harvest, "the angel thrust in his sickle...and gathered the vine of the earth, and cast it into the great winepress of the wrath of God" (v. 19). A winepress in ancient Israel was hewn out of solid stone. Grapes were cast into the press and crushed under foot until all the juice was squeezed out of them.

The harvest mentioned by the angel will take place at the Second Coming of Christ. With one word from His mouth, He will "smite the nations" (19:15) who have gathered in Israel for "the battle of that great day of God Almighty" (16:14), better known as Armageddon. The huge army that will be destroyed will look like grapes crushed in a winepress. The carnage will reach to "the horse bridles" (about five feet) and cover an area of "a thousand and six hundred furlongs" (about 200 miles, v. 20).

The world will then be ruled by the victorious Christ, who will set up His glorious universal Kingdom of peace and justice.

Endnote

[1] John F. Walvoord, *The Revelation of Jesus Christ* (Chicago: Moody Press, 1966), p. 217.

REVELATION 15:1-8

And I saw another sign in heaven, great and marvelous, seven angels having the seven last plagues; for in them is filled up the wrath of God. And I saw, as it were, a sea of glass mingled with fire, and them that had gotten the victory over the beast, and over his image, and over his mark, and over the number of his name, standing on the sea of glass, having the harps of God. And they sing the song of Moses, the servant of God, and the song of the Lamb, saying, Great and marvelous are thy works, Lord God Almighty; just and true are thy ways, thou King of saints. Who shall not fear thee, O Lord, and glorify thy name? For thou only art holy; for all nations shall come and worship before thee; for thy judgments are made manifest. And after that I looked and, behold, the temple of the tabernacle of the testimony in heaven was opened. And the seven angels came out of the temple, having the seven plagues, clothed in pure and white linen, and having their breasts girded with golden girdles. And one of the four living creatures gave unto the seven angels seven golden bowls full of the wrath of God, who liveth forever and ever. And the temple was filled with smoke from the glory of God, and from his power; and no man was able to enter into the temple till the seven plagues of the seven angels were fulfilled.

18

VISION OF GOD'S COMING WRATH

Revelation 15, although short in length, is not short in significance or importance. It provides a needed introduction to the final phase of God's wrath. In this chapter, John was given two glorious visions from heaven in preparation for the coming bowl judgments. First, he saw martyred saints, who were victorious over the Antichrist, singing the song of Moses and the song of Christ the Lamb. Then he saw seven angels proceeding from God's Temple in heaven with bowl judgments in hand, ready to pour out God's wrath.

The events of God's wrath are centered on the seven seals opened by the Lamb of God (6:1-17; 8:1). With the opening of the seventh seal, seven trumpet judgments were unleashed on the earth (8:1-9:21; 11:15). With the blowing of the seventh trumpet, and after a lengthy textual interlude including chapters 10 to 14, the seven bowl judgments are poured out just prior to Christ's Second Coming.

As told by Christ, the seal, trumpet, and bowl judgments will grow in intensity: "For then shall be great tribulation, such as was not since the beginning of the world to this time, no, nor ever shall be. And except those days should be shortened, there should no flesh be saved; but for the elect's sake those days shall be shortened" (Matthew 24:21-22). The Tribulation judgments will be cut off by the return of Christ. If this were not so, no life would survive on the earth.

Scene in Heaven

John recorded seeing "another sign in heaven, great and marvelous" (v. 1). The word "another" indicates that other signs preceded this one, two of which are mentioned in Revelation 12. The first sign refers to Israel, described as "a great wonder in heaven—a woman clothed with the sun, and the moon under her feet, and upon her head a crown of twelve stars" (12:1). The second sign was a "wonder in heaven...a great red dragon" (12:3) representing Satan. The third sign is a group of "seven angels having the seven last plagues" (15:1) of God's wrath. These three signs are "Great and marvelous" because they speak of the works of the "Lord God Almighty" (v. 3). This is the final expression of God's terrible wrath or anger on the beast's satanic system (13:8). These judgments are labeled "last" because they "filled up [completed] the wrath of God" (v. 1). This indicates that the preceding seals and trumpets are also to be seen as judgments. However, the "seven angels" (v. 1) who implement these judgments are a different group of angels from those previously mentioned.

In the heavenly vision, John saw, "as it were, a sea of glass mingled with fire" (v. 2). The "sea of glass" was first revealed in 4:6 and functioned as a mirror, reflecting God's glory and majesty. This sea is also symbolic of God's purity, holiness, and separation from creation. Here it is "mingled with fire," symbolizing the divine judgment that is about to be manifested from a holy God.

Next John saw Tribulation saints "that had gotten the victory over the beast, and over his image, and over his mark, and over the number of his name, standing on the sea of glass, having the harps of God" (v. 2). These victorious believers did not take the mark of the beast or worship his image. Rather, they suffered martyrdom for their faith (13:7-18). This group of faithful believers will receive their resurrected bodies and rewards just prior to the Second Coming of Christ and will come back to rule with Him during the Millennial Kingdom (20:4, 6).

Only four groups are mentioned as having harps in heaven: living creatures, elders (5:8), heavenly singers (14:2), and the martyred Tribulation saints (15:2). Harps were not given to all the martyred dead (cp. 7:9-17). The harpers have a privileged position before God's throne. They contribute greatly to the heavenly harmony of the chorus that the redeemed offer to God.[1]

Songs in Heaven

The martyred saints sang two songs. The first was "the song of Moses" (v. 3). There are two songs composed by Moses. The first, recorded in Exodus 15, celebrates Israel's victorious deliverance and triumph over Pharaoh's army, all of whom drowned in the Red Sea. The second, recorded in Deuteronomy 32, sets forth God's greatness, historical faithfulness to Israel, and ultimate victory over their enemies. Commentators are divided on whether one, both, or a combination of the two Mosaic songs is referred to in chapter 15. Evidence suggests that this passage refers to the song in Exodus 15.

Some commentators try to link the "song of Moses" with the "song of the Lamb" (v. 3). In so doing, there seems to be an effort to link Israel with the church. There are similarities between the two songs.

1. The theme of both songs is victory of believers over their enemies.

2. Both songs speak of the Lamb. The Passover lamb protected and delivered Israel from judgment. Christ, the Lamb of God, will pro-

vide a greater deliverance from judgment for Tribulation believers.

3. Both songs speak of the Lord's marvelous works and ways in deliverance (Exodus 15:6-7; Revelation 15:3).

4. Both songs speak of God's holiness (Exodus 15:11; Revelation 15:4).

5. Both songs mention similar plagues that would come upon the enemies of Israel and Tribulation believers.

6. Both songs express apocalyptic-type judgments on Egypt and the beast's kingdom.

7. Both songs refer to the nations' fear of God when they hear of His works.

8. Both songs speak of people giving triumphant praise to God for His glorious deliverance.[2]

Major differences do exist, however, indicating that these two songs are *not* the same.

1. The definite article "the" appears before the phrase "song of the Lamb," making this a distinct and specific song.

2. The "song of Moses" refers to a historical deliverance of all Israel from the captivity of Egypt, whereas the "song of the Lamb" commemorates the ultimate victory of Tribulation believers over sin and worship of the beast through faith in Christ, the Lamb of God.

3. John cited only the "song of the Lamb" in 15:3-4, leaving it to the reader's memory to make the proper connection to the "song of Moses" in Exodus 15.

Thus, they are two different songs, but both manifest the same theme—deliverance.[3]

These songs ascribe praise to God the Father and Christ the Son in a number of ways.

1. "Great and marvelous are thy works, Lord God Almighty" (v. 3). The great manifestation of God's omnipotence strikes astonishment in mankind.

2. God manifests His judgments in ways that are "just and true" (v. 3). He is perfectly righteous in what He determines and keeps His promises faithfully.

3. He is "King of saints [lit., nations]" (v. 3). This God, who sovereignly rules over the nations, is about to bring His wrath upon wickedness worldwide.

4. God's works and ways evoke two inevitable, rhetorical questions: "Who shall not fear thee, O Lord, and glorify thy name?" (v. 4). Although the nations living under the Antichrist's control will not fear God or give glory to His name during most of the Tribulation (16:9, 11, 21), they will do both during the Millennial Kingdom (Psalm 72:8-11; 86:9; Philippians 2:10-11).

5. They will sing, "For thou only art holy" (v. 4). One reason the nations will submit to Christ will be because He is "holy" (*hosios*). This is not the usual word for *holy*. It means that God is *devout* or *absolutely right* in vindicating persecuted believers and judging wicked earth dwellers.

6. They sang, "for all nations shall come and worship before thee" (v. 4). This will take place dur-

ing the Kingdom, when "all the nations" come to Jerusalem for worship (Zechariah 14:16). The reason for this worship is that God's "judgments are made manifest" (v. 4). The day will come when all people will acknowledge that God's wrath, which is about to be poured out, is deserved, righteous, and perfectly designed to achieve His holy purposes. It should be noted that the saints in heaven do not sing about their own victory over the beast, but about God's glory, sovereignty, and justice.

Sanctuary in Heaven

The scene changes as John is given another vision, focusing his attention back to the Temple of God in heaven and the seven angels holding bowls of judgment. He wrote, "And after that I looked and, behold, the temple of the tabernacle of the testimony in heaven was opened" (v. 5). The words "temple [Gr., *naos*] of the tabernacle of the testimony" refer to tablets of the Ten Commandments kept in the Ark of the Covenant that stood in the Holy of Holies where the presence of God dwelt.

John saw the veil of the Holy of Holies part, and out of the inner sanctuary of the Temple appeared "seven angels" (v. 6) who had been selected to administer God's bowl judgments. They are holding "the seven plagues, clothed in pure and white linen, and having their breasts girded with golden girdles" (v. 6). White linen is symbolic of the purity of the angels, their righteous character, and the righteous act of God in pouring out His wrath on the earth. Golden girdles held the linen garments in place and were worn by the priests as they ministered in the Temple. Gold is symbolic of God's riches, beauty, greatness, and majesty. Christ wore the same apparel when He appeared to John (cp. 1:13).

Seven Bowls in Heaven

John watched as "one of the four living creatures gave unto the seven angels seven golden bowls full of the wrath of God" (v. 7). These are not deep bowls, as often pictured by artists today, but are shaped like a saucer. The emphasis, however, is not on the saucers but on their contents—"full of the wrath of God" (v. 7). The word *full* addresses the comprehensive, complete, and totally devastating character of this final set of judgments from God. The word *wrath* is not the Greek word *orge* usually used for *wrath*, but *thymos*, meaning *anger*. In the Old Testament, this anger is pictured as a cup of hot, bitter wine, boiling to the point of overflowing, depicting violent wrath from God against sin.

This wrath will pour forth from God, "who liveth forever and ever" (v. 7). Although there seems to be a delay in the execution of God's wrath, that is not the case. He is everlasting and will perform His divine judgment at His appointed time.

Just before God's wrath is poured out, "the temple was filled with smoke from the glory of God, and from his power; and no man was able to enter the temple till the seven plagues of the seven angels were fulfilled" (v. 8). Smoke is frequently associated with God's glory and power. When God made a covenant with Abraham, He passed through the divided pieces of the sacrifice in the smoking furnace and burning lamp (Genesis 15:17). When Moses received God's law on Mount Sinai, God revealed His holiness with fire and smoke (Exodus 19:18). After Israel placed the Ark of the Covenant in the Tabernacle, God's presence was symbolized with smoke and fire (Exodus 40:34-35). In Solomon's Temple, the glory of the Lord filled the holy place in the form of a cloud (1 Kings 8:10-11). This is an ongoing reminder of God's holiness. God's glory is always manifested during the time of His judgment. Smoke from God's glory made entering the Temple impossible until His seething indignation was poured out. What a sign to the ungodly people on the earth, who chose to shun the worship of a holy God and, rather, to follow the beast.

The seven angels stand ready, awaiting the final signal to pour out God's wrath.

Endnotes

[1] John F. Walvoord, *The Revelation of Jesus Christ* (Chicago: Moody Press, 1966), p. 227.

[2] Robert L. Thomas, *Revelation 8-22, An Exegetical Commentary* (Chicago: Moody Press, 1995), p. 235.

[3] *Ibid*.

REVELATION 16:1-21

And I heard a great voice out of the temple saying to the seven angels, Go your ways, and pour out the bowls of the wrath of God upon the earth. And the first went, and poured out his bowl upon the earth, and there fell a foul and painful sore upon the men who had the mark of the beast, and upon them who worshiped his image. And the second angel poured out his bowl upon the sea, and it became like the blood of a dead man; and every living soul died in the sea. And the third angel poured out his bowl upon the rivers and fountains of waters, and they became blood. And I heard the angel of the waters say, Thou art righteous, O Lord, who art, and wast, and shalt be, because thou hast judged thus. For they have shed the blood of saints and prophets, and thou hast given them blood to drink; for they are worthy. And I heard another out of the altar say, Even so, Lord God Almighty, true and righteous are thy judgments. And the fourth angel poured out his bowl upon the sun, and power was given unto him to scorch men with fire. And men were scorched with great heat, and blasphemed the name of God, who hath power over these plagues; and they repented not to give him glory. And the fifth angel poured out his bowl upon the throne of the beast, and his kingdom was full of darkness; and they gnawed their tongues for pain, And blasphemed the God of heaven because of their pains and their sores, and repented not of their deeds. And the sixth angel poured out his bowl upon the great river, Euphrates, and its water was dried up, that the way of the kings of the east might be prepared. And I saw three unclean spirits, like frogs, come out of the mouth of the dragon, and out of the mouth of the beast, and out of the mouth of the false prophet. For they are the spirits of demons, working miracles, that go forth unto the kings of the earth and of the whole world, to gather them to the battle of that great day of God Almighty. Behold, I come as a thief. Blessed is he that watcheth, and keepeth his garments, lest he walk naked, and they see his shame. And he gathered them together into a place called in the Hebrew tongue Armageddon. And the seventh angel poured out his bowl into the air, and there came a great voice out of the temple of heaven, from the throne, saying, It is done. And there were voices, and thunders, and lightnings; and there was a great earthquake, such as was not since men were upon the earth, so mighty an earthquake, and so great. And the great city was divided into three parts, and the cities of the nations fell; and great Babylon came in remembrance before God, to give unto her the cup of the wine of the fierceness of his wrath. And every island fled away, and the mountains were not found. And there fell upon men a great hail out of heaven, every stone about the weight of a talent; and men blasphemed God because of the plague of the hail; for the plague was exceedingly great.

=== 19 ===

THE SEVEN BOWLS OF WRATH

In Revelation 15, John was given a detailed introduction to the bowl judgments. He saw seven angels proceeding from God's heavenly Temple with seven bowls in hand, ready to pour out God's wrath upon the earth.

As Revelation 16 opens, John's attention was still fixed on the heavenly scene. Suddenly the apostle heard a great voice out of God's Temple commanding the seven angels, "Go your ways, and pour out the bowls of the wrath of God upon the earth" (v. 1). Although the voice is not identified, most scholars agree that it is the voice of God. The seven angels were commanded not to pour out their bowls as a group. Each angel was to pour out his bowl, one by one, in quick succession, without further instruction. Without a doubt, what follows is the darkest chapter in the history of mankind.

Similarities between the trumpet and bowl judgments have led some scholars to believe that they will take place simultaneously. Others teach that the two series will occur successively. The successive view is correct for the following reasons:

1. There can be no overlap between the trumpet and bowl judgments because the latter will proceed from the seventh trumpet (11:15).

2. The bowl judgments will affect the entire earth, but the first four trumpet judgments will affect only one-third of the earth.

3. The bowl judgments will occur near the end of the Great Tribulation (cp. 15:1), but the trumpet judgments will begin at the midpoint of the Tribulation period.

4. The trumpet and bowl judgments will not follow in the same sequence.

The first four bowls will be poured upon nature and will affect mankind globally. The final three bowls will affect only the kingdom of the beast.

Four Bowls of Wrath

When the first angel "poured out his bowl upon the earth...there fell a foul and painful sore upon the men who had the mark of the beast, and upon them who worshiped his image" (v. 2). This judgment will involve a foul-smelling, malignant ulcer (like a boil) that is extremely painful and will not heal. It is similar to the sixth plague poured out upon Egypt (Exodus 9:8-12). The plague will be limited to those who took the mark of the beast and worshiped his image. Their destiny is damnation in the lake of fire. But before that torment, they will suffer from this judgment during the Great Tribulation (14:9-11).

When the second angel poured out his bowl, "the sea...became like the blood of a dead man; and every living soul died in the sea" (v. 3). This refers to all saltwater seas. The text does not say that the sea *became* the blood of a dead man, but became *like* the blood of a dead man. The sea will turn into a thick, coagulated mass producing a putrefying stench like that of a decaying corpse. This condition will cause unimaginable disease and death. This judgment is similar to the first plague upon Egypt (Exodus 7:19-21), when all the fish died. It is also similar to the second trumpet judgment, when a fiery mountain will be cast into the sea, turning one-third of the sea to blood and killing one-third of the sea life (8:8-9). All marine life will be destroyed, severely affecting the world's food supply.

When the third angel "poured out his bowl upon the rivers and fountains of waters...they became blood" (v. 4). This judgment will affect all of the world's freshwater springs, rivers, and lakes. This judgment is similar to the third trumpet judgment, when the meteor, Wormwood, will fall upon one-third of the freshwater, polluting it and rendering it poisonous. Many people who drink the water will die (8:10-11). Like the Egyptians (Exodus 7:24), people will dig for freshwater, only to find that it too has turned to blood and is unfit for human consumption. Without water, people will go mad and will stop at nothing to quench their thirst. We can only imagine the agony, panic, and death this pollution will create.

Then comes a great angelic proclamation: "Thou art righteous, O Lord, who art, and wast, and shalt be, because thou hast judged thus" (v. 5). Often people question God's judgment upon them, but the angels do not. The angels confirm that an eternal God is justified in pouring out His wrath upon the ungodly. Further confirmation is made on this point by "another out of the altar say[ing], Even so, Lord God Almighty, true and righteous are thy judgments" (v. 7). The angel also affirmed that the wicked are worthy to have "blood to drink" because "they have shed the blood of saints and prophets" (v. 6; cp. 7:14; 11:7-8). The *altar* in Revelation is often associated with the prayers of God's people, who are crying for vengeance and judgment on their persecutors.

The fourth angel "poured out his bowl upon the sun, and power was given unto him to scorch men with fire" (v. 8). This judgment, like the fourth trumpet, involves the sun, yet it is quite different. Under the fourth trumpet, one-third of the sun will be darkened (8:12). Here the sun's intensity will be supernaturally increased by God, causing it to scorch people with fire. The scorching heat will not result in unbelievers' crying out to God for mercy. They will blaspheme "the name of God, who hath power over these plagues; and they [will repent] not to give him glory" (v. 9). Not even God's wrath will produce repentance in the hardened hearts of wicked people.

Final Bowls of Wrath

The fifth angel "poured out his bowl upon the throne of the beast, and his kingdom was full of darkness; and they gnawed their tongues for pain" (v. 10). The throne of the beast is the one spot where Satan's power resides on earth. Up to this point, nothing will touch the throne of the beast, but now God will center on Satan's earthly seat of power. This bowl judgment is similar to the fifth trumpet (9:2) and the ninth plague upon Egypt (Exodus 10:21-23), with one exception: It will cover the entire earth. The darkness will be so thick that it will cause intense psychological pain to people already in physical agony due to festering boils and burning flesh. This will cause them to gnaw "their tongues for pain." This is a preview of the outer darkness of hell that unbelievers will suffer (Matthew 25:30). They will continue to blaspheme "the God of heaven because of their pains and their sores, and [will repent] not of their deeds" (v. 11).

When the sixth angel "poured out his bowl upon the great river, Euphrates...its water was dried up, that the way of the kings of the east might be prepared" (v. 12). The river is called "great" because of its significant location. It is the longest river in western Asia, flowing almost 1,800 miles from Syria to Babylon and emptying into the Persian Gulf. It forms a natural eastern boundary for the Roman Empire. The kings of the east will flood across the dried-up Euphrates River to take part in the battle of Armageddon.

The vision in verses 13-16 is not a parenthetical section between the sixth and seventh bowls, as some scholars teach. Rather, it provides needed insight into this gathering of nations for the battle of Armageddon. John saw "three unclean spirits, like frogs, come out of the mouth of the dragon…the beast, and…the false prophet" (v. 13). These demonic spirits will perform miracles that will entice all nations to bring their armies to Israel for "the battle of that great day of God Almighty" (v. 14).

The word *battle* (Gr., *polemos*) does not mean a single conflict, but a campaign of battles at the end of the Tribulation (cp. Daniel 11:45). This will set the stage for a climactic conflict with Christ at His Second Coming. Why will all the nations gather at Mount Megiddo (Gr., *Armageddon*, v. 16)? They will come to challenge the Antichrist's worldwide dominion, which will have begun to deteriorate, and to annihilate Israel. Mount Megiddo will be the staging area and focal point of the battle, but the conflict will extend for a radius of about 200 miles around Jerusalem (14:20). While the nations are engaged in conflict, Christ will suddenly appear and destroy them with the sword of His mouth (19:15).

A word of praise is given to the faithful saints during the Tribulation: "Blessed is he that watcheth, and keepeth his garments, lest he walk naked, and they see his shame" (v. 15). This is the third of seven beatitudes in Revelation. It is also a warning for the saints living in the Tribulation to stay alert in light of Christ's imminent return. The word *garments* is symbolic of the righteousness of the saints (cp. 19:8). Those who are walking in sin before God (cp. 3:18) and the world are considered to be spiritually naked. This is shameful at any time, but especially in light of the Second Coming of Christ. Believers must guard their lives from evil at all times and be clothed in God's righteousness.

When the seventh angel "poured out his bowl into the air...there came a great voice out of the temple in heaven, from the throne, saying, It is done" (v. 17). "It" is the completion of God's wrath being poured out prior to Christ's Second Coming.

Immediately, John heard "voices...thunders...lightnings; and...a great earthquake, such as was not since men were upon the earth" (v. 18). The great earthquake will affect the earth in four ways.

1. The earth will convulse (v. 18) in an unprecedented magnitude, causing great damage, disruption, death, and distress upon mankind.

2. Cities will be destroyed worldwide: "The great city was divided into three parts...cities of the nations fell; and great Babylon...[drank] the cup...of the fierceness of his [God's] wrath" (v. 19). The "great city" seems to be a reference to Jerusalem's destruction (cp. 11:8). It is possible that the new areas outside the old city walls of Jerusalem will be divided by the earthquake at Christ's return (Zechariah 14:4), but the old city itself may remain intact. People stand in awe at what mankind is able to create and construct, but one day it will all collapse and crumble when God pours out His wrath on the nations of the world.

3. Continents will be severely changed by the earthquake, as "every island fled away, and the mountains were not found" (v. 20). The earth's topography will be radically altered during the earthquake, causing massive flooding and great destruction.

4. Climatic changes will impact the earth, as "there fell upon men a great hail out of heaven, every

stone about the weight of a talent" (approxi-
mately 100 pounds, v. 21). The velocity of these
stones' peppering the earth will have a devastating impact on whatever is not destroyed by the
preceding judgments. This judgment will be
similar to the seventh plague upon Egypt
(Exodus 9:23-24) and the first trumpet judgment
(8:7). The consequences of these cataclysmic
changes will crush the Antichrist's kingdom, but
his followers will not repent. In fact, the opposite will take place: "men blasphemed God
because of the plague of the hail" (v. 21).

These descriptions concerning God's wrath being poured out
upon the earth are both awesome and terrifying. They should
cause all people to examine their priorities in life and their personal relationship with Christ. Only those who have put their
faith in Him will escape the wrath to come.

REVELATION 17:1-7

And there came one of the seven angels who had the seven bowls, and talked with me, saying unto me, Come here; I will show unto thee the judgment of the great harlot that sitteth upon many waters; With whom the kings of the earth have committed fornication, and the inhabitants of the earth have been made drunk with the wine of her fornication. So he carried me away in the Spirit into the wilderness and I saw a woman sit upon a scarlet-colored beast, full of names of blasphemy, having seven heads and ten horns. And the woman was arrayed in purple and scarlet color, and bedecked with gold and precious stones and pearls, having a golden cup in her hand, full of abominations and filthiness of her fornication; And upon her forehead was a name written, MYSTERY, BABYLON THE GREAT, THE MOTHER OF HARLOTS AND ABOMINATIONS OF THE EARTH. *And I saw the woman drunk with the blood of the saints, and with the blood of the martyrs of Jesus; and when I saw her, I wondered with great wonder. And the angel said unto me, Why didst thou wonder? I will tell thee the mystery of the woman, and of the beast that carrieth her, which hath the seven heads and ten horns.*

20

MYSTERY BABYLON

Lying silently in the shifting sands of time, Babylon is destined to rise from the ashes of the past to play a major role in end-time events. The name *Babylon* brings to mind incredible images of a wicked city-state with an abominable religious system. This wicked religious system will once again sweep across the world, corrupting everything it touches—religiously, politically, and economically.

In Revelation 17 and 18, John has outlined the rise and fall of Babylon during the Tribulation period. Events in these chapters represent an ecclesiastical, political, and commercial Babylonian system whose doom was prophesied earlier (14:8; 16:19). The events in chapter 17 *do not* follow the bowl judgments chronologically. They begin at the inception of Daniel's 70th week and will be fulfilled by the midpoint of the Tribulation. In chapter 18, Babylon is described as a powerful city with a prosperous commercial center that will be suddenly destroyed at the end of the Tribulation (18:10, 16, 19). Some scholars believe that the name *Babylon* in chapter 18 is to be interpreted symbolically, referring to Rome. Others believe that the city refers to a rebuilt Babylon. More about the city will be revealed in Revelation 18.

Announcing the Harlot

Because Babylon did not exist in John's day, the announcement of its destruction must have perplexed the apostle. One of
the seven angels who poured out the bowl judgments invited John
to witness the judgment of Babylon, described as a "great harlot"
(v. 1). The word *harlot* (Gr., *porneia*) means *fornication, adultery,* or *prostitution* and refers to Babylon's abominable religious
idolatry (cp. Jeremiah 23:17). Its perverted paganism is the epit-
ome of spiritual idolatry, and it will reach its peak during the first
half of the Tribulation.

It is pictured sitting on "many waters" (v. 1), later described
as "peoples, and multitudes, and nations, and tongues" (v. 15).
Captivated by its charm, the whole world will become intoxicated by its idolatrous religious system. "The kings of the earth have
committed fornication, and the inhabitants of the earth have been
made drunk with the wine of her fornication" (v. 2), writes the
apostle. Babylon will gain worldwide domination by permeating
every area of society—pagan religions, apostate Christianity,
political powers (cp. 14:8).

Alliance of the Harlot

The angel carried John away "in the Spirit" to a wilderness
area, where he "saw a woman sit upon a scarlet-colored beast,
full of names of blasphemy, having seven heads and ten horns"
(v. 3). This beast is the revived Roman Empire and, more specifically, its ruler (the Antichrist), who embodies the spirit of the
Roman Empire (13:1). He will control the political system within the empire. The "seven heads" are seven successive world
empires of the past, leading up to the final unveiling of the
revived Roman Empire. The "ten horns" are ten kings within the
confederacy of the revived Roman Empire, over whom the beast
will rule. The beast is robed in "scarlet," a color symbolic of
luxury and splendor.

The depravity of this woman is seen in her unholy alliance with such a despicable political ruler. Church and state will be wed together as the woman rides the beast (uses the political system to spread her false religious beliefs). In the first half of the Tribulation, each system will use the other to promote its ambition of world domination. At this point, the religious system will have a dominating influence over the political system.

Apparel of the Harlot

The woman riding the beast will be "arrayed in purple and scarlet color, and bedecked with gold and precious stones and pearls" (v. 4). "Bedecked [lit., *made gold*] with gold" is a play on words, emphasizing that she will be covered with gold from head to toe. Precious stones and pearls provide a look of ostentatious extravagance. Today, such an array of ecclesiastical pomp is seen in many religions. What a sharp contrast to the appearance of the bride of the Lamb, whose apparel consists of "fine linen, clean and white" (19:8).

This vile woman is pictured "having a golden cup in her hand, full of abominations and filthiness of her fornication" (v. 4). The word *abomination* is used in Scripture to express idolatrous worship and the immoral practices associated with it. In this passage, it expresses the woman's polluted character and idolatrous practices. Those who partake of the harlot's poisonous cup of idolatry are destined to perish with her.

The woman had written on "her forehead...MYSTERY, BABYLON THE GREAT, THE MOTHER OF HARLOTS AND ABOMINATIONS OF THE EARTH" (v. 5). Scripture does not specify if this identifying statement is in her flesh or on a headband like the ones worn by Roman prostitutes.[1] The word *mystery* (Gr., *mysterion*) is not part of her title. In the New Testament, the word *mystery* refers to a revelation hidden in the past but revealed in the present.

An in-depth study of Revelation 17 may leave students confused about the exact meaning of the phrase "BABYLON THE GREAT" (v. 5). Added to this confusion are the divergent interpretations held by Bible scholars. Most conservative scholars have embraced one of the following positions:

1. The word *Babylon* represents an ecclesiastical and political Babylon. *Ecclesiastical Babylon* refers to apostate Christendom (i.e., a one-world church including non-Christian religions) with headquarters in Rome (vv. 1-6). *Political Babylon* is a revival of the Roman Empire, the last form of Gentile world dominion, headed by the "beast" (vv. 7-18).

2. The word *Babylon* refers to the religious and political systems mentioned above, as well as to a rebuilt city of Babylon near the Euphrates River.

3. Revelation 17 refers to the rebuilt city of Babylon, whose end-time existence and subsequent annihilation were predicted by Isaiah, Jeremiah, and Zechariah. According to this interpretation, Babylon is a literal city of religious and political significance yet to be rebuilt. The text says, "the woman whom thou sawest is that great city, which reigneth over the kings of the earth" (17:18).

It is clear from chapter 17 that "MYSTERY, BABYLON" is linked to Rome religiously and politically, but it would seem from chapter 18 that Babylon may be rebuilt.

This diabolical religious system can be traced from Nimrod's establishment of the city of Babel (Genesis 10:8-10), later called Babylon. Nimrod built a huge tower, known as a *ziggurat*, made of sun-dried bricks, on the plains of Shinar (Genesis 11:4). The tower was recognized as a temple or rallying center and a symbol of mankind's pride and rebellion against God. Other nations followed suit and constructed similar towers in honor of their heathen deities. God poured out judgment on this rebellious act by confounding their language and scattering them across the face of the earth (Genesis 11:7-9).

However, this did not mean the demise of the Babylonian religious system. History records that Nimrod's wife Semiramis became the head priestess of an idolatrous system of secret religious rituals known as *Babylonian Mysteries.* Babylon became the fountainhead of idolatry and the mother of every pagan system that spread across the world.

Semiramis supposedly gave birth to a son named Tammuz, who was miraculously conceived by a sunbeam. He was presented to the people as a savior, in fulfillment of the promise made to Eve concerning her seed (Genesis 3:15). Tradition says that Tammuz was killed by a wild boar, but after the people fasted for 40 days, he was resurrected from the dead on the feast of Ishtar. This legend of a mother-son cult became part of the Babylonian Mystery ritual and was quickly included in other idolatrous religious practices worldwide. The mother-son cult was headed by a priesthood that promoted salvation by the means of sprinkling holy water, ceremonial cleansing, and purgatorial cleansing after death. Semiramis established an order of virgins dedicated to religious prostitution. She became known and worshiped as the "queen of heaven."

Ezekiel condemned the practice of Jewish "women weeping for Tammuz" (Ezekiel 8:14). Jeremiah condemned Judah for offering cakes and burning incense to the "queen of heaven" (Jeremiah 7:18; 44:17-19, 25). Zechariah personified wickedness as a woman who will be reestablished in the land of Shinar (Babylon) in the latter days (Zechariah 5:6-11).

After the Medo-Persian Empire took over Babylon, the city and temples were eventually destroyed. The Babylonian cult survived and found a new home in Pergamos of Asia Minor. It thrived under the name *Etruscan Mysteries* and eventually was headquartered in Rome. The chief priests wore miters shaped like the head of a fish, in honor of Dagon, the fish-god, the lord of life—another form of the Tammuz mystery. In Rome, the chief priest took the title *Pontifex Maximus*. When Julius Caesar became head of the Roman Empire, he took the name *Pontifex Maximus*, a title held by all of the Roman emperors down to Constantine the Great, who became head of both church and state. The title was later adopted by the Bishop of Rome. Over time, the church in Rome absorbed many of the Babylonian practices and idolatrous teachings, obscuring the true meaning of Scripture—such teachings as the worship of the virgin Mary and various festivals such as Easter, also known as Ishtar, one of the titles of the Babylonian queen of heaven. Many of these teachings can be attributed to Constantine, who combined paganism with Christianity when he adopted Christianity as a state religion.

In our day, a number of Protestant denominations have turned a blind eye to the anti-biblical teachings found in Roman Catholicism. They are cooperating in various religious functions with the Roman church and are even making overtures to reunite with it. Christendom will ultimately give birth to a one-world church after the Rapture of true believers.

Attack by the Harlot

John "saw the woman drunk with the blood of the saints, and with the blood of the martyrs of Jesus" (v. 6). This woman will not tolerate competition from other religious beliefs and will pour out her cruelties against the defenseless Tribulation saints. She will be drunk with human blood. This will inflame her insatiable lust for even more violence and inhumane savagery, as she attempts to destroy all recognition of Christ and His followers. The Antichrist will assist her by providing the political power to carry out this dastardly deed. This persecution will be against Tribulation believers, not the church, which will already have been raptured. The Tribulation saints will be massacred on a worldwide scale (cp. 6:9-11; 7:14; 11:7; 13:7) for faithfully proclaiming their belief in Jesus.

John was stunned by what he had just witnessed: "when I saw her, I wondered with great wonder" (v. 6). While John stood in astonishment, the angel responded, "Why didst thou wonder? I will tell thee the mystery of the woman" (v. 7). The next chapter will deal with the mystery of the woman and the beast who carries her.

We must be on guard against heretical religious systems, like "MYSTERY, BABYLON," which try to corrupt and subjugate us to their evil ways.

Endnote

[1] Robert L. Thomas, *Revelation 8-22, An Exegetical Commentary* (Chicago: Moody Press, 1995), p. 288.

REVELATION 17:7-18

And the angel said unto me, Why didst thou wonder? I will tell thee the mystery of the woman, and of the beast that carrieth her, which hath the seven heads and ten horns. The beast that thou sawest was, and is not, and shall ascend out of the bottomless pit, and go into perdition; and they that dwell on the earth shall wonder, whose names were not written in the book of life from the foundation of the world, when they behold the beast that was, and is not, and yet is. And here is the mind which hath wisdom. The seven heads are seven mountains, on which the woman sitteth. And there are seven kings: five are fallen, and one is, and the other is not yet come; and when he cometh, he must continue a short space. And the beast that was, and is not, even he is the eighth, and is of the seven, and goeth into perdition. And the ten horns which thou sawest are ten kings, who have received no kingdom as yet, but receive power as kings one hour with the beast. These have one mind, and shall give their power and strength unto the beast. These shall make war with the Lamb, and the Lamb shall overcome them; for he is Lord of lords, and King of kings, and they that are with him are called, and chosen, and faithful. And he saith unto me, The waters which thou sawest, where the harlot sitteth, are peoples, and multitudes, and nations, and tongues. And the ten horns which thou sawest upon the beast, these shall hate the harlot, and shall make her desolate and naked, and shall eat her flesh, and burn her with fire. For God hath put in their hearts to fulfill his will, and to agree, and give their kingdom unto the beast, until the words of God shall be fulfilled. And the woman whom thou sawest is that great city, which reigneth over the kings of the earth.

21

THE WOMAN AND THE BEAST

The woman sitting on the scarlet-colored beast was a spectacle to behold. John marveled at her ostentatious dress, her idolatrous practices, the murder of defenseless saints, and her alliance with pagan Rome. Understanding John's great wonderment, the angel rhetorically asked, "Why didst thou wonder?" (v. 7). He then proceeded to reveal the mystery of both the woman and the beast—a revelation that exposes much more about the beast than it does about the woman it is carrying.

Monster of Wickedness

The angel continued, "The beast that thou sawest was, and is not, and shall ascend out of the bottomless pit, and go into perdition" (v. 8). Commentators hold different interpretations of the beast's identity. This is understandable because previous chapters identify Satan, the Antichrist, and the revived Roman Empire as beasts.

Some scholars believe that the angel is speaking of the Antichrist who had a near-death experience, was raised back to full health (13:3), and became possessed by a great demon from the bottomless pit. Others teach that the phrase "yet is" (v. 8) refers to one who will be resurrected from the bottomless pit and become ruler of the revived Roman Empire. They mention Judas Iscariot, Nero, and Adolf Hitler as possible candidates. This is highly unlikely. Satan was never given power to raise anyone from the dead. Further, the wicked will not be resurrected until the Great White Throne Judgment (20:11-15). Still others believe this describes the revived Roman Empire. In the past, Rome *was* an imperial world power; today, it is not; but in the future Tribulation it will be satanically controlled by a great demon from the pit. This interpretation fits the context. All three beasts, along with their followers, are destined for "perdition" (v. 8), eternal destruction, and damnation in the lake of fire (cp. Matthew 25:41; Revelation 19:20).

During the Tribulation, even the unsaved on earth, "whose names were not written in the book of life from the foundation of the world," will wonder "when they behold the beast" (v. 8). The unsaved (whose names were never written in the book of life) will marvel at the swift establishment of the revived Roman Empire, as its charismatic leader conquers vast areas once held by ancient Rome.

The beast is further described as having "seven heads [that] are seven mountains, on which the woman sitteth" (v. 9). This verse has been interpreted in various ways and requires a "mind which hath wisdom" (v. 9), or special insight from God, to be properly understood.

Some scholars teach that the seven mountains refer to the city of Rome. Throughout its history, Rome has been called the "city of seven hills." There are three problems with this interpretation:

1. Rome encompasses more than seven hills.

2. The city sits on hills, not mountains.

3. The text identifies the "seven mountains" as "seven kings" (v. 10).

Others believe that the mountains refer to seven kings or rulers of ancient Rome: Julius Caesar, Tiberias, Caligula, Claudius, Nero, Domitian (the one who is), and the Antichrist (who is yet to come). This interpretation is also limited. It "does not connect well with the prophecies of Daniel which imply that world empires or extensive kingdoms are being suggested, rather than individual leaders....The beast with seven heads represents world government throughout human history and should not be relegated to the time of the apostle John."[1]

A similar view says that the seven kings are various forms of Roman government: kings, consuls, dictators, decemvirs, military tribunes, and emperors. The sixth—the "one is" (v. 10)—refers to the imperial form of government, which was destroyed and will reappear under Satan's control. The same objections apply to this position as to the previous view.

Still others hold a double prophetic significance: The seven mountains (v. 9) represent Rome, and the seven kings (v. 10) symbolize world empires. The same objections apply to this position as to the first view.

It is preferable to hold that the "seven mountains" and "seven kings" represent seven great world empires (kingdoms) throughout history. Up to John's day, "five are fallen [Egypt, Assyria, Babylon, Medo-Persia, and Greece], and one is [Rome], and the other is not yet come [revived Roman Empire]; and when he cometh, he must continue a short space" (v. 10). In Daniel's prophetic description of Gentile world rule, he used the terms *beast, king,* and *kingdom* interchangeably (Daniel 7:1-28). These seven empires cover the history of Gentile world rule until its destruction by Christ at His Second Coming. Then Christ's Kingdom, described as a mountain, will fill the whole earth (Daniel 2:34-35).

Further revelation is given about an eighth head: "And the beast that was, and is not, even he is the eighth, and is of the seven, and goeth into perdition" (v. 11). Thus, the seventh kingdom is the revised Roman Empire (a ten-nation confederacy) out of which the eighth king (the Antichrist) will rise, along with his kingdom. When the Antichrist takes over the ten-nation confederacy, he will manifest complete dictatorial power, which will introduce the eighth or final form of Gentile world rule. His destiny is "perdition" (v. 11). Both the eighth king and his kingdom will be destroyed by Christ at His Second Coming and will be cast into the lake of fire (19:20).

Next, the angel identified the beast's "ten horns" (v. 7) as "ten kings, who have received no kingdom as yet, but receive power as kings one hour with the beast" (v. 12). These kings will be appointed to rule over the kingdom of the Antichrist, which will be divided into ten administrative districts. There is no way that these kings can be literally or symbolically applied to any nation in the past because they will not receive a kingdom until Daniel's 70th week. They will not reign *successively* but *simultaneously* during the Tribulation. The beast will give them power for a very brief period of time—less than 42 months (13:5). These nations will not rule independently but will be of "one mind" with the beast and yield their "power and strength [authority] unto the beast" (v. 13). Their power will extend to the end of the Tribulation, when they will "make war with the Lamb [Christ], and the Lamb shall overcome them" (v. 14). Christ will accomplish the victory with ease at Armageddon (19:15) because "he is Lord of lords, and King of kings" (v. 14). Along with the Lord will be an army of Old Testament believers, the church, and Tribulation saints, properly identified as "called, and chosen, and faithful" (v. 14). These faithful believers will share in Christ's victorious conquest.

Murder of the Woman

The harlot's diabolical religious system (17:1-6) will have influence over the whole world by the midpoint of the Tribulation. Those whom she will impact are described as "waters," symbolic of "peoples, and multitudes, and nations, and tongues" (v. 15). The world's population will have become submissive to her seductive lure, being made drunk with the wine of her heathenish religious teaching and worship (17:2).

An abrupt turnabout will be made by the "ten horns" (v. 16) who follow the beast in uncompromising obedience. They will awaken from their drunken stupor with the woman, whose charm and seduction will have lost their lure. Love for the woman will turn to "hate" (v. 16) as the ten kings, along with the beast, destroy her just before the midpoint of the Tribulation. They will make "her desolate" (v. 16), or divest her of all the wealth she has confiscated. They will make her "naked" (v. 16), stripping away her personal support, position, power, and prestige, and thus exposing her moral corruption. They "shall eat her flesh" (v. 16), like wild dogs devoured the corpse of Jezebel (cp. 1 Kings 21:23; 2 Kings 9:30-37). They will "burn her with fire" (v. 16), totally eliminating any identity of the woman and her false religious system. Israel's law required that those who committed extreme acts of sin be burned with fire after their deaths to remove any symbol of their remembrance (Leviticus 20:14; 21:9; Joshua 7:15, 25).[2]

These hostile actions will be initiated by God: "For God hath put in their hearts to fulfill his will" (v. 17)—that is, to rid the world of her pseudo-religious system. At times, Satan is allowed to manifest his will through nations to accomplish God's purposes. This is seen in Revelation 16, when demons go forth to gather all nations to Israel for the battle of Armageddon (16:13-14). The kings will believe that they are carrying out their own program for conquest as they destroy the woman (harlot), but in actuality they will accomplish God's providential program.

With the woman destroyed, the Antichrist will unite the world's religious and political systems under his control. The ten nations will agree to "give their kingdom unto the beast, until the words of God shall be fulfilled" (v. 17). God's prophetic program will reach its intended goal as He sovereignly allows the kingdoms of this world to come under the beast's control until the end of the Tribulation.[3] At that time, the cup of wickedness will be full, and Christ will destroy the entire system upon His Second Coming.

The angel concluded his revelation by identifying the woman simply as "that great city, which reigneth over the kings of the earth" (v. 18). The early church believed that the city the angel was speaking of was Rome. Those living in the Middle Ages believed the verse was a reference to the ecclesiastical system of Rome. Many scholars today identify the city with Rome because of her ostentatious dress (v. 4), the reference to the "seven mountains" (v. 9), and the belief that Rome will be the religious center of the world during the Tribulation. Still others believe that John was anticipating the woman's fall and the religious emphasis' shifting from the woman to the beast. Thus, this great anti-God system will continue, both as power (political) and cult (religion), united in one figure—the Antichrist.[4] Some teach that the verse is not referring to the woman as a religious system but as the literal city of Babylon yet to be built on the Euphrates River. This city will become the center for a religious system that will oppose true Christianity. The system will gain tremendous influence during the Tribulation, until the beast and the ten kings determine that it is no longer useful to their worldwide rule and destroy it.[5]

A more plausible interpretation teaches that the woman is identified with the "great city" Babylon in its religious, not historical, significance. According to verse 5, "BABYLON THE GREAT" is not referring to the literal city of ancient Babylon, but to its diabolical religious system. As Babylon conquered cities politically, its religion dominated political states. Thus, the meaning cannot be confined to a city in the past or future, such as Rome or Babylon.[6] This verse refers to a trans-historical system of satanic evil, which is an extension of ancient Babylon, forming the one-world religious system during the

Tribulation. After the destruction of the woman, this religious system will reside in the Antichrist, who will manifest all of its satanic evils.[7]

Seeds of this diabolical, one-world system are beginning to sprout in Europe. A move is underway to forge nations into a European Economic Community. This could well be the fore-shadowing of the satanically orchestrated religious and political system mentioned in Revelation 17. Christians must be alert and warn others of these ominous events. In the midst of this bad news, however, there is good news: The Lord will take His church to glory before it happens.

Endnotes

[1] David Hocking, *The Coming World Leader: Understanding the Book of Revelation* (Portland, OR: Multnomah Press, 1988), p. 249.

[2] Robert L. Thomas, *Revelation 8-22, An Exegetical Commentary* (Chicago: Moody Press, 1995), p. 304.

[3] John F. Walvoord, *The Revelation of Jesus Christ* (Chicago: Moody Press, 1996), p. 257.

[4] Walter M. Dunnett, *King of Kings: Studies in Revelation 17-22* (Chicago: Moody Press, 1967), part 1, p. 10.

[5] *Op. cit.*, Thomas, p. 308.

[6] *Op. cit.*, Walvoord, p. 257.

[7] John Walvoord, *The Bible Knowledge Commentary: Revelation* (Wheaton, IL: Scripture Press Publications, Inc., 1983), p. 972.

REVELATION 18:1-24

And after these things I saw another angel come down from heaven, having great power, and the earth was made bright with his glory. And he cried mightily with a strong voice, saying, Babylon the great is fallen, is fallen, and is become the habitation of demons, and the hold of every foul spirit, and a cage of every unclean and hateful bird. For all nations have drunk of the wine of the wrath of her fornication, and the kings of the earth have committed fornication with her, and the merchants of the earth are grown rich through the abundance of her delicacies. And I heard another voice from heaven, saying, Come out of her, my people, that ye be not partakers of her sins, and that ye receive not of her plagues; For her sins have reached unto heaven, and God hath remembered her iniquities. Reward her even as she rewarded you, and double unto her double according to her works; in the cup which she hath filled fill to her double. How much she hath glorified herself, and lived luxuriously, so much torment and sorrow give her; for she saith in her heart, I sit a queen, and am no widow, and shall see no sorrow. Therefore shall her plagues come in one day, death, and mourning, and famine, and she shall be utterly burned with fire; for strong is the Lord God who judgeth her. And the kings of the earth, who have committed fornication and lived luxuriously with her, shall bewail her, and lament for her, when they shall see the smoke of her burning, Standing afar off for the fear of her torment, saying, Alas, alas, that great city, Babylon, that mighty city! For in one hour is thy judgment come. And the merchants of the earth shall weep and mourn over her; for no man buyeth their merchandise any more: The merchandise of gold, and silver, and precious stones, and pearls, and fine linen, and purple, and silk, and scarlet, and all thyine wood, and all kinds of vessels of ivory, and all kinds of vessels of most precious wood, and of bronze, and iron, and marble, And cinnamon, and incense, and ointments, and frankincense, and wine, and oil, and fine flour, and wheat, and cattle, and sheep, and horses, and chariots, and slaves, and souls of men. And the fruits that thy soul lusted after are departed from thee, and all things which were dainty and sumptuous are departed from thee, and thou shalt find them no more at all. The merchants of these things, who were made rich by her, shall stand afar off for the fear of her torment, weeping and wailing, And saying, Alas, alas, that great city, that was clothed in fine linen, and purple, and scarlet, and bedecked with gold, and precious stones, and pearls! For in one hour so great riches are come to nothing. And every shipmaster, and all the company in ships, and sailors, and as many as trade by sea, stood afar off, And cried when they saw the smoke of her burning, saying, What city is like unto this great city? And they cast dust on their heads, and cried, weeping and wailing, saying, Alas, alas, that great city, in which were made rich all that had ships in the sea by reason of her costliness! For in one hour is she made desolate. Rejoice over her, thou heaven, and ye holy apostles and prophets; for God hath avenged you on her. And a mighty angel took up a stone like a great millstone, and cast it into the sea, saying, Thus with violence shall that great city, Babylon, be thrown down, and shall be found no more at all. And the voice of harpers, and minstrels, and flute players, and trumpeters shall be heard no more at all in thee; and no craftsman, of whatever craft he be, shall be found any more in thee; and the sound of a millstone shall be heard no more at all in thee; And the light of a lamp shall shine no more at all in thee; and the voice of the bridegroom and of the bride shall be heard no more at all in thee; for thy merchants were the great men of the earth; for by thy sorceries were all nations deceived. And in her was found the blood of prophets, and of saints, and of all that were slain upon the earth.

22

THE FALL OF BABYLON

In the 1980s, Saddam Hussein started to rebuild portions of the ancient city of Babylon. Christians began to ask if Hussein's project had anything to do with Bible prophecy. This in turn rekindled the often-asked question, "Did prophecy predict the rebuilding of Babylon?"

Conservative scholars differ on what the Bible teaches concerning Babylon's future. Some teach that the city of Babylon will never be rebuilt for the following reasons:

1. Isaiah predicted that "Babylon...shall be as when God overthrew Sodom and Gomorrah. It shall never be inhabited, neither shall it be dwelt in from generation to generation; neither shall the Arabian pitch tent there; neither shall the shepherds make their fold there" (Isaiah 13:19-20).

2. Jeremiah predicted that no stone from the ruins of Babylon would be used to rebuild the city, and no one would dwell there (Jeremiah 51:26, 43).

3. In Revelation 17-18, the word *Babylon* is a symbolic description of a wicked religious, political, and commercial system, not a future rebuilt city.

The flip side for believing that Babylon will be rebuilt during the Tribulation includes the following:

1. Babylon was not suddenly and completely destroyed, as were the cities of Sodom and Gomorrah, nor did the city drink the last of God's wrath when it was taken by the Medo-Persian Empire in 539 B.C.

2. The area is still inhabited, and stones from the old Babylon are being used to rebuild the city.

3. Israel and Judah did not reunite, flee the city, come to the Lord in tears, or find rest from sorrow and fear (Isaiah 14:3-4; Jeremiah 50:4-5, 8) when Babylon was destroyed.

These unfulfilled prophecies seem to indicate that Babylon will be rebuilt with a commercial system that will function on a worldwide scale.

Revelation 18 opens with John stating, "And after these things I saw another angel come down from heaven, having great power, and the earth was made bright with his glory" (v. 1). The phrase "And after these things" indicates that John received a new revelation about future events. The angel was given "great power" or authority to execute God's judgment upon Babylon. His glory was so great that it illuminated the earth. The identity of the angel is not revealed, but he and his mission resemble the "mighty angel" mentioned in Revelation 10.

Babylon Destroyed

Although Babylon's destruction is yet future, in God's eyes it is already accomplished. With a strong voice, the angel cried, "Babylon the great is fallen, is fallen" (v. 2). Upon Babylon's demise, she will "become the habitation of demons, and the hold of every foul spirit, and a cage of every unclean and hateful bird"

(v. 2). This once-thriving city will become a wilderness, possessed with imprisoned evil spirits hovering over the area like
scavenger birds over their prey.

One reason for the city's fall is her decadent relationship with
"all nations" described as "fornication" (v. 3). In the Tribulation,
unbelievers, including kings and merchants (v. 3), will be wooed
into a wicked union with Babylon and will become intoxicated
with a passion for her wealth. Political and corporate leaders
will have "grown rich through the abundance of her delicacies
[luxuries]" (v. 3).

John "heard another voice from heaven" commanding true
believers to "Come out" of Babylon, so that they will not be "partakers of her sins" or "receive not of her plagues" (v. 4). They are
to disassociate themselves from this evil system of idolatry, luxury, and violence. Those who fail to do so will not be protected
when God destroys the city. The same admonition was given to
the Jewish people before the destruction of ancient Babylon
(Jeremiah 50:4-8; 51:6, 45).

God will remember the spiritual and moral evil of Babylon
and will judge her accordingly. Her sins will have "reached unto
heaven" (v. 5). The word *reach* means *to glue* or *weld
together*—that is, pile one on top of another, as bricks in a building. This is an allusion to the tower of Babel, which began the
wicked history of ancient Babylon (Genesis 11:3-9).[1] God will
permit sin to increase until the cup is full; then He will act in
divine judgment.

The angel calls for the law of retribution to be implemented
against Babylon: "Reward her...double according to her works;
in the cup which she hath filled fill to her double" (v. 6).
Babylon's cup—used to seduce others—will be filled with God's
undiluted wrath and used to destroy her. No mercy will be
shown. God will measure out twice as much judgment on
Babylon because of the enormity of her sin.

Another reason for the city's fall is her pride of wealth: "she hath glorified herself, and lived luxuriously" (v. 7). This phrase "denotes a luxurious lifestyle with the accompanying trappings of discourtesy, arrogance, self-indulgence, ruthless exercise of strength, and unruliness."[2] Her self-glorification will lead to self-sufficiency, self-deification, and finally self-deception. She will boast in her heart, "I sit a queen, and am no widow, and shall see no sorrow" (v. 7; cp. Isaiah 47:8-11). However, just the opposite is true. She will be deceived and will suffer all the sorrow of widowhood.

Although the kings of the earth glorify her with praise, she will be forsaken by God. Her destruction will be sudden and complete. In "one day" she will suffer "death, and mourning, and famine, and she shall be utterly burned with fire" (v. 8; cp. vv. 10, 17, 19). In 539 B.C., ancient Babylon was captured on the very night God prophesied her fall (Daniel 5).

Bewailing Dirge

A worldwide lament will rise from the earth dwellers as they see the smoke of Babylon's destruction. First, monarchs "who have committed fornication and lived luxuriously with her" (v. 9) will bewail the city's destruction. Afraid of being caught up in the same holocaust that consumed Babylon, these leaders are seen "Standing afar off for the fear of her torment" (v. 10). Their cry for the great city is, "Alas, alas [woe], that great city, Babylon, that mighty city! For in one hour is thy judgment come" (v. 10). The kings will wring their hands and weep over the loss of the power they enjoyed by participating in Babylon's wickedness and wealth. "They eulogize her with...praise, but there is a terrible hopelessness in their anguish; they marvel at the sudden destruction of that which they thought was gilt-edged security. They mourn as if lamenting the passing of a loved one."[3]

Second, the merchants will mourn their loss, "for no man

buyeth their merchandise any more" (v. 11). It would seem that doing business with Babylon will bring great riches to many people worldwide. These traders will profit enormously from doing business with Babylon. They will sell their souls to traffic in the items mentioned in verses 12-13: merchandise made of gold, silver, and precious stones; beautiful purple and scarlet fabrics of fine linen and silk; household furnishings of thyine wood, vessels of ivory, precious wood, bronze, iron, and marble (v. 12); exquisite spices, perfumes, ointments, and incense; food items such as oil, flour, wheat; cattle, and sheep for human consumption; "horses and chariots," modes of transportation affordable only to the wealthy; a multitude of slaves, whom they own body and soul (v. 13). All of this opulence and wealth, which they will lust after, will depart in one hour and will be found no more (v. 14). The merchants will respond as did the monarchs to the loss of Babylon (v. 15) with anguish and lamentation. These merchants are the same men who will take the mark of the beast so that they may buy and sell (13:17). The loss of Babylon will deny them the same right they denied to others.

Third, mariners will mourn over their loss: "And every shipmaster...and sailors...cried when they saw the smoke of her burning, saying, What city is like unto this great city?" (vv. 17-18). They expressed great grief, as the people in Old Testament times did: "they cast dust on their heads, and cried, weeping and wailing" (v. 19), echoing the lament of all the others. Once again, "in one hour" (v. 19) all will be lost.

Believers' Delight

In contrast to the monarchs, merchants, and mariners who lament the demise of Babylon, heaven, along with the "holy apostles and prophets" (v. 20), will rejoice over Babylon's destruction. They will rejoice because God, in His righteous judgment, "hath avenged" (v. 20) the blood of the saints. He will recompense Babylon with the same infliction she showed in martyring the saints (cp. 6:9-11).

A "mighty angel" appears for the third time in this chapter and takes "up a stone like a great millstone, and cast[s] it into the sea" (v. 21), symbolizing the sudden, swift, violent, total destruction of Babylon (cp. Jeremiah 51:61-64). The angel assures the world that Babylon "shall be found no more at all" (v. 21). The words "no more" are mentioned seven times in this chapter. No more will all the luxury items be found in Babylon. Neither will the "voice of harpers, and minstrels, and flute players, and trumpeters...craftsman...the sound of a millstone...light of a lamp...the voice of the bridegroom and of the bride" (vv. 22-23). Sounds of life will cease to exist in any form when God destroys Babylon. This will be a testimony to her total destruction, like that of Sodom and Gomorrah.

The enormity of Babylon's great sin, which will precipitate her demise, is once again mentioned in the closing verses of Revelation 18.

1. Merchants, "the great men of the earth" (v. 23), will not only be responsible for exporting their products worldwide, but for exporting the diabolical Babylonian system as well.

2. "By thy sorceries were all nations deceived" (v. 23). Babylon will use pseudo-magical arts to deceive *all* nations during the Tribulation and lure them into an immoral spiritual relationship with herself.[4]

3. "The blood of prophets, and of saints, and of all that were slain upon the earth" will be found in her (v. 24; cp. Jeremiah 51:35-36, 49). During the Tribulation, Babylon will not be the only one responsible for the martyrdom of prophets and saints. Her aggressive hatred for true believers

will be transmitted worldwide, as she inspires governments to martyr saints.

The sins of the Babylonian system are traced back to Genesis. Its demonic influence is threaded all through Scripture, touching every major area of human existence.

- Politically, Babylon symbolizes prideful rebellion against God. By trying to build a tower to heaven, Nimrod attempted to confederate the people into a city-state that would receive worldwide fame and recognition. This was in direct defiance of God's command to "multiply, and fill the earth" (Genesis 9:1). God destroyed this program by confusing their language and scattering the people.

- Religiously, Babylon symbolizes the mother of idolatrous religion and worship that has infected all nations with its satanic dogma and practice.

- Economically, Babylon symbolizes the pride of wealth and sensuality; the worship of money, power, and prosperity; the spirit of covetous commercialism that dominates worldwide commerce.

All of this will be destroyed at the Second Coming of Christ. The phrase "Babylon...shall be found no more" (v. 21) says it all.

Endnotes

[1] John F. Walvoord, *The Revelation of Jesus Christ* (Chicago: Moody Press, 1966), p. 269.

[2] Robert L. Thomas, *Revelation 8-22, An Exegetical Commentary* (Chicago: Moody Press, 1995), p. 325.

[3] Jack MacArthur, *Expositional Commentary of Revelation* (Eugene: Certain Sound Publishing House), p. 356.

[4] *Op cit.*, Thomas, p. 308.

REVELATION 19:1-10

And after these things I heard a great voice of many people in heaven, saying, Hallelujah! Salvation, and glory, and honor, and power, unto the Lord, our God; For true and righteous are his judgments; for he hath judged the great harlot, who did corrupt the earth with her fornication, and hath avenged the blood of his servants at her hand. And again they said, Hallelujah! And her smoke rose up forever and ever. And the four and twenty elders and the four living creatures fell down and worshiped God that sat on the throne, saying, Amen. Hallelujah! And a voice came out of the throne, saying, Praise our God, all ye his servants, and ye that fear him, both small and great. And I heard, as it were, the voice of a great multitude, and like the voice of many waters, and like the voice of mighty peals of thunder, saying, Hallelujah! For the Lord God omnipotent reigneth. Let us be glad and rejoice, and give honor to him; for the marriage of the Lamb is come, and his wife hath made herself ready. And to her was granted that she should be arrayed in fine linen, clean and white; for the fine linen is the righteousnesses of saints. And he saith unto me, Write, Blessed are they who are called unto the marriage supper of the Lamb. And he saith unto me, These are the true sayings of God. And I fell at his feet to worship him. And he said unto me, See thou do it not! I am thy fellow servant, and of thy brethren that have the testimony of Jesus. Worship God; for the testimony of Jesus is the spirit of prophecy.

=== 23 ===

THE MARRIAGE SUPPER
OF THE LAMB

On March 23, 1743, *The Messiah* was performed for the first time in London. In attendance was King George II of England. He was deeply moved as the "Hallelujah Chorus" was being sung, and at the words, "For the Lord God omnipotent reigneth," the king rose to His feet and stood until the end of the cantata. From that time to this, it has been customary to stand whenever the "Hallelujah Chorus" is performed. When Handel composed *The Messiah*, he was so immersed for the 23 days it took to write that he hardly ate or slept. At times he would run to the harpsichord, waving his arms and singing, "Hallelujah! Hallelujah!" Handel said, "I think I did see all heaven before me, and the great God Himself."[1]

In this passage, John did not see God, but he recorded a similar experience. "And after these things I heard a great voice of many people in heaven, saying, Hallelujah!" (v. 1). The phrase "after these things" refers back to Babylon's destruction in chapters 17 and 18, bringing the Tribulation to a close. The scene then shifts from earth to heaven.

Multitudes Singing

Heaven is invited to rejoice over Babylon's destruction, as John reports, "I heard a great voice of many people in heaven, saying, Hallelujah!"   *Hallelujah* is a transliteration of the Hebrew word *Praise the Lord*. It is found frequently in the Old Testament, but Revelation is the only place it is found in the New Testament, where it introduces four victory hymns in heaven (19:1, 3, 4, 6).

Let's examine the groups participating in these Hallelujah choruses.

1. "Many people in heaven" (v. 1) is a general statement but could be a specific reference to the martyred dead in the Great Tribulation (cp. 6:9-10; 7:9, 14).

2. "The four and twenty elders" (v. 4) represent the church and sing the song of redemption (cp. 4:4; 5:8-10).

3. The "four living creatures" (v. 4) are cherubim surrounding God's throne, associated with His presence, holiness, and power (4:6-9).

4. The phrase "his servants, and ye that fear him, both small and great" (v. 5) refers, not to a specific group, but to all the servants in heaven. They are encouraged to continue praising God for His mighty victory, no matter what their status.

There are five reasons for the servants' praise:

1. They praise God for deliverance: "Salvation, and glory, and honor, and power, unto the Lord, our God" (v. 1). This celebration is for God's great deliverance over the beast, Babylon, and

the Antichrist. This will take place just before Christ victoriously takes back the earth to establish God's Kingdom. He alone is due all the glory, honor, and power.

2. They praise God for judging Babylon, "the great harlot" (v. 2). This judgment will be "true [faithful] and righteous [fair]...for he hath...avenged the blood of his servants at her hand" (v. 2).

3. They praise God because Babylon's demise is final, complete, and irreversible: "her smoke [will rise] up forever and ever" (v. 3). The city's destruction is permanent, as is the eternal destiny of those connected with her. The 24 elders and the four living creatures "fell down and worshiped God [the Father] that sat on the throne, saying, Amen [so be it]. Hallelujah!" (v. 4).

4. They praise God for His sovereignty over heaven and earth. "Hallelujah! For the Lord God omnipotent reigneth" (v. 6). Their praise will reverberate throughout heaven "like the voice of many waters, and...mighty peals of thunder" (v. 6). The sound coming from the host of heaven will be deafening, like the noise of a mighty waterfall and the booming of thunder echoing throughout the sky.

5. The host of heaven encourage one another to "be glad and rejoice, and give honor" to God for the upcoming "marriage of the Lamb" because Christ's "wife hath made herself ready" (v. 7) for the wedding.

Marriage Service

The marriage of the Lamb is patterned after the Jewish marriage customs of Bible times.

- **Phase one is the *arrangement*.** After the fathers of the bride and groom consummated a match, the bride's father was given the *bride price* as a dowry. The bride price for God the Father was the blood of His Son (Ephesians 5:25).

- **Phase two is the *preparation*, or betrothal.** This phase would last for a year or longer, during which time the bride was observed to display her purity. During the year, the bridegroom would prepare a home for his bride, attached to his father's house. In like manner, Christ is in heaven preparing a place for His bride, the church (John 14:1-3). On the wedding day, the groom would leave his father's house to fetch his bride. After taking her from her home, the groom would then lead the bridal procession back to his own home. This is a beautiful picture of the Rapture of the church (1 Thessalonians 4:13-18) prior to Christ's Second Coming.

- **Phase three is the *marriage ceremony*.** Before the marriage, there was the writing of a legal wedding document called the *Ketubah*, signed by two witnesses not related to the bridegroom or bride. The document was a marriage covenant, a willing agreement between the bride and groom that included obligations of the husband and rights of the wife. The bride was beautifully adorned, like a queen (cp. 21:2), with precious jewels plaited in her hair and clothing and a long veil covering her face. In biblical times, the ceremony was conducted at the home of the groom, attended by the immediate family, two witnesses, and a few close friends. Today, the ritual and customs vary according to country. It is held under a *huppah* (*marriage canopy*) and begins with the benediction of betrothal recited over a cup of wine, partaken of by both the bridegroom and the bride. A ring is placed upon the bride's finger, the Ketubah is read, and Seven Blessings are recited by a rabbi over a second cup of wine. The ceremony concludes with the groom breaking a glass in memory of the Temple's destruction. In biblical times, the couple would leave the guests to actually consummate the marriage. This is a beautiful picture of the church (the bride of Christ) consummating the marriage of the Lamb (19:7-8).

- **Phase four is the *marriage feast*,** to which friends of the bride and groom were invited to rejoice at the marriage. After a week of feasting, the couple would settle into their new home, which had been prepared by the groom.

For a greater understanding of the marriage of the Lamb, a number of questions must be answered.

- **Who are the participants?** The Lamb is the Lord Jesus Christ, identified as such 28 times in the Book of the Revelation. The bride is the church betrothed to Christ. Some might object to this identification, saying that Israel is described as the wife of God (Isaiah 54:6; Jeremiah 31:31). It is true that Israel is called the wife of Jehovah, but she is a *wife*, not a *bride*. As a wife, Israel has been unfaithful to God throughout the centuries. She will be restored, cleansed, and display marital fidelity to God in the Millennial Kingdom. The New Testament pictures the church as a virgin waiting to be united with the bridegroom at His coming (2 Corinthians 11:2; Ephesians 5:25-32). This wedding union of Christ and the church will be consummated in the future.

- **How has the wife "made herself ready" (v. 7)?** For the past 2,000 years, God has been preparing His church. He made all the arrangements for the purchase of the bride by paying the bride price, the blood of His Son. The Lord is in the process of perfecting the church in order to present her as "a chaste virgin to Christ" (2 Corinthians 11:2). She is now undergoing a sanctification process by being washed with the water of God's Word (Ephesians 5:26). Complete sanctification of the church will take place at the Rapture, when believers are changed and presented to Christ. This will take place at the Judgment Seat of Christ, after which a glorious church will be presented to Christ without spot, wrinkle, or blemish (Ephesians 5:27).

- **How will the church be dressed?** She will be "arrayed in fine linen, clean and white; for the fine linen is the righteousnesses of saints" (v. 8). This is not a reference to righteousness imputed at the time of salvation, but to Christ's righteousness as produced in the inner life and character of believers. The fine linen represents the righteous deeds of godliness and goodness produced by the Holy Spirit. These are the good works unto which we are created in Jesus Christ (Ephesians

2:10), with which the believers are to adorn themselves in order to bring honor to Christ's name.[2] We will appear before God clothed in whatever righteous acts remain after our works have been tested by fire. During our earthly pilgrimage, we are weaving the wedding garments that will adorn us at the marriage supper.

Marriage Supper

At this point, John was instructed to write the fourth of seven beatitudes presented in Revelation: "Blessed are they who are called unto the marriage supper of the Lamb" (v. 9). Who are those "called unto the marriage supper"? Some scholars believe they are the church saints and saints from other ages. Others believe that the invited guests are saints from other ages, but not the church saints. This is the best view because the bride is definitely identified as the church, whereas those called to the supper are saints from other ages. The invitation is given to Old Testament saints, martyred Tribulation saints, and believers who survive the Tribulation. The statement, "These are the true sayings of God" (v. 9) confirms the veracity of all that has been revealed in Revelation 17:1-19:10.

Two major positions are taught concerning the time and location of the marriage supper. Some scholars believe that the marriage supper will be held in heaven while the seven years of Tribulation are taking place on the earth. They give the following reasons for their view:

1. The marriage supper mentioned here is related to Jewish marriage customs in the Bible.

2. The marriage did not take place in the bride's home but in the bridegroom's home after he brought her to that prepared place.

3. It was customary for the marriage supper, given

by the groom's father, to be held at the bridegroom's home on the same night as the marriage
ceremony.

4. The Old Testament teaches that there will be
another marriage supper at the beginning of the
Millennium, associated with a second marriage
of God the Father and the nation of Israel (see
Isaiah 25:6). Thus, the future marriage of God
the Father and the marriage of the Lamb have
two different brides. The bride at the marriage of
God the Father is the nation of Israel; the bride at
the marriage of Christ the Lamb is the church.

According to this view, the marriage supper of the Lamb will take
place in heaven after the Rapture of the church and will include
the church (the bride), along with Old Testament saints and martyred Tribulation saints as guests.[3]

Other scholars believe there is just one marriage supper, to be
held on earth after Christ returns with His bride, the church.
According to this position, the wedding feast will begin God's
earthly Kingdom and will take place during the 45 days mentioned in Daniel 12:11-12. The guests will include friends of the
bride and groom from every period of history. John the Baptist is
a good example of an invited guest. He did not consider himself
the bridegroom or the bride, but a friend of the bridegroom (John
3:28-30).

Upon receiving this revelation, John "fell at his [the angel's]
feet to worship him" (v. 10). The angel sharply rebuked John:
"See thou do it not! I am thy fellow servant" (v. 10). The angel
revealed that he and the other angels are simply bond slaves,
along with all Christians, in Christ's service. Angels and
Christians possess "the testimony of Jesus" (v. 10), which is
Jesus' own testimony of Himself. He is the one who provides
prophetic revelation of Himself in the Old and New Testaments

and propagates it through His servants.

Further explanation is given concerning the testimony of Jesus: "for the testimony of Jesus is the spirit of prophecy" (v. 10). John, along with other apostles, received prophetic insight and inspiration and gave testimony that their prophecies are intended to glorify Jesus Christ. The title of the book is "The Revelation of Jesus Christ" (1:1). Christ is the central figure of all revelation. In Revelation, prophecy is designed to unfold Christ's character, glory, purpose, and program. Therefore, "Worship God" and only God (v. 10)!

With these words, the scene is set for the manifestation of Jesus Christ as the glorified King of kings and Lord of lords. *Hallelujah!*

Endnotes

[1] Paul Lee Tan, *Encyclopedia of 7700 Illustrations* (Rockville: Assurance Publishers, 1979), pp. 326, 480.

[2] C. I. Scofield, *New Scofield Reference Bible* (New York: Oxford University Press, 1967), p. 1371.

[3] For a detailed interpretation of this view, see Renald Showers' article, "The Marriage and Marriage Supper of the Lamb," *Israel My Glory*, vol. 49, no. 3, June/July 1991.

REVELATION 19:11-21

And I saw heaven opened and, behold, a white horse; and he that sat upon him was called Faithful and True, and in righteousness he doth judge and make war. His eyes were like a flame of fire, and on his head were many crowns; and he had a name written, that no man knew, but he himself. And he was clothed with a vesture dipped in blood; and his name is called The Word of God. And the armies that were in heaven followed him upon white horses, clothed in fine linen, white and clean. And out of his mouth goeth a sharp sword, that with it he should smite the nations, and he shall rule them with a rod of iron; and he treadeth the winepress of the fierceness and wrath of Almighty God. And he hath on his vesture and on his thigh a name written, KING OF KINGS, AND LORD OF LORDS.

And I saw an angel standing in the sun; and he cried with a loud voice, saying to all the fowls that fly in the midst of heaven, Come and gather yourselves together unto the supper of the great God, That ye may eat the flesh of kings, and the flesh of captains, and the flesh of mighty men, and the flesh of horses and of them that sit on them, and the flesh of all men, both free and enslaved, both small and great. And I saw the beast, and the kings of the earth, and their armies, gathered together to make war against him that sat on the horse, and against his army. And the beast was taken, and with him the false prophet that wrought miracles before him, with which he deceived them that had received the mark of the beast, and them that worshiped his image. These both were cast alive into a lake of fire burning with brimstone. And the remnant were slain with the sword of him that sat upon the horse, which sword proceeded out of his mouth; and all the fowls were filled with their flesh.

24

CHRIST'S SECOND COMING

C hrist's Second Coming is a major doctrine throughout the Bible. It is the most dominant theme in the New Testament, next to the subject of faith. Christ's return, put simply, is *the personal, physical, visible return of the Lord to the earth in resplendent glory.*

There are some astounding statistics regarding the frequent mention of Christ's Second Coming in Scripture:

- One-fifth of the Bible is prophecy. One-third of those prophecies relate in some way to Christ's Second Coming.

- There are at least 333 prophecies concerning Christ in the Old Testament. Only 109 were fulfilled in His first advent, leaving 224— more than twice as many—to be fulfilled at His second advent.

- Of the 46 Old Testament prophets, less than ten speak of events in Christ's First Coming, while 36 speak of events connected with His Second Coming.

- There are 7,959 verses in the New Testament, 330 of which refer directly to the Second Coming.

- The Lord refers to His return 25 times.

- Throughout the New Testament, there are more than 50 exhortations for people to be ready for Christ's return.[1]

Often, the Rapture of the church is referred to as Christ's Second Coming. It is important to understand that the Rapture of the church and Christ's Second Coming are separate events. The Rapture is imminent; no prophecy must yet be fulfilled for this event to occur. The Rapture will take place at least seven years before Christ's Second Coming. In the Rapture, the church will be caught up to meet the Lord in the air and go to live with Him in heaven (John 14:1-3; 1 Corinthians 15:51-52; 1 Thessalonians 4:13-18). Christ's Second Coming will not take place until after the seven years of the Tribulation have been completed on the earth. Then Christ will return from heaven with His church to rule and reign on the earth for a thousand years.

Christ's Coming Revealed

John wrote, "And I saw heaven opened and, behold, a white horse" (v. 11). In Revelation 4, the apostle saw a door open in heaven, but in this passage he sees all of heaven open. What a revealing contrast to Christ's first advent! At His First Coming, Christ rode into Jerusalem in a lowly state, sitting on a colt, the foal of a donkey. He was given no throne, only a cross; His crown was thorns; His scepter was a reed. But here, the Lord is seated on a white horse, ready for departure from heaven as a Warrior-King. He is poised for battle array, coming "in righteousness [to] judge and make war" (v. 11) against the Antichrist, the False Prophet, and all who follow them.

Throughout this Age of Grace, the world has scoffed at the possibility of Christ's return. Christ has held back His righteous indignation on such indifference, giving people time to "come to repentance" (2 Peter 3:9). He has allowed wickedness to run its course, but, in Revelation 19, the cup of sin is full. It is time to judge the rulers of darkness and reclaim the earth from Satan's grip. When He comes in the clouds, "every eye shall see him, and they also who pierced him; and all kindreds of the earth shall wail because of him" (1:7).

Christ's coming on a white horse will symbolize His glorious victory over God's enemies. In Bible times, Roman generals always returned from victorious campaigns riding white horses. They and their legions would parade up the *Via Sacra*, the main street of Rome that led from the Forum to the Temple of Jupiter on the Capitoline Hill, mounted on white horses, to the jubilant cheers of the people.[2] It should be noted that the Antichrist will also come on a white horse (6:2). He will carry a bow without arrows, suggesting that he will conquer by peaceful means during the first half of the Tribulation. He will wear a victor's crown as the world leader, but his deceptive and demonic reign will mark him as a counterfeit. His reign will last only 42 months because Christ will destroy him at His Second Coming.

Christ's Characteristics Reviewed

Christ is described by a number of titles at His return.

1. He is called "Faithful" (v 11), meaning *trustworthy*, or one who can be *relied upon*. He is faithful to keep all of His promises. Jesus said, "Heaven and earth shall pass away, but my words shall not pass away" (Matthew 24:35).

2. He is "True" (v. 11)—that is, *genuine* or *real*, compared to that which is false. He promised to

bring peace and social and political justice to mankind, and He will perfectly deliver what He has promised. The rider of Revelation 6:2 is the exact opposite; he is dangerously deceptive and dishonest.

3. "He had a name written, that no man knew, but he himself" (v. 12). It seems that John was able to see the name, possibly written on Christ's garments, but it was incomprehensible to him, shrouded in mystery.

4. He is called "The Word of God" (v. 13). Christ is the eternal Word who became flesh and dwelt among mankind (John 1:1, 14). He is the complete personal manifestation of God and the full and final revelation of God. He who spoke the universe into existence will, at His Second Coming, destroy the beast and his empire by the Word of His mouth.

5. He has a name written on His vesture: "KING OF KINGS, AND LORD OF LORDS" (v. 16). This title is a summation of His rightful claim to reign and rule over all of creation in absolute sovereignty.

John described Christ's appearance at His return: "His eyes were like a flame of fire" (v. 12), indicating a penetrating gaze that flashed with intelligence, righteousness, and the look of divine wrath upon the wicked. His eyes will accurately expose and exterminate all unrighteousness (cp. 1:14; 2:18). Christ will wear "many crowns" (v. 12) on His head, denoting His royalty and majestic position as sovereign King of kings over heaven and earth.

Christ's Retribution

Armies will accompany Christ at His return. "And the armies that were in heaven followed him upon white horses, clothed in fine linen, white and clean" (v. 14). The armies will include the holy angels (Matthew 25:31), church saints (v. 8), Old Testament believers (Jude 14-15; Daniel 12:1-2), and Tribulation saints martyred for their faith (7:13-14; 20:4). They will return with Christ in their glorified bodies. The "fine linen, clean and white" symbolizes Christ's righteousness produced in the inner life and character of believers (v. 8).

Upon seeing Christ appear, "the beast, and the kings of the earth, and their armies, [will gather] together to make war against him...and against his army" (v. 19; cp. Psalm 2:2). "Out of his mouth goeth a sharp sword, that with it he should smite the nations" (v 15). The sword is more like a javelin, which is large, long, thin, and light enough to be thrown like a spear. The sword is symbolic, referring to Christ's Word that proceeds from His mouth. Christ, as the Warrior-King, will simply speak and consume the Antichrist and his army with the Word of His mouth (2 Thessalonians 2:8).

His "vesture [is] dipped in blood" (v. 13). This is not His own blood, shed on the cross, but the blood of His enemies. First, His garments will become blood-spattered when He delivers a remnant of Israelis living in Bozrah, who will flee to the land of Edom and hide in Bozrah to escape the wrath of the Antichrist (Isaiah 63:1-6). Then His garments will become even more blood-spattered as He destroys the armies at Armageddon (v. 15; cp. 14:14-20). In contrast, the garments of His armies will not be stained with blood. Christ alone will fight and gain this victory.

After the avenging Lord smites the nations, "he shall rule them with a rod of iron" (v. 15). His rule over the nations will be unyielding and in total authority, demanding that every nation conform to His righteous standards. Lawlessness will be handled swiftly and justly, insuring continued peace throughout the world. The word *rod* means *to shepherd*. The shepherd uses his rod to bring correction and comfort to sheep

(Psalm 23:4). Here the rod is made of iron and will be used to conform the world to order and justice and to put down all manifestation of wickedness. Christ is the "good shepherd" (John 10:11), the "great Shepherd" (Hebrews 13:20), and the "chief Shepherd" (1 Peter 5:4) who will rule the world through those returning with Him.

Christ's destruction of the armies is further described: "and he treadeth the winepress of the fierceness and wrath of Almighty God" (v. 15). This imagery portrays grapes being trampled under foot until all the juice is squeezed out of them. Here blood, not grape juice, will spurt from the winepress of God's wrath (cp. 14:14-20). The soldiers' flesh will "consume" (Zechariah 14:12) from their bodies while they are still standing. The word *consume* means *to rot* and has the idea of *wasting away*, as does the flesh of a leper. At Armageddon, the flesh will rot away at the Word of the Lord, instantly falling from the victims' bodies to the ground while they are still standing.

Christ's Conquest Realized

John "saw an angel standing in the sun; and he cried with a loud voice, saying to all the fowls that fly in the midst of heaven, Come and gather yourselves together unto the supper of the great God" (v. 17). The word *fowl* is not the general word for *bird*, but speaks of a *vulture*. Vultures are voracious eaters who descend swiftly upon carrion and devour it in minutes. Their task is to eat the "flesh of kings...captains...mighty men...horses and...all men...free and enslaved...small and great" (v. 18). The army of the Antichrist will include all classes of people who will be totally consumed by the vultures. Seeing these ugly birds feed on the decaying carcasses of millions of men in a 200-mile radius of Jerusalem will be a terrifying spectacle, beyond human imagination.

What a contrast between the two suppers mentioned in Revelation 19. At the first supper, believers are called to rejoice and feast with Christ in heaven (v. 7). At the second supper, unbelievers will be made the meal of scavenging birds (vv. 17-18).

The final destiny of this satanic confederacy is certain: "And the beast was taken, and with him the false prophet...and them that worshiped his image. These both were cast alive into a lake of fire burning with brimstone" (v. 20). Dr. Harry Ironside wrote,

> A thousand years later they are still said to be suffering the vengeance of eternal fire, thus incidentally proving that the lake of fire is not annihilation, and that it is not purgatorial either, for it neither annihilates nor purifies these two fallen foes of God and man after a thousand years under judgment. The lake of fire differs from the abode of Satan, in that, the abode is only temporary, the lake of fire is their final eternal destiny.[3]

More will be said about the lake of fire in the next chapter.

John concluded the description of the Lord's Second Coming by relating what will happen to the survivors of the Great Tribulation who follow the Antichrist. "And the remnant were slain with the sword of him that sat upon the horse, which sword proceeded out of his mouth; and all the fowls were filled with their flesh" (v. 21).

After Christ returns, He will judge the nations. Those who are righteous will enter the kingdom prepared for them from the foundation of the world. The wicked survivors of the Great Tribulation, who followed the Antichrist, will be condemned to death and destined to spend eternity in the everlasting fire prepared for the Devil and his angels (Matthew 25:31-46).

After the Lord has completed this judgment, He will establish His Millennial Kingdom on the earth. Those returning with Him will be made priests of God and will reign with Him in the Millennial Kingdom.

Endnotes

[1] John MacArthur, Jr., *The Second Coming of the Lord Jesus Christ* (Panorama City, CA: Word of Grace Communications, 1981), p. 1.

[2] John F. Walvoord, *The Revelation of Jesus Christ* (Chicago: Moody Press, 1966), p. 274.

[3] Harry A. Ironside, *Revelation* (New York: Loizeaux Brothers, 1946), p. 330.

REVELATION 20:1-10

And I saw an angel come down from heaven, having the key of the bottomless pit and a great chain in his hand. And he laid hold on the dragon, that old serpent, who is the Devil and Satan, and bound him a thousand years, And cast him into the bottomless pit, and shut him up, and set a seal upon him, that he should deceive the nations no more, till the thousand years should be fulfilled; and after that he must be loosed a little season. And I saw thrones, and they sat upon them, and judgment was given unto them; and I saw the souls of them that were beheaded for the witness of Jesus, and for the word of God, and who had not worshiped the beast, neither his image, neither had received his mark upon their foreheads, or in their hands; and they lived and reigned with Christ a thousand years. But the rest of the dead lived not again until the thousand years were finished. This is the first resurrection. Blessed and holy is he that hath part in the first resurrection; on such the second death hath no power, but they shall be priests of God and of Christ, and shall reign with him a thousand years. And when the thousand years are ended, Satan shall be loosed out of his prison, And shall go out to deceive the nations which are in the four quarters of the earth, Gog and Magog, to gather them together to battle; the number of whom is as the sand of the sea. And they went up on the breadth of the earth, and compassed the camp of the saints about, and the beloved city; and fire came down from God out of heaven, and devoured them. And the devil that deceived them was cast into the lake of fire and brimstone, where the beast and the false prophet are, and shall be tormented day and night forever and ever.

25

THE MILLENNIAL KINGDOM

U Thant, former Secretary General of the United Nations, addressed 67 scholars and statesmen on the requirements for world peace. He asked these questions:

> What element is lacking so that with all our skill and all our knowledge we still find ourselves in the dark valley of discord and enmity? Why is it that, for all our professed ideals, our hopes, and our skills, peace on earth is still a distant objective seen only dimly through storms and turmoils of our present difficulties?[1]

U Thant was not able to answer his own questions. But the Scriptures have answered them.

Will there ever be world peace? Yes. Christ has promised that He will return to the earth and establish world peace. That time is called the *Millennium*, a Latin word meaning *thousand years*—a thousand-year reign of peace, prosperity, and plenty never before experienced in history, all orchestrated by Jesus Christ.

Theologians differ on their views of the Millennium. *Amillennialists* believe there will be no earthly reign of Christ before or after His Second Coming. *Postmillennialists* believe that the whole world will be Christianized, submitting to the gospel a thousand years *before* Christ's return. They see Christ's return taking place *after* the Millennium. *Premillennialists* believe that Christ will return *before* the Millennium to reign on the earth for a *literal* thousand years.

Chapter 20 provides a great summary of many end-time events. It reveals Christ's Millennial rule on earth, Satan's destruction and destiny, the destiny of the Tribulation saints, the order of various resurrections presented in the Bible, and details on the Great White Throne Judgment. Evidence in this chapter proves that the Premillennial interpretation is the correct view.

Restraint of Satan

After the awesome destruction at Armageddon, Satan will be consigned to the bottomless pit. John wrote, "And I saw an angel come down from heaven, having the key of the bottomless pit and a great chain in his hand" (v. 1). A special place called "the bottomless pit" has been prepared for Satan and demons (9:1-2, 11; 11:7; 17:8). This is *not* hell, where the wicked dead reside, but is a separate location of suffering.

Who is this angel? Some scholars have identified him as Christ, but there is no evidence to confirm this interpretation. The Lord has given this angel great authority to implement His mission. This authority is signified by a "key" to lock and unlock the opening of the abyss. A "great chain" was given to the angel with which to shackle Satan. Scripture does not define the make-up of the chain, but it will render Satan inactive for a thousand years in the abyss.

The angel "laid hold on the dragon, that old serpent, who is the Devil and Satan" (v. 2)—the angel strong-armed Satan, seizing and holding him firmly. Only God-given authority can sub-

due Satan. Then the angel "cast him into the bottomless pit, and
shut him up, and set a seal upon him, that he should deceive the
nations no more, till the thousand years should be fulfilled" (v. 3).
The incarceration, chaining, and sealing guarantee that the dragon will be rendered incapable of deceiving or interrupting the
peace promised by Christ in the Millennial Kingdom.

Peace will prevail on the earth during this time for two reasons:

1. Satan and his demonic host will be sealed, unable
   to deceive the world.

2. Christ will rule on the earth with a rod of iron
   (19:15), allowing no wickedness to be manifested.

Then, "he must be loosed a little season" (v. 3) after the thousand years have run their course. Note that the duration of his
confinement is "a thousand years" (v. 2). This is not a symbolic
number, but a literal thousand years.

Resurrection of Saints

John is given a revelation concerning those who have part in
the first resurrection. The apostle said, "And I saw thrones, and
they sat upon them, and judgment was given unto them" (v. 4).
This statement is vague, lacking specifics about who is sitting on
the thrones and what judgment they will carry out. Identification
of the group is somewhat easier because it is reported that they
have part in the "first resurrection" (v. 5). Some scholars believe
they could be the 24 elders who represent the church (4:4) and
will reign on the earth (5:10). But there is no mention of the 24
elders or 24 thrones in this context. Others identify the saint
occupants of the thrones as the apostles (Luke 22:29-30), but
there is no mention of the apostles in this context. Still others
believe the occupants could be all the saints who comprise the
armies of Christ in 19:14. This view is supported by the promises given to the bride of Christ (2:26-28; 3:21) and all saints.

Those who return with Christ in glorified bodies will be the Old Testament saints, church age saints (the bride of Christ), and Tribulation saints martyred for their faith ("the souls of them that were beheaded for the witness of Jesus, and for the word of God, and who had not worshiped the beast, neither his image, neither had received his mark," v. 4). All these will "reign with him a thousand years" (v. 6).

Paul teaches that there are various stages to the first resurrection (1 Corinthians 15:20-24). In verse 23, he stated that each person is to be resurrected "in his own order." The church will be resurrected before the Tribulation begins. The Old Testament saints and the Tribulation saints will be resurrected just before the Second Coming of Christ, after the Great Tribulation. "But the rest of the dead lived not again until the thousand years were finished" (v. 5). This is the bodily resurrection of all unsaved people who ever lived, all of whom will be resurrected at the end of the Millennium.

Those who take part in the first resurrection are called "Blessed and holy" (v. 6). This is the fifth of seven beatitudes mentioned in Revelation. "Blessed" speaks of joy, satisfaction, complete and fulfilled peace within believers. On such people "the second death hath no power [authority]" (v. 6). There are two deaths mentioned in Scripture—physical and spiritual. Believers in Christ will experience only physical death—unless, of course, they are caught up alive in the Rapture of the church. The "second death" is both physical and spiritual and will be experienced by unbelievers (Matthew 10:28). The first death results in burial, but those facing the second death will be physically resurrected at the proper time and cast alive into the lake of fire (20:14). It is second only to the physical death previously mentioned. This is an eternal death, which means that people will be separated from God forever, cast into outer darkness, and suffer eternally in the lake of fire. The second death does not mean annihilation.

People will be conscious during their eternal torment in the lake of fire (v. 10; see Luke 16:22-25).

Righteous believers "shall be priests of God and of Christ, and shall reign with him a thousand years" (v. 6). Being priests of God and Christ will entitle believers to unlimited access and intimate fellowship with God. Resurrected saints will be given the privilege of ruling with Christ on the earth for the entire Millennium. The form this rule will take is not revealed in Scripture. It will not be limited to the Millennium but will extend into the eternal state (22:3, 5).

Release of Satan

The angel revealed that once again when "the thousand years are ended, Satan shall be loosed out of his prison, And shall go out to deceive the nations which are in the four quarters of the earth" (vv. 7-8). Why will God allow Satan this last opportunity to deceive the people born in the Kingdom? Scripture is silent on this question, but it is not difficult to speculate on some of the possible reasons.

- Mankind, living in the most favorable social, religious, and political order, when given their own choice, will manifest sin because of their depraved and ungodly nature. Mankind's problem is not environmental—it is a heart problem. This was clearly seen when Adam and Eve sinned in the Garden of Eden.

- It will reveal that God's sentence against Satan and those who follow him is just.

- God's nature is holy and just, and all His judgments are eternally consistent with His righteous character.

Who are the ones Satan will deceive within the nations? The offspring of righteous saints who will enter the Millennium in their natural bodies. They will be reared in a perfect environment, but many will not receive Christ during the Kingdom age. They will be easily deceived by Satan.

Revolt of Sinners

"The nations which are in the four quarters of the earth" (v. 8) are not the same as those that will take part in Armageddon. These are nations formed during the Millennial Kingdom. The number of unbelievers during the Millennium will be the largest the world has ever known—they will be "as the sand of the sea" (v. 8). This will be because during the Millennium, the curse will be lifted from the earth, allowing peace among nations, longevity of life, elimination of disease, and enormous food production.

The nations "in the four quarters of the earth" are described as "Gog and Magog" (v. 8) without any explanation. The words *Gog* and *Magog* are first used in Ezekiel 38-39 to identify a confederation of nations coming down from the north to invade Israel. Although the names *Gog* and *Magog* are the same as those used in Ezekiel 38-39, this is not the same battle. This battle is different in time and details, although agreeing in character and object.

- The Ezekiel battle will take place during the first half of the Tribulation; the Revelation battle will take place after the Millennium.

- In Ezekiel 38-39, the nations will not come from the four quarters of the earth, as they will in Revelation.

- After the Ezekiel battle, the dead will be buried; in Revelation they will be devoured by fire from heaven.

- Satan will lead the army mentioned in the Revelation battle, but he is not mentioned in the Ezekiel battle.

Dr. John Walvoord explains that, "The words Gog and Magog are used symbolically, 'much like the term Waterloo' to express a disastrous battle, but one not related to the historic origination of the term."[2] Thus, the terms are symbolically used for the unsaved people whom Satan will gather together to try and overthrow the Lord's rule on earth.

Satan will lead this enormous army against "the camp of the saints...and the beloved city" (v. 9). The beloved city is Jerusalem, which will be the capital of the world from which the Lord will reign in righteousness (Jeremiah 3:17). The Lord will allow Satan to bring this huge army to Jerusalem for their own destruction. Once the army is gathered to do battle, "fire came down from God out of heaven, and devoured them" (v. 9). The picture is similar to the great destruction of Sodom and Gomorrah, when God rained down fire on those wicked cities. The destruction of Satan's feeble attempt to overthrow God and His universal rule will be forever put to rest.

John describes the destiny of Satan: "And the devil that deceived them was cast into the lake of fire and brimstone, where the beast and the false prophet are, and shall be tormented day and night forever and ever" (v. 10). Satan, the great deceiver, who began his deception before the world was created (Ezekiel 28:15), will find his ultimate destiny in the lake of fire. The satanic trinity of the Devil, the beast (Antichrist), and the false prophet will be tormented in the lake of fire "day and night forever and ever" (lit., *to the age of ages*). It cannot be made any clearer. Any idea of annihilation of the wicked is forever put to rest with those words.

Each person must make a major choice in life: Receive Jesus Christ and enjoy eternal life in the Millennium and beyond, or reject Christ and suffer in the lake of fire.

Endnotes

[1] Michael P. Green, *Illustrations for Biblical Preaching* (Grand Rapids: Baker Book House, 1982), p. 260.

[2] John F. Walvoord, *The Revelation of Jesus Christ* (Chicago: Moody Press, 1966), p. 303.

REVELATION 20:11-15

And I saw a great white throne, and him that sat on it, from whose face the earth and the heaven fled away, and there was found no place for them. And I saw the dead, small and great, stand before God, and the books were opened; and another book was opened, which is the book of life. And the dead were judged out of those things which were written in the books, according to their works. And the sea gave up the dead that were in it, and death and hades delivered up the dead that were in them; and they were judged every man according to their works. And death and hades were cast into the lake of fire. This is the second death. And whosoever was not found written in the book of life was cast into the lake of fire.

26

THE GREAT WHITE
THRONE JUDGMENT

On July 8, 1741, Jonathan Edwards preached his famous sermon, "Sinners in the Hands of an Angry God." Edwards held the manuscript so close to his face that the congregation was unable to see his expression as he read every word. The people, so terrified by his words, gripped the backs of their pews, feeling that the ground below was about to open and swallow them into hell. One man rushed down the aisle crying, "Mr. Edwards, have mercy!"

That was *then*; this is *now*. Hell is not taken very seriously today. Martin Marty, American church historian, summarized the attitude of our day: "Hell disappeared, and no one noticed."[1] The Bible clearly validates the existence of hell. Jesus spoke more about hell than anyone in the Scriptures. But hell is not the final destiny of the damned. Worse than hell is being judged at the Great White Throne and then cast alive into the lake of fire to suffer eternally.

Why is this called the "great white throne" (v. 11) judgment?

- It is *great* because of the rank and dignity of the judge, the size and extent of the judgment, the vast number of people throughout world history who will be judged, and the fact that it will seal the eternal destiny of unbelievers.

- It is *white* because it displays and emphasizes the infinite purity and righteousness of Christ, who is the holy judge.

- It is a *throne* because Jesus Christ sits in sovereign majesty, using His authority to consign the wicked to eternal damnation.

Place of Judgment

John said, "I saw a great white throne, and him that sat on it, from whose face the earth and the heaven fled away, and there was found no place for them" (v. 11). The location of the throne is in *space* because the old heaven and earth will be destroyed. Scholars differ on whether the physical elements of heaven and earth will be totally destroyed (into nothingness) and newly created, or merely renovated (a remake of the present heaven and earth). A close study of Scripture would opt for a totally new creation of heaven and earth prepared for the eternal state.

The location of this throne in space is not given. The judge sitting on the throne is Christ: "the Father judgeth no man, but hath committed all judgment unto the Son" (John 5:22; cp. Acts 17:31).

People Judged

John said, "And I saw the dead, small and great, stand before God....And the sea gave up the dead that were in it, and death and hades delivered up the dead that were in them; and they were judged every man" (vv. 12-13). Believers are referred to as "the dead in Christ," but the unsaved are simply called "the dead." The Bible mentions three deaths:

1. The "spiritually dead" (those who are not saved).

2. The "physical death" (referring to the death of the body).

3. The "second death" (referring to the unsaved who will be resurrected to be judged at the Great White Throne and whose destiny will be eternal punishment in the lake of fire).

All unsaved, "small and great" in life, must face Christ in judgment. A person's age, position, prestige, power, popularity, great wealth, or poverty will make no difference—they will *all* be there.

John said that "death and hades delivered up the dead that were in them" (v. 13). "Death" claims the physical body of the deceased, and "hades" is where the soul and spirit of an individual reside in torment, awaiting the Great White Throne Judgment. The word *hell* (KJV) is translated by three different Greek words.

1. *Geenna* means *Valley of Hinnom* and appears 12 times in the New Testament. It is the place where King Manasseh offered Jewish children to the heathen god Molech (2 Chronicles 33:1-6). During New Testament times, a fire burned continually in this valley. It was used as a garbage dump to burn rubbish, dead animals, and the bodies of criminals. Jesus often used this term to give a pictorial image of what hell-fire would be like. Geenna is referred to as the "lake of fire" in verse 15.

2. The Greek word *Tartaros* is translated "hell" in 2 Peter 2:4. Tartaros was used in Greek mythology to refer to the unseen world where evildoers were punished. Peter used this word in reference to the subterranean abyss, where some

of the fallen angels are chained, awaiting their final judgment.

3. The word *Hades* is used ten times in the New Testament. It refers generally to the place of the departed dead, but it is more often used to describe the temporary abode of the wicked dead prior to the final judgment. The story in Luke 16:19-31 of the rich man and Lazarus provides the best insight of what the wicked dead experience in hades. The rich man was able to see, hear, speak, thirst, feel torment, pray for mercy, argue with Abraham, and remember his past life. From his Jewish upbringing, he knew about God, Moses, and the prophets, and he believed in miracles. He believed that if Lazarus witnessed to his five lost brothers, they would be saved from hades. Jesus indicated that the rich man was permanently separated from God and from all righteous people in paradise. He had no communication with earth and no possibility of having his sins forgiven. Furthermore, a person who is not persuaded to believe in God during his or her lifetime will not believe the witness of one coming back from the dead.

Premise for Judgment

The premise for God's judgment is based on what is recorded in various sets of books. First, the "book of life" (v. 12) was opened. This book contains a record of the names of all people who have received Jesus Christ as their Savior. The names of unsaved people are not found in the book of life because they rejected Jesus Christ during their lifetime. Thus, their destiny will be the lake of fire. Some scholars teach that the book of life contains the names of all people born into the world and that God blots out the names of the unsaved at their death. Other passages of Scripture indicate that only the saved have their names recorded in the book of life (3:5; 13:8; 17:8).

Second, "the books were opened....And the dead were judged out of those things which were written in the books, according to their works" (v. 12). People are always judged according to their works. The books will contain the "secrets of men" (Romans 2:16) because all things are naked and opened before the eyes of God (Hebrews 4:13). No experience is ever forgotten. The subconscious mind stores all the thoughts and experiences of life, and they can be recalled by the conscious mind under the right conditions. When facing death, people often speak about their entire lives flashing before them. God keeps such a record of all of a person's words and deeds. John said twice that people are judged "according to their works" (vv. 12, 13).

At the final resurrection of the unsaved "the sea gave up the dead that were in it, and death and hades delivered up the dead that were in them; and they were judged every man according to their works" (v. 13). Every speck of dust that comprises the bodies of the unsaved will be regathered and reformed into the bodies of the individuals, and they will stand face to face before Christ at His throne of judgment. "Every man" (v. 13) means that this judgment will be all-inclusive and individual in nature.

How will the unsaved be judged from the books?

1. By how they *responded* to the Word of God (which they rejected). Jesus said, "He that rejecteth me, and receiveth not my words, hath one that judgeth him: the word that I have spoken, the same shall judge him in the last day" (John 12:48). Even if people never read the Word of God, they will still be without excuse (Romans 1:20; 2:12) because God's

law was written in their hearts (Romans 2:14-16), and the revelation of God could be discerned in their consciences from creation (Romans 1:19-20).

2. Their own *words* will judge them: "I say unto you that every idle word that men shall speak, they shall give account of it in the day of judgment" (Matthew 12:36).

3. Their own *works* (v. 13) will judge them. All the evil that people thought, said, or did will be manifested and properly rewarded in that day. Concerning the wicked, one writer put it this way: "Back they will come, with faces wrecked and ruined by sin and with souls knotted and gnarled, shriveled and shorn by lust and hate, envy and scorn, passion and pride, iniquity and crime. Back they will come to be judged—according to their works."[2] The Bible is clear: "be sure your sin will find you out" (Numbers 32:23).

Someone may ask, "Is it fair to send to eternal damnation a person who never had an opportunity to hear the gospel or accept Christ as Savior?" God, who is perfect and possesses infinite knowledge, will judge each person righteously and fairly. "For there is no respect of persons with God. For as many as have sinned without law shall also perish without law; and as many as have sinned in the law shall be judged by the law" (Romans 2:11-12).

Although the unsaved will be punished throughout eternity, Scripture indicates that there will be degrees in the severity of their punishment. Jesus said, "And that servant, who knew his lord's will, and prepared not himself, neither did according to his will, shall be beaten with many stripes. But he that knew not, and did commit things worthy of stripes, shall be beaten with few stripes" (Luke 12:47-48).

The Great White Throne Judgment will *not* be similar to our court of law. There will be no defense attorney, no jury, no plea bargaining, no appeal, and no leniency. This judgment concerning a person's guilt and the severity of punishment will not be arbitrary but determined from his or her recorded deeds. Thus, the person's destiny is sealed before he or she stands before the judge. Christ, the judge, will pass sentence according to the record established by the defendant.

Punishment After Judgment

John continued, "And death and hades were cast into the lake of fire. This is the second death" (v. 14). Hades (hell) is not the final destiny of the unsaved; the lake of fire is their final destiny. What is meant by the "second death"? The first death results in the burial of the body, but those facing the "second death" will be physically resurrected at the proper time and cast alive into the lake of fire. This is second only to the physical death. It is an eternal death; the individual will be separated from God forever, cast into outer darkness, and suffer eternally in the lake of fire.

This section closes with the simple words, "And whosoever was not found written in the book of life was cast into the lake of fire" (v. 15). Language like this leaves no room for any form of universal salvation, soul sleep, an intermediate state of purgatory, a second chance, or annihilation of the wicked. This is the eternal infliction of punishment resulting in the physical and mental misery mentioned by Jesus (Matthew 25:41, 46). The wicked will be tormented without rest, day and night, forever (14:11). Remember, "it is appointed unto men once to die, but after this the judgment" (Hebrews 9:27).

Endnotes

[1] Erwin W. Lutzer, *One Minute After You Die* (Chicago: Moody Press, 1997), p. 97.

[2] John Phillips, *Exploring Revelation* (Chicago: Moody Press, 1974), p. 258.

REVELATION 21:1-8

And I saw a new heaven and a new earth; for the first heaven and the first earth were passed away, and there was no more sea. And I, John, saw the holy city, new Jerusalem, coming down from God out of heaven, prepared as a bride adorned for her husband. And I heard a great voice out of heaven saying, Behold, the tabernacle of God is with men, and he will dwell with them, and they shall be his people, and God himself shall be with them, and be their God. And God shall wipe away all tears from their eyes; and there shall be no more death, neither sorrow, nor crying, neither shall there be any more pain; for the former things are passed away. And he that sat upon the throne said, Behold, I make all things new. And he said unto me, Write; for these words are true and faithful. And he said unto me, It is done. I am Alpha and Omega, the beginning and the end. I will give unto him that is athirst of the fountain of the water of life freely. He that overcometh shall inherit all things, and I will be his God, and he shall be my son. But the fearful, and unbelieving, and the abominable, and murderers, and fornicators, and sorcerers, and idolaters, and all liars, shall have their part in the lake which burneth with fire and brimstone, which is the second death.

27

THE NEW CREATION

The subject of eternity piques people's interest as no other theme in Scripture. People intuitively know that there is a more fulfilling existence beyond this life because the transitory events on earth do not satisfy. But to affirm the reality of eternity requires, not intuitive speculation, but a source that transcends mankind itself. God has affirmed throughout Scripture that all believers will live forever. In the last two chapters of Revelation, God provides mankind with an overview of what eternity will be like.

The Creation Declared

With the Great White Throne Judgment completed, John's gaze is focused on a new creation. Three times in chapter 21, the apostle said, "I saw." He saw a "new heaven and a new earth" (v. 1), a "new Jerusalem" (v. 2), and the spiritual state of the new Jerusalem (v. 22). Scholars are divided over whether this is a total renovation of heaven and earth or a discarding of the old before replacing it with a new creation. When all the evidence is studied, Scriptures seem to teach the dissolution of the old heaven and earth in favor of a new heaven and earth. This is reasonable because the old heaven and earth are tainted by the curse of sin.

Although John provides an overview of the new heaven and earth, little information is given in Scripture concerning their structure and makeup (see Isaiah 65:17; 66:22; 2 Peter3:13). The fact that there is no definite article before the words "heaven" and "earth" stresses the qualitative nature of the new heaven and earth, rather than their identity.

The Bible is silent concerning the earth's atmosphere, as well as the structure of planets in the universe, except to say that there is no need for the sun or the moon (v. 23). Neither is any information given on the new earth's form, color, or vegetation. John goes on to reveal that the new earth has "no more sea" (v. 1), indicating the removal of large bodies of water that are present today. The earth will take on a very different look, considering that presently three-fourths of the earth's surface is covered with water. Mankind in its glorified state will not need water to sustain life.

Often Bible teachers have confused the eternal state with the Millennial Kingdom. This is understandable because sometimes both states are mentioned in the same verse without revealing the time gap between them. The same is true when reading verses about Christ's first and second advents in Isaiah 61:1-2 (cp. Luke 4:17-19). Another example is Isaiah 9:6-7, where both Christ's birth and Second Coming are mentioned. The first part of verse 6 refers to Jesus' birth, but the remaining part of verse 6 and verse 7 point to His Second Coming. The prophets often saw Christ's coming, but they did not understand that there were two comings with many intervening events. Chapters 21 and 22 refer to the eternal state, not to the Millennial Kingdom.

The City's Descent

Although the new heaven and earth must have been awe-inspiring to John, his attention was riveted on "the holy city, new Jerusalem, coming down from God out of heaven" (v. 2).

The words "holy city" emphasize the character of the city because it is "the city of...God" (3:12), which has not been tainted by sin.

There has been much discussion about whether this city will be visible during the Millennial Kingdom. Some scholars teach that it will be like a satellite city orbiting or hovering above the earth during that time. Those holding this view believe that the new Jerusalem is being prepared as the dwelling place of the church (Christ's bride) during the Millennial age (Hebrews 12:22-24). Dr. John Walvoord states,

> The possibility of Jerusalem being a satellite city orbiting or hovering over the earth during the millennium is not specifically taught in Scripture. At best, it is only an inference based on the implication that the city has been in existence prior to its introduction in Revelation 21. The city's characteristics are presented in chapter 21, however, they are related to the eternal state rather than to the Millennial Kingdom.[1]

This city is said to be "prepared as a bride adorned for her husband" (v. 2). Because the church is called the bride of Christ, some believe that the new Jerusalem will be the exclusive home of the church throughout eternity. There are a number of problems with this view:

- The Bible does not say that this city is prepared for the church only.

- The Bible does say that the city is prepared "as" a bride—that is, gloriously arrayed like a beautiful bride prepared for her husband.

- Throughout Scripture, the figure of marriage is used in reference to *both* Israel and the church.

- Abraham looked for a heavenly city "whose builder and maker is God" (Hebrews 11:10-16).

- Finally, at the inception of the eternal state, this city will descend to the new earth, and all redeemed people will have access to it (21:24-27).

As John gazed on the new Jerusalem, he suddenly heard a great (loud) voice out of heaven: "Behold, the tabernacle of God is with men, and he will dwell with them, and they shall be his people, and God himself shall be with them, and be their God" (v. 3). The word "tabernacle" points to the tabernacle in the wilderness, where God dwelt with His people in the holy of holies. Earlier, John had seen the tabernacle in heaven (13:6; 15:5). In eternity, God will "dwell" (i.e., tabernacle) on earth in the new Jerusalem, symbolizing His fellowship with and blessing of the redeemed, who will experience a new, intimate relationship and fellowship with the Lord. Such fellowship is unfathomable today, far beyond the scope of a believer's comprehension.

The Citizens' Delight

Every believer's experiences on earth will vanish, never to be remembered in eternity. "God shall wipe away all tears from their eyes" (v. 4). This image portrays God's great compassion. There will be no tears shed in eternity over the sin and sorrow of this life, nor pain for loved ones who are eternally separated from Christ. The text goes on to say, "and there shall be no more death, neither sorrow, nor crying, neither shall there be any more pain" (v. 4). Dwelling in the midst of the redeemed, God will provide a perfect state of eternal peace, blessing, and uninterrupted bliss because the former things—such as Satan, sin, and the old heaven and earth—are "passed away" (v. 4). Not only will they be removed, they will "not be remembered, nor come into mind" (Isaiah 65:17).

People will not live in a vacuum in eternity. God described what will replace the former things. "And he that sat upon the throne said, Behold, I make [form] all things new" (v. 5). The word "Behold" introduces what follows as a special pro-nouncement—not just to John but to all the redeemed throughout time. The reader is to give careful attention to the coming revelation.

The apostle was instructed, "Write; for these words are true and faithful" (v. 5). John was so mesmerized by the revelation that he had to be aroused to take pen in hand and record what was to follow. The apostle was assured that the information he was about to receive was true and trustworthy, resting upon the veracity of God Himself.

The one sitting on the throne speaks again: "It is done. I am Alpha and Omega, the beginning and the end" (v. 6). The words "It is done" are in the perfect tense, indicating that God's program for the world—from its inception at creation through eternity—will be brought to completion. This assures believ-ers that God will accomplish all that He has planned for mankind. God is the "beginning [first] and the end [finisher]" of all things and will faithfully guide the destiny of His cre-ation to its designated conclusion.

Not only will the eternal state and the new Jerusalem be a splendid place, it will be a satisfying place. First, God promis-es, "I will give unto him that is athirst of the fountain of the water of life freely" (v. 6). Thirst is used in the Bible to express spiritual need (see Isaiah 55:1; John 4:13-14; 7:31-39). The redeemed who have a spiritual thirst to know God in His full-ness will have their souls totally satisfied in eternity. Spiritual water will be abundantly and freely bestowed upon all redeemed people.

A second promise is given: "He that overcometh shall inher-it all things" (v. 7). It is beyond our finite ability to comprehend what this will include. We do know, however, that it will encompass the new heaven and earth and all the glories of the new Jerusalem. This will apply to all believers, for all true believers are overcomers (1 John 5:4-5). Dr. Erwin Lutzer put this promise into perspective when he wrote,

> The universe is 20 billion light years in diameter, and if there are stars millions of times greater than our earth, man is but a speck of dust on the cosmic landscape. The discovery of the immensity of the universe does not diminish but actually magnifies man's role in the cosmos. For if Christ is to rule over all things and we are to reign with Him, then we will be ruling over all the galaxies, affirming Christ's Lordship over the whole universe. In a way that we cannot comprehend, all things will be in subjection to Christ, and we shall be a part of His eternal rule.[2]

Finally comes a promise that exceeds them all: "I will be his God, and he shall be my son" (v. 7). Here John transferred the Messianic formula of intimate relationship, which God the Father has with Christ, to the glorified saints. Such a statement is even more incomprehensible!

In verse 8, with a stroke of his pen John abruptly mentioned eight categories of people who will not inherit eternity.

1. The "fearful" are cowardly individuals who, because of fear, will not confess Christ openly when confronted with persecution (see Hebrews 10:38-39).

2. The "unbelieving" are those who deny faith in Christ by their conduct and speech.

3. The "abominable" are those polluted by gross acts of idolatry.

4. "Murderers" are malicious, savage killers (especially those who kill the Tribulation saints).

5. "Fornicators" are those who practice sexual immorality.

6. "Sorcerers" are those who mix drugs with the practices of spirit worship, witchcraft, and magic.

7. "Idolaters" are worshipers of idols and images (this practice will be prevalent when the world bows to the Antichrist's image).

8. "All liars" are those who habitually deceive others.

None of the aforementioned people will have access to the new Jerusalem. They will spend eternity "in the lake which burneth with fire and brimstone" (v. 8), along with Satan, the beast, and the false prophet (19:20; 20:10, 14-15). This is called "the second death" (v. 8), and is second only to the physical death these individuals will suffer. This is an eternal death (not annihilation), which means that these people will be separated from God, cast into outer darkness, and suffer eternally in the lake of fire.

Eternity should motivate all believers to become serious about our commitment to the Lord during a relatively short time on earth. Dr. J. I. Packer, as quoted by Ron Rhodes, said it well: "Lack of long, strong thinking about our promised hope of glory is a major cause of our plodding, lackluster lifestyle."[3] Setting our affections on the glories that await us in eternity will renew and motivate us to greater service for our Lord in this present age. Christians should purify themselves afresh before the one who sits enthroned eternally.

Endnotes

[1] John F. Walvoord, *The Revelation of Jesus Christ* (Chicago: Moody Press, 1966), p. 313.

2 Erwin W. Lutzer, *Your Eternal Reward* (Chicago: Moody Press, 1998), pp. 156-157.

3 Ron Rhodes, *Heaven: The Undiscovered Country* (Eugene, OR: Harvest House Publishers, 1996), p. 179.

REVELATION 21:9-22:5

And there came unto me one of the seven angels who had the seven bowls full of the seven last plagues, and talked with me, saying, Come here, I will show thee the bride, the Lamb's wife. And he carried me away in the Spirit to a great and high mountain, and showed me that great city, the holy Jerusalem, descending out of heaven from God, Having the glory of God; and her light was like a stone most precious, even like a jasper stone, clear as crystal; And had a wall great and high, and had twelve gates, and at the gates twelve angels, and names written on the gates, which are the names of the twelve tribes of the children of Israel: On the east three gates; on the north three gates; on the south three gates; and on the west three gates. And the wall of the city had twelve foundations, and in them the names of the twelve apostles of the Lamb. And he that talked with me had a golden reed to measure the city, and the gates of it, and its wall. And the city lieth foursquare, and the length is as large as the breadth; and he measured the city with the reed, twelve thousand furlongs. The length and the breadth and the height of it are equal. And he measured the wall of it, an hundred and forty and four cubits, according to the measure of a man, that is, of the angel. And the building of the wall of it was of jasper; and the city was pure gold, like clear glass. And the foundations of the wall of the city were garnished with all manner of precious stones. The first foundation was jasper; the second, sapphire; the third, chalcedony; the fourth, emerald; The fifth, sardonyx; the sixth, sardius; the seventh, chrysolite; the eight, beryl; the ninth, topaz; the tenth, chrysoprasus; the eleventh, jacinth; the twelfth, amethyst. And the twelve gates were twelve pearls; each one of the gates was of one pearl; and the street of the city was pure gold, as it were, transparent glass. And I saw no temple in it; for the Lord God Almighty and the Lamb are the temple of it. And the city had no need of the sun, neither of the moon, to shine in it; for the glory of God did light it, and the Lamb is the lamp of it. And the nations of them who are saved shall walk in the light of it, and the kings of the earth do bring their glory and honor into it. And the gates of it shall not be shut at all by day; for there shall be no night there. And they shall bring the glory and honor of the nations into it. And there shall in no way enter into it anything that defileth, neither he that worketh abomination, or maketh a lie, but they who are written in the Lamb's book of life.

And he showed me a pure river of water of life, clear as crystal, proceeding out of the throne of God and of the Lamb. In the midst of the street of it, and on either side of the river, was there the tree of life, which bore twelve kinds of fruits, and yielded her fruit every month; and the leaves of the tree were for the healing of the nations. And there shall be no more curse, but the throne of God and of the Lamb shall be in it, and his servants shall serve him; And they shall see his face; and his name shall be in their foreheads. And there shall be no night there; and they need no lamp, neither light of the sun; for the Lord God giveth them light, and they shall reign forever and ever.

28

THE NEW JERUSALEM

To most people, the thought of home brings a feeling of warmth and comfort, a sense of security. It is a place where one can shut out the cares of life and find a refuge for the soul during the pilgrimage through life. For Christians, however, this world is not our home; our citizenship is in the heavenly Jerusalem. Although we are not home yet, our gaze is firmly fixed on that new Jerusalem, the final home awaiting us in heaven. In this section of Revelation, John was given a description of the new Jerusalem, the residence of each believer in eternity.

A Sanctified City

Having introduced the eternal state, "one of the seven angels who had the seven bowls full of the seven last plagues" approached John and said, "Come here, I will show thee the bride, the Lamb's wife" (v. 9). This could be the same angel who revealed the vision of Babylon to the apostle (17:1).

The angel revealed that he would show John "the bride, the Lamb's wife" (v. 9), which is identified as "the holy Jerusalem, descending out of heaven from God" (v. 10). Why is the new Jerusalem called the bride, the wife of the Lamb?

1. The city is beautifully adorned, as will be the church, Christ's bride, at the marriage supper of the Lamb (19:7).

2. The city will be spotless and pure, like Christ's church after it is glorified.

Thus, the city is being compared to a bride in its beauty and intimate relationship to Christ, the Lamb of God. It should be understood that John is not saying that the bride is the new Jerusalem, but it is being characterized as "the bride, the Lamb's wife." The bride is a figure for a material city yet to come, as well as for the inhabitants of that city. The bride figure cannot be limited to the individuals who will live in the city. It must also include the literal city with its physical characteristics.[1]

Some scholars believe that the new Jerusalem presented here is a description of the city during the Millennial Kingdom, rather than in the eternal state. This section cannot apply to the Millennium for the following reasons.

1. There is a chronological progression from Revelation 19:11-22:21 that would mediate against such a position.

2. Sin and sinners will be present in the Millennium, but sin will be absent in the new Jerusalem.

3. The curse (22:3), which will continue in the Millennium (20:8-9), will be absent.

4. The sun, moon (21:23), and night (21:25), which will continue in the Millennium, will be absent.

5. There will be a Temple (Ezekiel 40-48) during the Millennium, but not in the new Jerusalem (21:22).

6. Features of the new Jerusalem in 21:2 match the description in 21:9, so they must be the same.[2]

7. The holy city will descend to the new earth,
    not in the Millennium (21:2, 10-11), but in the
    eternal state.

Prophecies governing the millennial earth do not allow for
such a city on earth. The new Jerusalem is presented here as it
will be in the eternal state, not in the Millennium.

Some scholars believe that the new Jerusalem, as presented
here, will descend from heaven and hover over the Millennial
Kingdom as a satellite city of the glorified church during
Christ's thousand-year reign. Scripture offers no evidence for
this position.

The angel carried John "away in the Spirit to a great and
high mountain and showed [him] that great city, the holy
Jerusalem, descending out of heaven from God" (v. 10). John
was supernaturally transported out of the material world fully
awake (in a trance-like state) to receive the revelation and
record a description of the new Jerusalem.

The city's description is not a symbolic expression of the fulfillment of God's promises, but a real material city that will exist
throughout eternity. John's description of the new Jerusalem far
exceeds our ability to perceive and understand it in its fullness
because it is the creation of an infinite God. What John saw tran-
scended any earthly experience known to mankind.
Nevertheless, it is an accurate description of a literal city because
it was revealed by the Holy Spirit.

The city will shine with "the glory of God" (v. 11), like the
Shekinah glory that filled the holy of holies in the Tabernacle
and Temple, because of God's divine presence. Also, it will be
illuminated by the light of Jesus, "the Lamb" (v. 23). In like
manner, believers in Christ do not generate the light of Christ
but reflect and transmit His glory to the world. Its brightness
"was like a stone most precious, even like a jasper stone, clear
as crystal" (v. 11). The jasper stone is like transparent crystal,

similar to a diamond, whose facets sparkled with every color found in the rainbow. The jasper stone is "most precious" because of its beauty and cost and will be extensively used in making the new Jerusalem (v. 19).

A Spacious City

After presenting the general appearance of the new Jerusalem, John described the various components of the city. He began with its walls, which are described as "great and high" (v. 12). The material used in the walls "was of jasper" (v. 18) to reflect the glory of God. It is obvious that high walls will not be needed for defense because the city will have no enemies. The walls will be symbolic of God's protection and security and the exclusion of all that is evil (cp. v. 8).

The city will have "twelve gates, and at the gates twelve angels" (v. 12). Each gate will be inscribed with the name of one of the tribes of Israel (v. 12). The many gates symbolize freedom to enter the city from all sides. Angels will act as honor guards, functioning as watchmen, stressing the security of both the city and God's glory. The text does not reveal the order in which the tribes' names will be placed on the gates of the new Jerusalem, but it could correspond to the pattern presented in the millennial Jerusalem (v. 13; cp. Ezekiel 48:31-34). Abraham "looked for a city which hath foundations, whose builder and maker is God" (Hebrews 11:10). That city will have his descendants' names engraved on its gates to show Israel's direct role in God's program in eternity.

The city will have "twelve foundations, and in them the names of the twelve apostles of the Lamb" (v. 14). The foundations indicate that the city will be on the earth throughout all eternity. Although the twelve apostles came out of Israel, the mention of one of the twelve apostles on each foundation links the church to a major role in the new Jerusalem. Although Israel and the church are brought together in the New

Jerusalem, they will have distinct identities in eternity and should not be lumped into one group. Scripture clearly indicates that God has an eschatological role for both groups in the new creation.

The angel measured the "city...gates...and...wall" with a "golden reed" (v. 15). Its size will be "twelve thousand furlongs" (v. 16). It will be shaped in a perfect cube of almost 1,400 miles on each side and 1,400 miles in height (rounded off to 1,500 miles by many commentators). Dr. David Jeremiah writes,

> To grasp something of the enormity of the city, consider that this figure is 40 times the area of England, 20 times that of New Zealand, and 10 times the area of Germany or France. The ground floor alone would provide enough living space for far more people than have ever lived in the history of the world. And this is just the first floor; there are around 1,500 miles of additional floors above it.[3]

Although the city is described in square dimensions, nothing is revealed regarding its shape. Some scholars believe it to be a pyramid whose sides slope upward to form a peak at its apex. Others, like J. Vernon McGee, suggest that the city will be like a cube within a crystal sphere floating in space. Most interpreters hold that the city will be a perfect cube, just like the cube-shaped holy of holies in Solomon's Temple (1 Kings 6:19-20).

Next the angel measured the city walls, which were "an hundred and forty and four cubits, according to the measure of a man" (v. 17). Assuming that a cubit is 18 inches, the wall would be only 216 feet high—extremely small for a 1,400-mile-high city. The measurement may apply to the wall's thickness rather than its height. Although this will be a literal wall around the city, it will only be symbolic of defense, since there will be no enemy against whom to defend it.

John was given a description of the materials used to construct the city. "And the building of the wall of it was of jasper; and the city was pure gold, like clear glass" (v. 18). The walls of jasper and the city of pure gold would look like a sparkling diamond in all its crystalline beauty, designed to reflect the effulgence of God's radiant glory in every area of the city.

A further description was provided of the materials making up the foundations, gates, and streets of the city. There will be twelve foundations, "garnished with all manner of precious stones" (v. 19). Eight of these stones appear in the breastplate of the high priest (Exodus 28:17-20). Each foundation will be made of one of the following stones, layered on top of the next, extending around the city, as described in verses 19-20:

1. The jasper stone is clear crystal, like a diamond, and refracts all the colors of the spectrum in wondrous brilliance.

2. The sapphire is blue in color (possibly flecked with gold).

3. The chalcedony is a translucent milky or grayish quartz with colored stripes running through it.

4. The emerald is a brilliant, grass-green, transparent variety of beryl.

5. The sardonyx is an onyx stone with alternating brown and white bands running through it.

6. The sardius is a red translucent stone, like a ruby.

7. The chrysolite is gold in color, resembling a yellow beryl or a golden jasper stone.

8. The beryl is a translucent bluish or sea-green colored stone.

9. The topaz is a translucent yellow or yellow-green stone.

10. The chrysoprasus is a translucent apple-green stone.

11. The jacinth is a translucent, bluish-smoke, violet-colored stone.

12. The amethyst is a brilliant purple or violet transparent stone.

Although stones can take on different hues or colors, it is clear that the twelve foundations will be structured to refract the effluence of God's glory and holiness. Such beauty will transcend anything mankind has seen since the inception of God's creation.

There will be "twelve gates" (v. 21), each made of one huge pearl, attached to the city walls. They will open into streets made of "pure gold, as it were, transparent glass" (v. 21). Pearls were highly valued in the ancient world for their natural beauty. Each pearl gate will bear the name of one tribe of Israel, and these gates will never be closed.

A Spiritual City

After describing the dimensions of the city, John detailed some of the city's distinctives. He said, "And I saw no temple in it; for the Lord God Almighty and the Lamb are the temple [sanctuary] of it" (v. 22). This is a major distinction from the Millennial Kingdom, which will possess a Temple. In eternity, there will be no need for a Temple because God Himself will dwell in the midst of His people, who will have direct, immediate, and intimate communion with Him.

The city will have no need of creative light from the sun or moon because "the glory of God did light it, and the Lamb is the lamp of it" (v. 23). God's glorious presence in the city will illuminate every corner of the new Jerusalem; nothing will be hidden. Scripture does not say that the sun and moon will be absent in eternity, but that there will be no need for them.

All the "nations...who are saved shall walk" in the physical and spiritual "light" (v. 24) of God's glory. The word *nations* means *Gentiles* and is used, not in a political sense, but referring to saved Gentiles living in the eternal state who are not part of Israel or the church. At that time, "the kings of the earth do bring their glory and honor into" the new Jerusalem (v. 24). Those holding positions of honor among the saved Gentiles in eternity will give their glory and honor, once it is bestowed upon them, to God the Father and Jesus Christ.[4] Like the 24 elders mentioned earlier in Revelation, those kings in positions of honor will recognize the Lord as the source of that glory and honor.

John recapped what had already been alluded to: "And the gates of it shall not be shut at all by day; for there shall be no night there. And they [kings] shall bring the glory and honor of the nations into it" (vv. 25-26). The city will be open to all, for only redeemed people will be living in the world at that time. They will experience only daytime because the glorious effulgence of God's radiant presence will eliminate the darkness of night.

Nothing of an evil nature will ever enter the city. John wrote, "And there shall in no way enter into it anything that defileth, neither he that worketh abomination, or maketh a lie" (v. 27). Only the redeemed, whose names "are written in the Lamb's book of life" (v. 27), will be there.

A Sinless City

John then divulged the paradise qualities of the new Jerusalem. The city will exhibit paradise restored. That which was lost in the Garden of Eden, because of mankind's sin, will be recreated by Jesus Christ. The angel revealed to the apostle "a pure river of water of life, clear [i.e., bright and shining] as crystal, proceeding out of the throne of God and of the Lamb" (22:1). This is not the same river that will flow from the

Millennial Temple (Ezekiel 47:1, 12), nor is it the living water that will flow from Jerusalem (Zechariah 14:8) during the Millennial Kingdom. This will be a life-giving river, providing those living in the city with a deeper quality of spiritual life and symbolically portraying the eternal life manifested to them in eternity. Jesus likened the Holy Spirit present within each believer to a river of living water (John 7:37-39), which is only a foretaste of the fuller life that will be experienced in eternity. This river will flow "out of the throne of God and of the Lamb" (22:1), indicating that Christ will be enthroned with God the Father in eternity.

John's attention was then drawn to "the tree of life" (v. 2) located in the middle of the street, whose branches will be large enough to spread on both sides of the river of life. This tree has no relation to the trees mentioned in the Millennial Kingdom (Ezekiel 47:12). The "tree of life" will bear "twelve kinds of fruits, and [yield] her fruit every month" (v. 2). This tree will be different from any tree known today because it will produce an annual harvest of twelve different fruits. The mention of twelve months would indicate that time will be calculated in eternity. The text gives no indication that mankind, in their glorified bodies, will partake of the fruit; it will not be necessary to sustain life. Christ ate and drank with the disciples in His glorified body, but it was not necessary for Him to nourish His body. Since the fruit will not be needed to sustain life, its purpose in bearing twelve types of fruit may be to stand as a continual reminder of the eternal and abundant life enjoyed by the redeemed in eternity.

Leaves from the tree will provide "healing [for] the nations" (v. 2). The word *healing* comes from a Greek word that means *therapeutic* or *health giving*. There will be no disease in the new Jerusalem because the "curse" (v. 3) will be removed; therefore, the leaves will, in some unknown way, enhance the joy of life in eternity.

John said, "the throne of God and of the Lamb shall be in it [the new Jerusalem], and his servants shall serve him" (v. 3). With God sovereignly residing and ruling on the new earth and the curse upon mankind and the earth removed (Genesis 3:16-19), there will be nothing to hamper believers in their service for God. Eternity will not be a place of idleness, boredom, or wearisome labor, but one of joyful service and worship.

In eternity, believers will be able to "see his [God's] face" (v. 4). God told Moses, "Thou canst not see my face; for there shall no man see me, and live" (Exodus 33:20). On the other hand, Jesus said, "Blessed are the pure in heart; for they shall see God" (Matthew 5:8). Jesus said, "No man hath seen God at any time; the only begotten Son, who is in the bosom of the Father, he hath declared him" (John 1:18). Believers today are unable to see the face of God, but they will be able to look on His face in the new Jerusalem because they will be in their glorified bodies. Believers will be easily identified because God's "name shall be in their foreheads" (v. 4). This is a seal of ownership, showing that they are God's possession, identifying them as citizens of the new Jerusalem.

John reiterated a condition already mentioned: "And there shall be no night there; and they need no lamp, neither light of the sun; for the Lord God giveth them light" (v. 5). In 21:23, the emphasis was on the physical makeup of the new Jerusalem—it will have no need for the light of the sun or moon. Here, the purpose is to show how delightful the city will be for its citizens as they experience life in the illumination of God's Shekinah glory.

John concluded by revealing the greatest privilege of all for glorified believers: "And they shall reign forever and ever" (v. 5; cp. 3:21; 5:10; 20:4, 6). What a glorious promise to believers! Only eternity will reveal the exact role and responsibility of glorified believers in ruling and reigning over the universe. What a blessed new home awaits believers in eternity!

Endnotes

[1] Robert L. Thomas, *Revelation 8-22, An Exegetical Commentary* (Chicago: Moody Press, 1995), p. 460.

[2] *Ibid.*, p. 458.

[3] David Jeremiah with C. C. Carlson, *Escape the Coming Night: Messages from the Book of Revelation* (Dallas: Word Publishing, 1990), vol. 4, p. 73.

[4] John F. Walvoord, *The Revelation of Jesus Christ* (Chicago: Moody Press 1966), p. 327.

REVELATION 22:6-21

And he said unto me, These words are faithful and true; and the Lord God of the holy prophets sent his angel to show unto his servants the things which must shortly be done. Behold, I come quickly. Blessed is he that keepeth the words of the prophecy of this book. And I, John, saw these things, and heard them. And when I had heard and seen, I fell down to worship before the feet of the angel who showed me these things. Then saith he unto me, See thou do it not; for I am thy fellow servant, and of thy brethren, the prophets, and of them who keep the words of this book. Worship God. And he saith unto me, Seal not the words of the prophecy of this book; for the time is at hand. He that is unjust, let him be unjust still; and he that is filthy, let him be filthy still; and he that is righteous, let him be righteous still; and he that is holy, let him be holy still. And, behold, I come quickly, and my reward is with me, to give every man according as his work shall be. I am Alpha and Omega, the beginning and the end, the first and the last. Blessed are they that wash their robes, that they may have right to the tree of life, and may enter in through the gates into the city. For outside are dogs, and sorcerers, and fornicators, and murderers, and idolaters, and whosoever loveth and maketh a lie.

I, Jesus, have sent mine angel to testify unto you these things in the churches. I am the root and the offspring of David, and the bright and morning star.

And the Spirit and the bride say, Come. And let him that heareth say, Come. And let him that is athirst come. And whosoever will, let him take the water of life freely.

For I testify unto every man that heareth the words of the prophecy of this book, If any man shall add unto these things, God shall add unto him the plagues that are written in this book; And if any man shall take away from the words of the book of this prophecy, God shall take away his part from the tree of life, and out of the holy city, and from the things which are written in this book.

He who testifieth these things saith, Surely, I come quickly. Amen. Even so, come, Lord Jesus.

The grace of our Lord Jesus Christ be with you all. Amen.

29

GOD'S FINAL MESSAGE

A ll the purposes of God, from the inception of creation to the close of human history, have been completed. Christ has assumed His sovereign rule and reign over creation and has restored creation to the original holy state for which it was intended. Mankind, redeemed from its fallen state through the shed blood of Jesus Christ, has been resurrected to enjoy God's perfect creation in all its beauty and holiness.

No other words in the Bible carry more significance than Revelation 22:6-21. Herein lies the testimony of angels, of God the Father, of the Lord Jesus Christ, and of John himself to the validity and genuineness of this prophecy and the imminent return of Jesus Christ. A close comparison of the prologue in chapter 1 and the epilogue in this section reveals that they have a great deal in common. The prophecy...

- Comes from God the Father and Jesus Christ (1:1; 22:6).
- Tells of things that must shortly come to pass (1:1; 22:6).
- Is signified by an angel to John (1:1; 22:6, 8, 16).

- Was given to John to write (1:1; 22:8).

- Promises blessing to all who read it (1:3; 22:7) and judgment to all who reject God and this prophecy (1:7; 22:11-12, 18-19).

- Revolves around Jesus Christ (1:2, 5, 9; 22:16, 20).

- Reveals His glorious titles (1:5, 8; 22:13, 16).

- Speaks of His imminent return (1:3, 7; 22:7, 10, 12).

Confirming Words

The angel reminded John of four truths concerning Revelation. First, he affirmed its veracity: "These words are faithful and true" (v. 6). This emphasizes the completeness and certainty of all that had been revealed to John: "faithful" in the sense of its accuracy, reliability, and trustworthiness; "true" in the sense of being the whole truth from God. The reader should have complete confidence in this revelation and in no way try to reduce it to allegory or meaningless symbols.

Second, the angel verified that the revelation was from "the Lord God of the holy prophets [who] sent his angel to show unto his servant the things which must shortly be done" (v. 6). This directly contradicts the position held by many scholars that the Book of the Revelation is an imponderable mystery for which no key is available to unlock its true teaching today. To the contrary, the writing is God's Word, not John's vague imagination. Its purpose is to describe future events, and it can be properly understood when interpreted literally by those taught by the Holy Spirit, applying the proper interpretation, even though much of it is written in symbolic form.

Third, the angel affirmed Christ's imminent return: "Behold, I come quickly" (v. 7). The word *quickly* means *soon*. This is according to God's reckoning of time, not mankind's (see 2 Peter 3:9). The context would indicate that Christ is speaking concerning the Rapture—His coming for the church—rather than the Second Coming, although both are in the larger context.[1] Christ's coming will be sudden, without warning. Then will come the Tribulation with all its horrors. If people are not ready—that is, if they do not believe in Christ—they will be left to enter the Tribulation.

Fourth, the angel affirmed that Christ promised a special blessing to all who read and heed the words of this prophecy: "Blessed is he that keepeth the words of the prophecy of this book" (v. 7; cp. 1:3). This is the sixth of seven beatitudes given in Revelation to faithful believers. Those who keep the promises of this book—that is, exalt Christ—will find inner peace, happiness, and, above all, spiritual contentment. The word *keep* means *to guard, watch over, protect, observe, pay attention to,* or *give heed to.* Those who personally apply the truth found in this book will experience special blessing from the Lord. This is not a promise to those who *defend* the words of this book, but to those who *keep* them. Nor is it a promise to those who speculate about the time element involved in this book. The responsibility of believers is to keep or observe the sayings of this book. In order to do this, they must read, study, and live by its standards.

Christ to be Worshiped

This revelation totally overwhelmed John. He wrote, "And when I had heard and seen, I fell down to worship before the feet of the angel who showed me these things" (v. 8). Earlier, the apostle had responded to the angel's revelation in the same way (19:10) and was rebuked in like manner. Here the angel quickly responded, "See thou do it not; for I am thy fellow servant, and of thy brethren, the prophets, and of them who keep the words of this book" (v. 9). Sad to say, many who hear God's

Word proclaimed today focus on the ability and delivery of the messenger rather than on the content of Scripture. The angel minced no words in his response to John. Tersely he commanded, "Worship God" (v. 9). God alone, and no other, is the focal point of worship.

If people are to be blessed by reading this book, it must be open to them. Indeed, this is the case. The angel told John, "Seal not the words of the prophecy of this book" (v. 10). The opposite was true of Daniel; he was instructed to seal up his prophecy. The revelation he received was to be "sealed till the time of the end" (Daniel 12:4, 9) because people would not understand his prophecy until the end times. But the prophecy given to John was in the process of being fulfilled in his day, and in ours as well, because it concerned the church and those living on the earth after the church has been raptured. This was emphasized by the angel: "for the time is at hand" (v. 10). It is mandatory that people be properly prepared for the Lord's return—they must live with eternal values in view.

Comments to the Wicked and the Worthy

Abruptly, John gave a frightful and fatal warning to those who refuse to become faithful followers of Jesus Christ. At this period in history, the time and opportunity to receive Christ are running out because of His soon return. "He that is unjust, let him be unjust still; and he that is filthy, let him be filthy still; and he that is righteous, let him be righteous still; and he that is holy, let him be holy still" (v. 11). This verse has baffled some interpreters because it seems to encourage those who are unjust and filthy to continue these practices. Scripture confirms that God would never condone or encourage people to do evil (see 2 Peter 3:9; James 1:13). This is not a promotion of evil. It is a warning to the wicked.

1. People will continue doing evil until the end of this present earth.

2. The unjust will become more wicked because of their ungodly character.

3. The wicked must immediately read and heed the warning of this prophecy and come to Christ while there is still time.

4. Those who refuse to forsake their wickedness will be sealed in a state of sinfulness for eternity. Thus, the wicked have sealed their own destiny by personally rejecting Christ.

On the other hand, the same rule applies to the righteous. The implication of this verse is to make the right choice now, before it is too late, for Christ's return is imminent: "And, behold, I come quickly, and my reward is with me, to give every man according as his work shall be" (v. 12). Thus, judgment for both groups is certain. The ungodly will stand before the Great White Throne Judgment, be condemned, and be cast into the lake of fire. The righteous will stand before the Bema Judgment, be given rewards according to their works, and enter into the Kingdom age, which will eventually merge into the eternal state. Note that all final judgments of punishment and reward are based on an individual's works.

The one making this pronouncement is none other than Christ Himself. He alone is qualified to judge both the wicked and the righteous. What are His qualifications?

1. He is the "Alpha and Omega" (v. 13; cp. 1:8, 11, 17; 2:8; 21:6); there is nothing before or after Jesus Christ.

2. He is "the beginning and end" (v. 13) — the one who created, controls, and will consummate all things.

3. He is "the first and the last" (v. 13). He was before creation in eternity past and will be present in eternity future—the author and finisher of all things (Hebrews 12:2).

These statements are true about both God the Father and Jesus Christ.

Christ then pronounced the seventh and final beatitude in Revelation, which is for those who put their faith in Him as Savior and Lord: "Blessed are they that wash their robes, that they may have right to the tree of life, and may enter through the gates into the city" (v. 14). The blessed ones are blood-washed believers (cp. 3:5; 7:14) who do God's bidding. They alone will have access to the holy city (21:27) and the tree of life (22:2).

In contrast, unbelievers will be "outside" the city and will have no access to the tree of life: "dogs, and sorcerers, and fornicators, and murderers, and idolaters, and whosoever loveth and maketh a lie" (v. 15). This is the third and final mention of unsaved people whose character is described as that of a dog (cp. 21:8, 27). Dogs were considered unclean scavengers and objects of great contempt in biblical times.

Christ's Witness

Jesus attests to, affirms, and authenticates that the content of this book was inspired and revealed by Him: "I, Jesus, have sent mine angel to testify unto you these things in the churches" (v. 16). This strong personal testimony from Jesus leaves no doubt that He is the one who authored Revelation. He "sent" (commissioned) His "angel" to deliver the contents of Revelation to John and "the churches." This is the first occurrence of the word *church* since chapter three. The church was not mentioned or alluded to in chapters 4 through 18, indicating that the church will not be involved in the time of Tribulation.

Jesus certified His claim by providing credentials of His Messiahship with the right to inaugurate the Kingdom promised to David. He said, "I am the root and the offspring of David, and the bright and morning star" (v. 16).

1. The Lord referred to Himself as the "I am," a term first used of God the Father (Exodus 3:14) to proclaim Himself as the self-existent and sufficient sovereign of the universe. Jesus called Himself the "I am" seven times in John's Gospel and ten times in Revelation.

2. He is the "root" or source of David's life and line of descendants.

3. He is the "offspring of David," or a descendant from the line of David that established His humanity.

4. He is the "bright and morning star," the brightest star that shines just before dawn. He is the star that shatters the spiritual darkness and signals the bright and glorious day mentioned in chapters 21 and 22.

Call to Watchfulness

In response, Jesus said, "the Sprit and the bride say, Come" (v. 17). This is an invitation from the Holy Spirit and the church for Christ to come for His church, which awaits redemption and the consummation of the marriage of the Lamb.

A second petition was made: "And let him that heareth say, Come" (v. 17). Those in the first-century churches, where the Book of the Revelation was read, were to repeat the call for Christ's return (cp. 1:3; 22:7, 12).

The third petition is an invitation for the unsaved to receive Christ: "And let him that is athirst come. And whosoever will, let him take the water of life freely" (v. 17). Time is running out to receive Christ in this Age of Grace because His return and judgment are imminent. All who come will receive the "water of life freely" (cp. Isaiah 55:1; John 6:35; 7:37). The word *come* is a present imperative meaning *come now* or *come today.*

Christ's Warning

Christ then gave a warning to anyone who would tamper with the prophecy presented in this book: "For I testify unto every man that heareth the words of the prophecy of this book" (v. 18). The warning was twofold.

1. To those who add to the book: "If any man shall add unto these things, God shall add unto him the plagues that are written in this book" (v. 18). The penalty for doing so will be to suffer the seal, trumpet, and/or bowl judgments of the Tribulation.

2. Of equal severity is the judgment upon those who take away from God's Word: "if any man shall take away from the words of the book of this prophecy, God shall take away his part from the tree of life, and out of the holy city, and from the things which are written in this book" (v. 19). This verse does not teach the loss of salvation, thus denying a person a part in the new Jerusalem and eternity. This pronouncement is to the unsaved who deny the Scripture in this book regarding the Lord Jesus Christ. It is assured that those who deliberately add to or take away from this book despise the Word of God, indicating that they are not saved.

Jesus, who testified of this solemn warning, closed His revelation with the words, "Surely, I come quickly" (v. 20). He affirmed and confirmed that His return is certain.

John responded, "Amen. Even so, come, Lord Jesus" (v. 20). Today this is the heart cry of so many believers who often utter, "Maranatha!" They begin each day with the thought, *Perhaps today*, looking expectantly for Christ's return.

Christ began His message to the church with a prayer of grace (1:4) and closed it with the same: "The grace of our Lord Jesus Christ be with you all. Amen" (v. 21). The Old Testament closes with a curse (Malachi 4:6). The New Testament closes, as it begins, with grace. The Book of the Revelation does pronounce a curse on all who reject God's love and salvation provided through Christ, but it also sets forth the blessing of God on all who put their faith in Him for salvation. No more fitting conclusion can be given to this volume than John's closing words in the Book of the Revelation: "Even so, come, Lord Jesus."

Endnote

[1] John F. Walvoord, *The Revelation of Jesus Christ* (Chicago: Moody Press, 1966), p. 333.

ABOUT THE AUTHOR

DAVID LEVY was born and reared in Dayton, Ohio. He received Jesus as his Messiah through the witness of a Hebrew Christian in November 1960. He is a graduate of Moody Bible Institute, the University of Illinois, and Trinity Evangelical Divinity School. David spent ten years pastoring in Illinois.

Since 1974, David and his faithful wife Beverly have been on the staff of the highly respected, New Jersey-based Friends of Israel Gospel Ministry. He serves as the Foreign Field Director, overseeing workers in nine countries. In addition to his administrative and personnel responsibilities, he is in demand throughout the world as a conference speaker. David travels extensively representing The Friends of Israel in Eastern and Western Europe, Israel, New Zealand, Australia, and North and South America.

David has been Associate Editor of The Friends of Israel's highly acclaimed bimonthly publication, *Israel My Glory*, since 1977. His expositional articles appear in each issue of the publication and in many other international magazines. He has authored a number of books, including *Joel: The Day of the Lord; Malachi: Messenger of Rebuke and Renewal; The Tabernacle: Shadows of the Messiah; Guarding the Gospel of Grace;* and *When Prophets Speak of Judgment.*

CITY	EPHESUS REV. 2:1-7	SMYRNA REV. 2:8-11	PERGAMUM REV. 2:12-17
CHRIST	Hold 7 Stars Walks in Midst of Candlesticks	First and Last Dead and Alive	Sharp Two-edged Sword
COMMENDATION (I KNOW THY...)	Good Works Labor, Patience, Hate Deeds of Nicolaitans	Works Tribulation Poverty	Works, Hold Fast My Name, Not Denied My Faith
CONDEMNATION	Left First Love	None	False Teacher Balaam and Nicolaitans
COUNSEL	Remember Fall Repent Do First Works	Fear None of These Things Thou Shalt Suffer, Be Thou Faithful Unto Death	Repent
CONSEQUENCE	Give to Eat of the Tree of Life	Not Hurt by Second Death	I Will Fight Against Them with Sword of My Mouth
CONQUEROR (OVERCOMER)	Give to Eat of the Tree of Life	Not Hurt by Second Death	Give Hidden Manna and White Stone
CHURCH (TYPE)	Apostlic Church	Persecuted Church	Indulged Church

THYATIRA REV. 2:18-29	SARDIS REV. 3:1-6	PHILADELPHIA REV. 3:7-13	LAODICEA REV. 3:14-22
Eyes Like Flame of Fire, Feet Like Burning Brass	Seven Spirits of God	Holy, True, Key of David	Amen, Faithful and True Witness, Beginning of Creation
Works, Love, Service, Faith, Patience	Works, Hast a Name That Thou Livest	Works, An Open Door, Little Strength, Kept My Word, Not Denied My Name	None
Jezebel to Teach Idolatry Compromise	Ready to Die, Works Not Perfect	None	Lukewarm, Wretched, Miserable, Poor, Blind, Naked
Hold Fast Till I Come	Be Watchful, Strengthen Things That Are Ready to Die, Remember How Thou Hast Received and Heard, Hold Fast and Repent	Hold Fast That Which Thou Hast, That No Man Take Thy Crown	Buy Gold Tried in the Fire, Buy White Raiment, Anoint Thine Eyes with Salve, Be Zealous Therefore, and Repent
I Will Give Unto Every One of You According to Your Works	I Will Come on Thee as a Thief in the Night	Kept From the Hour of Tribulation	I Will Spew Thee Out of My Mouth
Power Over Nations, Rulership, Give Morning Star	White Raiment Given, Will Not Blot Name Out of Book of Life, Confess His Name Before God the Father and Angels	Make Him a Pillar in the Temple of God, Write on Him the Name of God, New Jerusalem, Jesus' New Name	Sit with Christ on His Throne
Pagan Church	Dead Church	Church Christ Loved	Apostate Church